Nights Are Longest There

Nights Are Longest There

A MEMOIR OF THE SOVIET SECURITY SERVICES

A. I. ROMANOV

Translated by Gerald Brooke

Little, Brown and Company • Boston • Toronto

102533

FIRST AMERICAN EDITION

T10/72

Library of Congress Cataloging in Publication Data

Romanov, A   I
    Nights are longest there.

    1. Secret service--Russia--Personal narratives.
I. Title.
HV8224.R613 1972   363.2'0947   72-4033
ISBN 0-316-755702

PRINTED IN THE UNITED STATES OF AMERICA

Preface

THIS BOOK has been in my mind for many years, but during the lifetime of my parents and of a few of their Service friends could be neither completed nor published. Only recently, when I was certain that my actions would not harm anyone in Soviet Russia, I decided to go ahead with publication under the pseudonym I have chosen. In bringing certain details up to date, and for general advice, I received most valuable suggestions from Wing Commander Asher Lee, Leonid Vladimirov, Kenneth MacGowan and Steven Constant, to all of whom I am most grateful. The final form of the book is, of course, entirely my own responsibility. Mr. Gerald Brooke, who was commissioned to translate the book, has, I am convinced, done his work excellently. I am also grateful to Sir Robert Lusty, due to whose encouragement the book now appears.

'This will last out a night in Russia,
When nights are longest there.'

Measure for Measure

I

THE TOWN WHERE I was born stands in a hilly area between two rivers, not far from the Don. Nearby magnificent coniferous forests, whose every precious pine has the makings of a fine mast, still stand untouched. It was probably because of them that Peter the Great chose my home town as the place to build the Russian fleet. From then onwards it became an important centre both for industry and agriculture, in the south-east part of the Russian black earth (*chernozyom*) zone, although the time when the last naval vessel was built there has long since been forgotten. On my father's side I come from a very old Cossack family, which had in its time given the Emperor of Russia many a faithful soldier and servant. The name of one of my remote forbears became well known throughout Russia for his exploits during the Napoleonic Wars. By the time that my father was born, the family followed a more peaceful way of life. The family's fame had declined accordingly. My father was the youngest member of the family and had two brothers, both of whom perished, or, to be more precise, simply vanished, during the Civil War which followed the Revolution. From snatches of grown-ups' conversation I recall that one of my uncles was last heard of fighting on the White side somewhere in the south. I never saw either of my paternal grandparents. They were probably dead when I was born. While still a student in Petersburg (Leningrad), my father made contact with revolutionary circles and broke with his parents, preferring to manage without their financial help. He went on with his studies and earned his keep partly by giving private lessons and partly by unloading barges on the wharves of the Neva. I recall from what he told us that by the time the Revolution took place he was a firm Bolshevik.

I remember quite distinctly my father's first post after the Revolution, in the Astrakhan-Caspian Sea area, because he was constantly supplied with black caviar. In those very early days my father was working for Kirov,[1] and for weeks on end he and his friends ate nothing but the most expensive fish and black caviar. When I was a little boy this story of my father's filled me with both acute envy and delight. The fact that at that time Astrakhan and the Caspian were cut off from the rest of the country by war and devastation didn't even enter my head. I couldn't grasp that there had been a terrible famine and, since there was no bread or potatoes to be had, my father had had to eat black caviar (which was produced locally) because there was nothing else. In any case, unlimited quantities of black caviar did not bring health and happiness. At that time my father suffered a terrible attack of typhus which he survived only by a miracle. It left him with a bad heart for the rest of his life. He often reminisced about Kirov, whom, unlike black caviar, my father continued to love and respect. He kept in touch with 'Mironych'[2] by letter, and whenever he was in Leningrad was always a guest at his house, right up to the day of the latter's tragic death.

My mother's family, on the other hand, had nothing in common with the Revolution, not to speak of its leaders. One evening my father happened to bring home a pre-Revolutionary directory: *Who's Who in Our Province.* My father and my maternal grandfather perused its pages for a long time with great amusement. Of course, the book came into my hands for a time as well. As far as I remember, Grandfather was a Councillor of State[3] and the head of a number of agricultural finance companies. I remember my grandfather possibly more clearly than I do any of the other people surrounding me then. He had already reached a venerable age, but took a lively interest in everything and everybody. Despite my mother's protests, he regularly attended the church by the river, which had survived the Revolution. My father, who respected the old man greatly, never objected. My grandfather would often reminisce with great pleasure about his trips to Germany (I remember particularly the town of Trier). But Grandfather's favourite country, Russia excepted—for Russia occupied a special place in his affections—was England. He used to spend hours telling me about England; the London fogs, the Stock Exchange, and particularly about the English themselves: their

[1] Kirov, Sergei Mironovich (Kostrikov), a secretary of the CC, who was in charge of the Party organisation of Leningrad, and was said to be the only man capable of replacing Stalin. He was killed in suspicious circumstances on 1st December 1934.
[2] Mironych—Kirov.
[3] A high civil rank in Czarist Russia, roughly equivalent to that of colonel.

politeness, and first and foremost their honesty. I remembered 'an Englishman's word is his bond' (of course, I had no idea what a bond was any more than I could conceive of kings and queens existing outside packs of cards). I realised that honesty and decency were the qualities in people which Grandfather valued most highly. I found out, by piecing isolated facts together, that to some extent Grandfather had survived the Revolution because of this very sense of decency, since he had supposedly treated his workers very fairly and had even on occasions hidden people from the Czarist police. I have no means of telling whether or not this is true. I am quite sure, however, that the fact that my father married his daughter played no small part in Grandfather's being left in peace, his surviving all the purges and dying in his own bed in his small room in my father's flat. As far as England was concerned I had irrefutable evidence to substantiate Grandfather's stories: a Royal Enfield bicycle with a huge sprocket-wheel, which made riding up hills very difficult (but how you went down them!) and an overcoat from some of grandfather's 'real English cloth', which was specially altered to fit me. I was terribly proud of both these things and flaunted them in front of the other boys. The English overcoat and the bicycle were left in my home town, as it burned after a German air raid on a hot July day in 1942.

All that, however, was a long way ahead. For the time being, if we discount typical boyish ups and downs, I had a bright, cloudless childhood. The whole world was full of things to be enjoyed. They began right in the yard of our apartment block for senior officials. For as long as I can remember my father was undoubtedly senior: a Central Committee representative (or CC Party organiser), for example, at the site where a large factory was being built, a hundred or so kilometres from the town. He lived there the whole year round and the rest of us—that is Grandfather, Mother and I—used to spend the summer with him. One could bathe in the river, fly kites, spend nights out of doors looking after the horses from the building site which were being pastured in the meadows, and sleeping by a campfire. After that Father filled in as Director of an Institute of Aviation. Although the institute was not military, it had its own uniform. He wore a single broad gold stripe on each sleeve of his dark blue tunic (this was equivalent to the rank of a naval captain or a colonel in the army). My mother, or perhaps it was my governess, gave way to my demands and sewed identical stripes to the sleeves of my jacket.

The yard, which had a fair-sized garden, was splendid. Once I had started school I discovered places in it where I could hide to avoid doing my homework. It was ideal for playing war games, for playing at Cossacks and brigands, at firemen, and heaven knows what else. In the evenings I could hide away in my room and read. Although it was no bigger than my grandfather's, it was still my own.

At a very early age I found I had a passion for books. At first I used to read everything: a handbook on breeding horses, tips for the young housewife, a flying manual. I later became more discriminating. I had my favourite books about heroes of the Civil War, there were foreign authors too, Fenimore Cooper, Gustav Umar, Mark Twain, Walter Scott. I was particularly fond of Seton Thompson's *Animal Heroes* and, of course, Dumas' *The Three Musketeers* which I knew almost off by heart. Mother and Nanny used to interfere, or I might have spent the whole night reading. Father hardly ever came home before midnight. He used to shrug this off by saying that some plenary session or conference had sat through yet another evening. Late at night, as I lay in bed doing my illicit reading, I would hear the noise of an approaching car—Father had come home.

From my earliest years I was strongly drawn first to literature, then a little later to history and geography. I took an immediate dislike to mathematics and the other exact sciences and just managed to get by in them somehow or other. I remember, too, that I devoted very little of my time to schooling in general but spent it on what I considered to be more useful and naturally more pleasant pursuits. As a rule I really got down to my studies only at the end of each quarter and at the end of the school year just before we moved up into the next class. My old friends—a few boys from the same class—agreed with me completely. My most loyal friend right up to the day we parted was a certain Yoska, the son of the director of a railway supply company. He was never down-hearted, and always full of ideas. I was also very close to his parents, who turned a blind eye, as did my own father, to our escapades. I remember his father as Uncle Abram and his mother was known in their family circle as 'Crazy Rosa'. I don't know who gave her this nickname (perhaps Yoska or his father). Of course, she was far from being crazy and on the contrary spent most of her time worrying whether Yoska and I had had enough to eat (I was one of the family in their house, just as Yoska was in ours) and constantly begging us to be a little more careful about what we got up to out of doors.

Yoska lived three blocks from our house and we always progressed (this word best describes it) to the school together. Some time earlier a pleasant innovation had appeared at the street intersections in the town—policewomen who directed the traffic. The traffic in our town was really quite something! Now and then a tramcar would rumble by in a cloud of sparks, a lorry or two might go shooting past, there were carts either involved in transportation or bringing *kolkhoz* produce to the market, even the occasional private car. The excellence of these ladies, however, lay in quite a different field from the usefulness of their work. In the summer these traffic policewomen wore tight-fitting white tunics, fairly short dark skirts and short neat boots. This sort of uniform was altogether to our taste, as it emphasised their figures. Among the policewomen were some pretty reasonable samples of their sex, particularly when, as they directed the traffic, they stood up on tiptoe and moved their arms about. One could easily spend quite a long time standing on the corner feasting one's eyes on them. The girl would become embarrassed and blush as a result of our lingering glances and loud sighs, but could not, of course, leave her post. Our pleasure often came to an end when a policeman appeared and said to us unceremoniously, 'Move on, what are you staring at, it's not a circus.'

Yoska and I had another way of amusing ourselves. This involved picking out a policewoman who was on the young side and rather more attractive than the general run. We would approach her respectfully and ask her in a voice at once polite and anxious, 'Comrade Policewoman, please tell us the way to Revolution Avenue.' The girl saluted (as bidden by the Police Code) and gave us detailed directions. Then one of us, more often than not Yoska, would say—'And where can one get a quick lay?' At this point we would wave 'bye-bye' and move on.

Well, here we were at school. Yoska and I were already very late for the first lesson. That didn't matter, it was only art and technical drawing. The teacher was a very kind man who was alas very hard of hearing. While he was standing with his back to the class, executing a drawing on the board, we staged a concert for him. This was very straightforward. One of us (often me, as I liked singing) would start to sing, in a stage whisper, some jazz song, for example 'Steamship' from the repertoire of the famous Soviet jazz musician Leonid Utyosov. 'Oh my dreams did not deceive me, and my eyes were true to me. She comes to meet us, like a white swan gliding through the water.' There were more girls in the class than boys and they too joined in with the last word of the song, *Steamship*!!! This made the teacher jump and he quickly turned round from the board. We were all sitting there quietly, respectfully, with serious faces and our pencils in our hands. He stared at us for a few moments, then shrugged his shoulders, turned round to the board and continued the drawing. Someone would start up the second verse of 'Steamship' and so it went on, a simple routine, but we enjoyed it. Of course, once in a while the headmaster, who had been lurking nearby, burst into the class. He was called 'Cross-eyed Kostya' and in actual fact his name was Konstantin and he did have a slight squint. Then followed a deadly dull 'funeral service', as we called his homilies, and strict reproof for us all. After all, just imagine trying to find out who started the singing. Almost the whole class was involved.

By now it was almost break time. Some work had got to be done here, as the second lesson was the maths we detested, and we could be asked for our homework. I'd better scrape it together quickly; i.e. copy it from some diligent girl or other. In the main break, as soon as we'd snatched a quick sandwich in the school cafeteria (we used to get the money from our parents), our group—Yoska, myself and five or six others—would decide what to do next. There was no hurry, as we needn't be on time for the next lesson. We would prepare for an attack on 'Budyonnovka'.[1] She actually served as something or other in the legendary First Cavalry Army under the command of Budyonny, Civil War hero and now a Marshal of the Soviet Union. She was a woman no longer young and always slightly tipsy. Her grey hair was cut short and she wore a rosette of red ribbon on her mannish-looking jacket.

We sometimes simply cut a lesson altogether. The result would be a 'funeral service' from 'Cross-eyed Kostya', the headmaster. At the very worst he would send for our parents. Kostya used to disturb my father only on very special occasions, especially after my father was put in charge of people's education for the whole region. I was very proud that my father occupied such important posts, for it was evidence that he was climbing the social ladder. The only thing wrong was that he didn't seem elated by this himself. On the contrary he became more and more tired and careworn and often came home only in the small hours of the morning.

I once went to see him at work (I often went to see him to beg for money) and went straight in to his office, bypassing his secretary. I could hear the sound of sobbing and two voices—a woman's and my father's. I froze in the doorway.

[1] Budyonnovka—a female soldier in the First Cavalry Army in the Civil War, which was commanded by Semyon Budyonny.

'Can't you understand,' the woman's voice was saying, 'I, who worked with Nadezhda Konstantinovna[1] and knew Ilych[2] well . . . have been expelled from the Party, in the Party Bureau itself, do you know what that means? . . . You will be doing my job, poor thing . . . and tomorrow, likely as not this very night . . .'

At this point they noticed me. To my astonishment I recognised the woman. She was the head of the Department of People's Education, an old Bolshevik, who had always treated me very affectionately. She and her husband, who was also a long-standing Party member and a professor, were close friends of my father. Her tear-stained face twisted into an agonised smile!

'Goodbye, Titch,' (my old nickname).

She kissed me on the cheek and walked unsteadily out of the office. My father was as white as chalk. The only other time that I had seen him look like that was on the day that his old boss, Kirov—'Mironych' —had been murdered.

Something odd was going on at school too. A number of boys and girls had disappeared both from our class and the next one to it. These included the children of both the commander and commissar of the local air force station, the son of the head of the NKVD Administration and several other children, all from the families of important officials. At home I happened to hear part of a conversation between my mother and her sister.

'. . . you can imagine what a dreadful situation it is, he' (i.e. my father) 'is now left in charge of the whole . . .'

Why is that dreadful? I thought, unable to understand. The more highly placed he is, the better. That means we'll have an even smarter car. How far I was from the truth! Though I did know what was what when it came to cars. I could tell you straight off what sort of cars each of the bosses had, just as could Yoska or any other of the kids. On the days of meetings and congresses we often stood near the huge building of the Regional Party Committee with its marble columns and admired the cars of the various regional and municipal leaders as they drove up. I even knew (I can tell you some of them now) the registration numbers of all those cars. They all ended with the figures '06' to make it easier for the various policemen on duty in the town to recognise them.

One day turned out to be particularly lucky. As I knew from my father, a special Regional Party meeting was taking place. The First

[1] N. K. Krupskaya, Lenin's widow.
[2] V. I. Lenin.

Secretary of the Regional Committee's dark blue Buick drove up,
then the emerald-green Zis of the Garrison Commander. In the doorway of the Regional Committee building a group of men in military
uniforms was bustling about. Their caps had fiery red bands and sky
blue crowns. They were Chekists[1] from the NKVD, clearly expecting
somebody important. A dark blue Buick which none of us recognised
glided softly up to the building. Perhaps it wasn't a Buick at all but
a Packard, for our town boasted no Packards. A Chekist leapt towards
it and flung the doors open, revealing a face we knew from portraits:
high forehead, pince-nez, a small toothbrush moustache—it was
Molotov. Flanked by two Chekists like the sausage in a hot-dog, he
entered the building. Then came another car we didn't recognise,
although it belonged to the local NKVD administration. It was a
dark green Lincoln and on its radiator was the silver figure of a hunting dog about to pounce. A small, slightly stooping man in a light
grey raincoat, gleaming boots and a red and blue military cap,
emerged from it. Limping slightly, he mounted the steps without
acknowledging the salutes of the Chekists who were standing by and
also disappeared into the building. Then came a black Zis with the
registration number oo-o6. This was the head of our local NKVD.
I was quite used to seeing the rhombus on his colour facings. He too
was wearing a light blue cap. What a day that was!

'Do you know,' exclaimed Yoska, 'it was Yezhov, that one in the
grey raincoat who came in the Lincoln!'

But of course! Why hadn't I guessed? The iron People's Commissar on Internal Affairs, Stalin's faithful comrade-in-arms, of
course it was he. I had even seen a cartoon of him in *Krokodil*. Beaming, blooming, rosy-cheeked, in that same raincoat and cap, he was
crushing in his huge hand, which was protected by a spiked glove,
some slimy green Trotskyite reptile. I remember too the caption on
the cartoon which said 'Yezhov's mittens',[2] but, for some reason or
other, on this particular day he (Yezhov) looked neither beaming,
blooming nor rosy-cheeked. He probably worked too hard like my
father. Shortly after this conference both our regional and municipal
authorities changed almost completely. My father became the head
of our Municipal Executive Committee. His friends jokingly dubbed
him the Lord of the Town, although in those days they joked very
rarely. My father himself, the Lord of the Town, was a very sorry

[1] From the Russian *Cheka,* founded in 1918 by Dzerzhinsky. The Chekists
were the first Soviet Secret Police.
[2] A pun on the word *yezh,* Russian for hedgehog.

sight. His skin had become parchment yellow and his eyes dull and red-rimmed. He was almost always accompanied by a man in uniform wearing a cap with a sky blue crown and a bar on his colour facings. He was a lieutenant in the State Security Service. He often dined at our house and I chatted with him about school matters and dances.

My school, or, rather, out-of-school, distractions went on as before. As always, there were men driving round the town catching stray dogs, but the dogs they caught were often not strays at all. One girl in our class came to a lesson in tears. Her favourite little puppy had been caught and taken away to the soap factory. This item of news reached our gang.

'Don't worry,' we assured the girl, 'we'll make them sorry they every laid hands on him.'

The dog-catchers were a couple of peasants. One of them used to sit perched on a high seat behind a horse drawing a large cage on the back of a cart. The other walked nearby with a rope noose on a long stick. Whenever he noticed a dog which was standing gaping at some-thing or other in the street he would creep up towards it, lasso it, overwhelm the yelping animal and drag it off to the cage. Then he would open the door from the side, kick the fright-crazed dog into the cage and release the noose. These were the mechanics of the operation.

We followed what they were doing and, one at a time, so as not to draw attention to ourselves, slowly closed in on them from behind. There were already some five or six dogs in the cage. That was one of us for each dog, but the peasants, particularly the catcher, were hulking devils. We chose a remote, deserted street. Five of us approached the catcher. When we came up to him we started a fight, but this was no ordinary fight. One of us closed with another, shout-ing as he did, 'I'll show you, you lout!' However, the person who received a heavy blow in the stomach was the catcher. Another member of our group yelled out, 'Don't you dare lay hands on my friend, you bugger!' But once again it was the catcher who caught the blow, this time on the neck. Then a third member of our gang threw himself at the catcher's legs, knocking the rogue's feet from under him, sending him flying face first into the dust and making him drop the stick with the lasso. Once the stick was in our hands we wasted no time in smashing it in half. At this point the last and strongest of our group, who till then had taken no part in the fight, rushed the driver, who was sitting round the corner on his high seat, and knocked him down on to the horse's rump with a cry of 'Kiss the mare's arse!' We had no time to look whether he kissed the mare or not. We hurled ourselves on to the cage, smashed off the bolt, flung wide the door and chased the dogs away in all directions. By this time, they had gone quite berserk, they left the scene at the speed of light—and we left almost as fast. From behind we could hear the voices of the catcher and driver who were beginning to come round. They were honouring us and our mothers with every expression they knew.

There was no chance to repeat this kind of operation. There were no more than three cages to cover the whole town. Of course, the crews of each of them knew of the sad mishap which had overtaken their colleagues and they all glared balefully at any lads walking in the streets, so that it was impossible even to get near them. I must confess that I didn't take part in this affair out of any particular fondness for the girl who had lost her dog. Nor did I do it out of love of animals. It was just that at that time I was bursting with unremitting high spirits.

This same spirit pushed me into a prank involving a refuse cart which could have had a very unhappy ending. Most of the houses in our town, the older ones in particular, had no inside lavatories. Such lavatories as they had were for the most part wooden or more occasionally stone buildings standing usually in the yard at the back of the house. From time to time the refuse collectors, known familiarly as the goldsmiths, emptied the contents of the midden, with the help of a special long-handled ladle, into large barrels standing on the back of carts. The contents of the barrels were then removed to certain places outside the town. This particular incident happened at the beginning of November (I can no longer remember the year) just before the October Revolution holiday. In preparation for this, the houses had been touched up with fresh paint, and red flags were hung out, or, if the house was a little larger, even whole slogans. All these jobs were the responsibility of the caretaker, a person without whom no Soviet communal house could function. Our caretaker was a tall, lean peasant with twirling gingery moustaches—a very obliging fellow. As my grandfather explained to me, before the Revolution the caretaker had served in Petersburg (Leningrad) in a regiment of horse guards. I had the vaguest possible notion of what horse guards were, thinking that they were probably somewhat similar to Budyonny's dashing cavalry, but belonging to Czarist times. Despite my bad behaviour, I was on fair terms with the caretaker. You could call them 'armed neutrality'. On this particular day, with the assistance of the man from the boiler room, he was hanging out flags, portraits of the leaders and slogans like 'Hail to the great October Revolution',

'Thank you, Comrade Stalin, for our happy life!' and so forth. Yoska and I were skulking nearby.

At this point a convoy of refuse carts with two or three barrels came round the corner. I let them go past, then taking a firm grip of my nose grabbed a red flag which was standing by the wall and jammed it into a hoop of the last barrel. The flag was caught by the wind and began to float proudly above the convoy. The next thing I heard was the stifled cry of the caretaker, who was quite beside himself with horror. Leaping like a tiger, he caught up with the barrel and, with hands that were trembling with fear, wrenched the flag from the hoop. Later I realised I had exposed a completely innocent caretaker to considerable danger. Usually in autumn one could see in the town so-called 'Red Waggon Trains' which were bringing grain and other produce from the collective farms for delivery to the State. These waggon trains were decked out with red flags and slogans of the same kind that the caretaker had been hanging on our house. Doubtless for waggon trains of this kind it was all very right and proper . . . but I had hung a flag on a waggon train which was bearing produce of a less salubrious nature.

That very evening, or more accurately in view of the time that my father came home from work, that night, the ex-horse guard-cum-caretaker waited up for him and for the first time ever complained to him about me. My father gave me a severe telling off.

'Didn't you realise what a stink you could have caused him?' It suddenly struck my father that he had used a rather inappropriate expression. I tried to pun my way out of the situation by saying that not just the caretaker but everybody, myself included, would have got a whiff of the stink I had created. The whole effect of the ticking off was spoilt and a glimmer of mirth appeared in my father's eyes.

Turning his head away he continued, 'You idiot! The things you get up to!'

Grandfather who was sitting nearby, did not share my father's merriment.

'You were a little fool, exposing somebody to danger like that. Don't you forget it!'

On the other hand the lieutenant of the State Security Service who had dinner with us on the following day looked at me rather strangely and snorted so much with laughter that he almost choked over his soup. However, I am quite convinced that my father, had this affair turned into anything other than a laughing matter, would have used all his influence to save the caretaker.

Soon my schemes were directed into another, rather purer, sphere. I attended a school which like all others of the same type was co-educational. Until then my friends and I had acted on the assumption that girls existed mainly so that we could pull their pigtails, trip them up at the skating rink and execute for their benefit on the blackboard before lessons rude drawings of things like dogs mating. We now began to see them as members of the opposite sex. In physical-training lessons, when we all wore nothing but shorts and a vest, we became very interested in the girls. Borrowing a piece of completely official terminology, we called those parts of the maiden anatomy which interested us, 'Socialist property'. We examined in the greatest detail the 'property' of one or another of our female classmates. A habit developed among us of arranging parties to which we all went, at the flats of various male pupils, particularly when their parents were not at home. At these parties one could have a glass or two of wine from a bottle that had been smuggled in as lemonade. There was also the chance to get some girl you fancied into a dark corner and give her a bit of a cuddle and a kiss. Later we discovered that in school too there were corners which could serve the same purpose. Sometimes we would end up with our cheeks burning from where the girls had slapped us and sometimes everything went smoothly. I had already become a veteran of such parties and a specialist in kissing and fumbling, but that was as far as it had gone.

The late spring, my sixteenth on this earth, was turning into summer. All the municipal gardens and suburban parks were already open. The annual exams at school were almost over and only the less important subjects remained to be taken. In the preceding quarter a new girl had appeared in our class whom I shall call Nonna. Her father had been transferred to work in our town. Till then I had had no permanent ties. I made do with 'what God sent'. This was how Yoska summed up the situation, though he acknowledged neither God nor the devil. But Nonna took my fancy straightaway. She had large grey eyes with soft delicate lashes, chestnut hair with just a touch of ginger in it drawn up into a plait on top of her head, and I gaped at her throughout the physical training lessons and most of the other lessons as well. I lived in a world of my own and gave all the wrong answers to the teachers' questions. Fuel was added to the flames of my passion by the fact that Yoska's girl friend, a girl from the next class, had totally capitulated to him. He told me that they were enjoying a 'happy family life' together. Yoska was a born comedian and borrowed this expression, like many others he used, straight from

Soviet official jargon. Of course, my envy knew no bounds. Eyeing Yoska's girl friend, I decided that she wasn't too bad at all. I then set my imagination to work on the problem of how Nonna would fit into the 'happy family' situation and, of course, she came out streets ahead of Yoska's intended or anybody else for that matter. The only question was how should I make my dreams a reality. Of course, there had been certain moves in the right direction. By this stage Nonna did allow me to take her home from the skating rink and was prepared to listen to my foolish chatter. I was beginning to undermine her resistance with my fine words.

To mark the end of the school year, Yoska and I planned a picnic with a drop to drink and a girl or two, in the Kaganovich[1] Park of Culture and Relaxation. In this very day I treasure the fondest memories of both that park and Kaganovich himself, and I am sure that my feelings are shared by many of the soldiers and NCOs of our town garrison. Both they and I often used this park for the same purpose. It occupied about ten acres of heath and woodland. Beyond it fields and woods stretched as far as the eye could see. There was enough room there for most things, including both culture and relaxation.

Unexpectedly, our far-reaching preparations for the picnic came to a dead end as we had no money. In view of my own none-too-resounding examination successes, my father had declined to offer any further financial subsidies. Neither were Yoska's roubles particularly thick on the ground. But he was not one to be down-hearted.

'My poor child,' he exclaimed after a brief pause for thought, 'we are saved from starvation! Nikolai Petrovich will come to our rescue.'

Just as Jaroslav Hasek's brave soldier Schweik knew many Ferdinands, I knew a host of Nikolai Petrovichs.

'Which one? And why on earth should he help us?'

'Everything will be all right if you just listen to me,' Yoska insisted. He then slipped off somewhere, returned with a brief-case and beckoned to me to follow him.

He took me into a public garden named after the pre-Revolutionary poet Koltsov, who had lived in our parts. We stood in the bushes and Yoska made me put on a red Pioneer's neckerchief, which he produced from his pocket.

'What's the matter with you? Are you nuts!' I said, tapping my forehead. After all, I was a Komsomol. I was too old to be a Pioneer

[1] A member of the Politbureau and at that time People's Commissar for Transport.

and even when I had been one the only time I'd worn a neckerchief like that was in January during the Lenin days.[1]

'Shut up and fasten your neckerchief,' said Yoska.

He then pinned a Komsomol badge (a small red metal flag) on to his chest.

'Well, how's that? Will it do?' he asked with some concern.

'It depends what you want it to do for,' I said.

Yoska was in fact wearing a browny-grey suit and I had·on a dark blue jacket with padded shoulders and grey trousers. We were both wearing good shoes. Yoska had an imposing leather brief-case in his hand.

'Come on then, only you keep quiet. I'll do the talking,' said Yoska.

We made our way towards the new hotel on the corner opposite the garden. Yoska had a good look at the small number of cars that were parked there. Satisfied with the result of his examination, Yoska declared, 'Well, that's all right.'

'We're going to see Nikolai Petrovich Kamanin,'[2] he whispered, as we approached the doors of the hotel.

I had seen Kamanin many times. He was a small cheerful man with a large forehead, who wore the gold star of a Hero of the Soviet Union on his chest, but, of course, I did not know him personally and was equally sure that Yoska didn't know him either. Noticing the expression of protest on my face, Yoska whispered: 'Shut up, leave the talking to me and everything will be all right!' We went into the hotel and were confronted by the manager who was standing at the reception desk.

'We're from the Municipal Komsomol Committee,' said Yoska, 'and we've come to see Nikolai Petrovich Kamanin about a speech that he's going to make at a rally of the town's Pioneers. We've already made arrangements with him by telephone and he's waiting for us. We know which room he's in.'

The receptionist nodded his head and we went over towards a broad red-carpeted staircase. When we reached the third floor Yoska pushed me into a bathroom, came in himself, closed the door and

[1] Those days when Lenin's death was commemorated.
[2] At that time a pilot with the rank of captain. He was decorated with the title of Hero of the Soviet Union for bringing to safety the members of a Polar expedition who had been shipwrecked on the *Chelyuskin*. At the moment he is a colonel-general in the air force and in charge of all Soviet astronauts.

dropped the catch. He opened the brief-case, produced a screwdriver and took a look around.

'If anybody knocks at the door,' he said quietly, 'then say what the parrot said in that joke.'

Of course, I knew the joke about the parrot. In a communal flat, bursting at the seams with tenants, the only place to hang the parrot's cage was by the door of the only lavatory in the flat. The wise bird sat there in its cage for years on end. When the parrot acquired a new owner, a young actress, she hung its case in a place of honour in her drawing-room. She was often visited by young gentlemen admirers. This would have been fine apart from the fact that every time someone knocked at her door the parrot shouted loudly in a voice full of irritation 'Engaged, engaged' and emitted the sounds 'Heh, heh! Pooh, pooh!' I had no opportunity to enjoy the joke, however, as Yoska, handling the screwdriver deftly, began to remove chromium-plated coat hooks, soap dishes, toothbrush racks and even the handle from the lavatory chain. This was nothing more or less than the stealing of real 'Socialist property'.

'Shut up,' Yoska hissed, 'you want to have Nonnka but who do you think's going to pay for the food and drink? Pushkin! You'd do better just to take these things and pack them neatly into the brief-case. Put them inside the textbooks so they don't rattle.'

Having made a clean sweep in one bathroom he dragged me up on to the fourth floor.

'All right,' I said, once we were behind the bolted door of another bathroom, 'pass that screwdriver and if anybody knocks this time it's your turn to do the parrot act.'

'Catching on at last,' says Yoska, and his eyes were full of laughter.

That was all there was to our visit to Nikolai Petrovich. We proceeded sedately past the receptionist, greeting him with a non-chalant, friendly wave of the hand. Once back in the park we divested ourselves of the Pioneer's neckerchief and the Komsomol badge and slipped them into our pockets. Then off we went to the rag market, a sort of bazaar held out in the open air. In a matter of minutes we had disposed of all our goods, since they were things that the man in the street found hard to get. They brought us a fair sum of money which resolved the financial side of the picnic.

We had no trouble in obtaining either food or alcohol. My family bought the food it needed in a closed shop for senior Party and State officials. This shop bore no sign on its door, but always had a police-man standing outside. I told him my father's name and we went in.

Several of the assistants there knew me. We bought a few bottles of vodka and wine, a selection of refreshments, sweets (for the girls), some packets of Palmyra of the North cigarettes (the ones Stalin himself smoked). There seemed no reason why we shouldn't smoke them too. Yoska suddenly remembered that we had better pay a visit to the chemist's.

On the day of the picnic our gang took a number five tram, which stopped right by the gates of the Kaganovich Park of Culture and Relaxation. From there we had to walk a further two kilometres to get right away from everybody and everything. It was regrettable, as we had two heavy cases of bottles and parcels to carry, but there was no point in asking Father to lend me the car for a jaunt like this. If I were going to the doctor or the dentist then, of course, it would be different. I took a sidelong glance at Nonna and I could see that she too was very excited. We sat down by a stream under a large tree. After the long walk we offered round what we described as a 'refreshing drink for children'. It was actually cherry juice generously diluted with vodka with a touch of mint powder to remove the smell. We were particularly solicitous in pressing this on the girls. We all drank some, refilled the cups and then had something to eat.

There were about eight of us in all. We split up into pairs and wandered off in different directions. Yoska and his girl friend stayed on guard by the cases. Just as if he were making a speech, Yoska wished those who were about to wander off 'Success in the building of socialism'.

I suggested to Nonna that I should show her a place where one could catch enormous pike. I couldn't vouch for the pike, but I did know that the place was really pleasant and secluded. I said that I was tired and sat down. Nonna dropped down beside me and 'serious' kissing commenced. I unbuttoned her blouse and tugged her brassière upwards. There were two tight little mounds, firm like stones. 'No, no . . .' whispered Nonna, but I didn't sense any serious resistance. There was the same ringing in my ears as when I leapt from a parachute training tower. Overcome by my yearning for her, I fell upon her. Nonna's cry, 'It hurts Sashka, it hurts!' brought me to myself. I felt her teeth biting my ear. I whispered, 'At first it hurts, then it's nice.' Nonna covered her face with her hand and fell silent. Brushing her hand aside I sank my lips into hers. Our mouths became one rhythm.

Only afterwards when we had already got up and straightened our clothes did Nonna say, all the time avoiding my eyes, 'Oh, there's some blood on the lobe of your ear, just a moment I'll put a plantain leaf on it.'

We returned to where the cases were. Several couples had already come back and there was a camp-fire burning. Yoska at once noticed the tiny wound on my ear.

'I caught it on the branch of a tree,' I remarked indifferently.

'Yes,' said Yoska, 'some trees do have very sharp teeth.'

Nonna was still avoiding looking at me and, of course, Yoska latched on to this as well. Imitating the voice of Leonid Utyosov he crooned, 'When she goes by, my darling's so proud that she doesn't look at me.' I let him have it with my foot. But there was nothing even he could do to affect my excellent mood. That evening, as I was hugging Nonna in the entrance to her block of flats, it became even better because when I asked her 'Are you angry?' she gave a negative shake of the head and kissed me quickly. I can safely say that on that evening I felt better than I did either when I was commissioned as a lieutenant or when Lieutenant-General Strokach[1] invested me with the Order of the Great Patriotic War First Class. I kept in close contact with Nonna, in fact with the passage of time we became even closer in some respects, right up to the time when she was evacuated from our town.

Although then one often heard people say, 'Hitler and Ribbentrop should bugger off,' there was no sign of that actually happening. Indeed, far from it. Stalin himself had received Ribbentrop in Moscow. My grandfather was far from delighted with our new allies.

'Now if it were the English, then I'd feel a lot better about it,' he used to say, 'but with those . . .'

The war with Finland broke out, though at first it didn't affect me in any way. Of course it seemed rather odd that such a tiny country not only didn't want to swap a small amount of territory near Leningrad for a much larger piece in Karelia, but even dared to open fire on us. This was what our newspapers and radio were saying, although to be quite frank at that time I hardly ever read the newspapers and the only thing I listened to on the radio was light music. What information I felt I needed I found out either directly from my grandfather (he not only listened to the radio and read the press, but even drew his own conclusions) or by listening to conversations between him and my father. I once heard my father's voice through the open door of the dining-room.

[1] People's Commissar (Minister) for State Security in the Ukraine.

'. . . of course it's a disgrace, it's a disgrace and a shambles . . . if Mironych (Kirov) had been alive he would never have let things get to this state!'

I recall my father using almost exactly the same words at a much later date when we were in Kiev and discussing the Leningrad blockade which cost such a number of lives. There was good reason for the fact that during the blockade a poem called 'Kirov is with us' was very popular. Zhdanov,[1] who was actually on the spot, could not rival him in popular appeal. Many folk, right at the end of their tether, with tears in their eyes, recalled this plain man who could always find time for everybody who wanted to see him.

One day the Komsomol secretary of our school, a tow-haired, unlikable youth, handed me an envelope with my name on it. The reason we couldn't stand this secretary was because he fawned on the headmaster and never took any part in our pranks. The envelope contained an invitation: 'The Regional Administration of the NKVD invites you to a meeting between the town's best Komsomol members and officials of the Commissariat.[2] The meeting will take place in the NKVD club.' Yoska got an identical invitation. Anybody who included us among the town's best Komsomols must have had a very keen sense of humour.

'Well,' he said, with feigned horror, 'if we've got to go, we've got to go, as the sparrow said when the cat caught it by the tail.'

There were about eighty people in the NKVD club, all of them boys from the upper classes of school. The platform party included one girl (she was the only female present), who was the second secretary of the Municipal Komsomol Committee. We were addressed by a thickset man who had two bars on the colour facings of his collar. I knew him, as I'd met him both at our country house and various parades. His name was Makarov and he was one of the deputies of Sergey Filipovich Pismensky, the head of our local NKVD. Sergey Filipovich used often to play billiards with my father. Makarov uttered truths that were known to us all.

'Our Party, as our great leader, Comrade Stalin, has said, is strong because of its permanent links with the people itself. . . . For this reason too are we strong, we disciples of the great Stalin—we Soviet Chekists . . .!'

I began to look around me in search of distraction, but there was

[1] A secretary of the Central Committee, who succeeded Kirov as the First Secretary of the Leningrad Regional Committee of the Party.
[2] The People's Commissariat for Internal Affairs.

nothing suitable, as the whole audience was made up of boys just like myself.

'What are you fidgeting for?' whispered Yoska, who was sitting beside me. 'Have you got a pin sticking in your arse or something?'

I tried to look straight at the platform.

'. . . watching over the people's serene and noble labour. What can be more honourable.'

These were the words that rolled from the platform. I began to fix my attention on the girl secretary. Not a bad bit of property, nice round little knees, shapely legs and probably . . .

'No, we Chekists declare to all enemies . . .' Makarov continued.

I imagined how she would look in a bathing suit, or, even better, without one, like Nonna looked . . .

'Hey,' said Yoska, giving me a dig in the ribs, 'listen to what he's saying!'

'Our groups are altogether different from the Auxiliary Police Youth Brigades. . . . They will have to carry out responsible tasks of a secret nature!'

By now I was listening to every word Makarov was saying.

The whole thing was carried out very simply. During the following week all the people who had been at the meeting in the club were summoned one by one to a grey building decorated with reddish marble which was the NKVD's new premises. There, in the Secret Political Branch, we signed an undertaking to join an Auxiliary NKVD Group. The groups themselves were under the aegis of the Operational Branch. I met the head of this branch, Yakovlev, in the corridor. It struck me that now he was my boss too. On his colour facings he wore the two bars of a first lieutenant in the State Security Service.

'Well,' said he, laughing, 'it'll be a bit more complicated than organising a "Red Waggon Train" this time.'

'Good God,' I thought, resorting to words my grandfather would have used, 'how does Yakovlev know about my epic deed with the red flag?' I consoled myself with a phrase that was then in fashion, 'The NKVD knows everything.'

I very quickly got my first job for the NKVD. Late one evening the members of our group were loaded into a large bus. Off we went to the station, not to the passenger station that I knew so well, but to a special goods station which was surrounded on all sides by a high fence. By the gates stood a sentry from the NKVD forces with a rifle and fixed bayonet. A long passenger train was standing at the platform. All the windows were lit up with white blinds drawn across them. An officer in NKVD uniform, whom I did not know, spoke to us. He told us that we would be transferring from the train officers and men of our army who had arrived from the Finnish front. This operation was secret. We were not even to tell members of our own families about it. I remember how proud I was to think that I had information secret even from my father. I was, however, deeply mistaken. As I learned subsequently, it was my own father who had been responsible for preparing special hospital premises in the town for soldiers who had returned from Finland suffering from wounds and frostbite. So far as I can recall, about a thousand such officers and men were sent to our town. Of course, I have no idea how many were sent elsewhere.

This work was very dull and I was soon fed up with it. Fool that I was, I thought that I would discover from the men who arrived a whole lot of accurate information about the war with Finland. This was far from being the case. The wounded either joked with us or simply fobbed us off with answers like 'First rate', 'Wonderful', 'Everything's going according to plan', and so on. I have never liked it when people have treated me like a fool or a child. I remember that I consoled myself by thinking that they had no right to reveal military secrets since we might have been overheard by enemy agents. I was nevertheless left with a feeling of dissatisfaction. I took part in operations like this three or four times. Soldiers of the NKVD forces worked alongside us but there were no representatives of our town's large army garrison.

I had made very impressive plans for the summer of 1941. It had been decided that I would spend the time up to the beginning of August with my grandfather at our house in the country and then go with my father to the Crimea so as to spend part of the so-called 'velvet season' (the best time is August and September) there. It didn't turn out that way. Around midday on the 22nd June I went into my grandfather's room. He was standing before his favourite icon, a tiny one of St. Nicholas (Grandfather always used to refer to him as the defender and patron saint of the Russians). I just caught the last few words of his prayer. '. . . save and preserve Russia'. Grandfather told me that Germany had attacked the Soviet Union. I couldn't wait to find out the details and began to bombard him with questions.

'What will happen?' Grandfather said, repeating my question slowly. 'It'll be a hard and difficult struggle, but in the end, and don't you ever forget it, my boy, we shall win. No one will ever conquer Russia.'

I still remember those words very clearly. I realise now that Grandfather always intentionally avoided words like 'Soviet power', 'the building of socialism' and 'the Party'. With hindsight I can guess that he never took seriously either the Revolution or the new regime, but simply regarded them as transitory unpleasant necessities. He had boundless faith in Russia and the Russian people. I think he had just as much faith in England. When he heard Churchill's first speech after the German attack his face was transformed and radiant. Crossing himself, my grandfather murmured, 'May the Lord help and preserve him.'

When my father came home to dinner we noticed an unusual bulge at the bottom right-hand side of the back part of his jacket. On lifting up the hem, I discovered a brown leather holster containing a pistol of an unfamiliar make.

'Well,' said my father, smiling sadly as he answered our unspoken questions, 'as you see all the main Party and civic functionaries have been armed. In case the worst comes to the worst,' he added vaguely.

Grandfather said nothing. About three weeks later, however, I heard a conversation between him and my father which shook me to the depths of my shallow inexperienced being. My mother was at Pyatigorsk in the south. My ex-nanny was with her relatives in the country and the servants were only in during the daytime. We men were quite by ourselves. Actually, the youngest of these men, myself, ought to have been in bed, as it was after two o'clock in the morning. I wasn't asleep, however, and heard almost everything. My father, who had just come home and taken off his boots (at this period he wore semi-military dress), was pacing up and down the large room in his stockinged feet, unwinding after the day's work. Grandfather had made some tea and was sitting at the table in the same room. I would be telling a lie if I said I had committed to memory every sentence of that conversation, but this is the gist of it.

Our army was retreating, in places in total disorder, leaving behind both equipment and weapons, losing entire units. The top brass had completely lost control of the situation, not knowing even where the front line was. Was there a shortage of men? Not enough weapons or equipment? Weren't there enough competent officers? These were the questions that Grandfather was putting. To all of them Father produced the same stereotyped answer, 'No, it's not that.' As far as I could understand we had sufficient of all these things and in some respects were even better off than the Germans, though there was indeed a shortage of experienced commanders (I did not then know why this was so). This, however, was not the root of the trouble. The situation was far worse: a very large percentage of the population did not want to fight for Soviet power and for the communists. In their millions! they had gone over voluntarily to the Germans, killing Party workers first and then laying down their arms.

'Why else do you think,' my father's voice went on, 'they lumbered me with this ridiculous pop-gun.' Then I heard the sound of something flying across the room and landing on the sofa with a dull thump. My father had obviously taken off his gun-belt. 'For my personal safety,' he went on bitterly. 'You see, I'm a commissar too and one who learnt his trade with Kirov into the bargain. Who's that gun supposed to save me from? From my own people! The shame of it. What a balls-up they've made of it!'

I can remember my father then coming out into the hall, holding the teapot in his hand. When he saw my half-open door he came into my room and flicked on the light. I was sitting on the bed making no attempt to conceal the fact that I had not been alseep and stared straight at him.

'Don't worry, son, everything'll get sorted out. We just need a bit of time.' And that was more or less all he said to me.

All this, of course, was astonishing news to me. I experienced a mixture of feelings. In the first place I was both hurt and fearful for my father. He who had done so much for the people now had to protect himself from them! I knew that he had long been a commissar —a regimental commissar in the reserve.[1] I'd always been very proud of this. After all, there was even a well-known song whose words ran, 'The Commissar is the father of a Division . . .' And now I heard that commissars were being beaten up.

Fresh events, however, distracted me from these disturbing thoughts. I graduated from my ten-year school. I couldn't wait to get to the front to fight the Germans. My father wouldn't hear of it and he fixed me up on a preparatory course in the Department of History at our local university. The most important thing that happened then was that I said farewell to Yoska. He was leaving to enter a technical school for troops in armoured forces, somewhere near Chelyabinsk. He held a farewell dinner at his home for his

---

[1] All major officials had titles like this, e.g. Brezhnev was a brigade commissar, but when shoulder boards were introduced he was demoted and given only the rank of colonel.

closest friends. I was both astonished and moved by the fact that my father came, though only for half an hour. My father and Uncle Abram retired into a corner so that we could only catch the odd word of what they were saying. Strange as it may seem, my father, who had long been on very good terms with Yoska's father, was talking about Jews. Once when I was still quite a child I had started to poke fun at an Armenian shop assistant by imitating the way he spoke. My father had taken me out of the shop and told me off very angrily. I had learnt then once and for all that a man's nationality is completely unimportant. The only thing that matters is whether a man is a decent individual or a scoundrel. Now, however, my father was talking angrily to Uncle Abram about something to do with Jews!

'. . . if it were within my power I'd load them all up and evacuate them from the town to the east . . . you just can't imagine what happened over there in the western part of the country . . .'

Uncle Abram was saying something about ignorant, uneducated people. My father was asserting that all that any Jew could expect was derision and death. 'But at whose hands?' I thought in puzzlement. I couldn't have cared a damn whether a man was a Jew or not.

As a matter of fact I had been slightly involved in Jewish matters. A few years earlier Yoska had dragged me off to a synagogue not far from the street where we lived. All the men in the synagogue were singing something which was both pleasant and rather sad. We found ourselves a place at the back and began singing too. I seem to remember our singing 'Silva, you no longer love me' from the operetta by Kalman. Of course, we were thrown out of the synagogue in disgrace. Although, being rather proud of my voice, my deepest feelings were wounded by this incident I did not become an anti-Semite. Sometimes too Yoska would tell me Jewish stories. He gave a superb imitation of two Jewish women neighbours having a quarrel which made me laugh so much that I felt I had to check my trousers afterwards to make sure that I hadn't let everything go. When he bade Yoska goodbye my father said that he hoped he would next see him in an officer's uniform.

'I can't promise that,' Yoska answered modestly, 'but I shall definitely become a general.'

All this time I was constantly busy in my Auxiliary NKVD Group. We always seemed to work at night. We travelled round the town in a large lorry in the charge of two Chekists in plain clothes. The lorry was loaded with sacks of cement, spades and small galvanised boxes.

We would drive up to certain houses and one of the plain-clothes men would wake the caretaker, and wave an NKVD warrant card in his face. The caretaker was told that a communication apparatus for the town anti-aircraft defence service was to be set up in the basement of his building. Sometimes other similar pretexts were used. He would always get a stern warning that this was a highly secret matter (he would there and then sign a paper, undertaking not to divulge anything of what he knew). The caretaker was ordered to ensure that neither the tenants of the house nor outsiders should wander about in the basement any more than was absolutely necessary, after which he was told that he was free to go to bed. The lorry then crawled slowly into the yard of the house. Then things began to happen all over the place. Guards were set up by the door into the yard and the basement itself. Some of the cement and boxes were unloaded and a bucket of water was obtained. The second of the plain-clothes men then began deftly inserting objects into the small niches which had been made for them either in the walls or in the floor. These objects were longish pipes with protruding wires soldered on to each end, or sometimes so far as my memory serves me, had the appearance of sealed metal dinner plates. The niches were then made good with cement and all that remained to mark the spot were special signs, which were well concealed from prying eyes. We would then set off for another address. All the other members of the group were as well aware as I was that these objects were not communication devices at all, but explosives and delayed-action mines. 'Why?' one might ask. We were not supposed to ask such questions and none of us did.

It was almost the 7th November, the anniversary of the October Revolution, and a day when a traditional military parade was held. I had loved these parades since I was a boy. I used to go not only to the parades themselves but also to the dress rehearsals, which took place at night on the days immediately preceding the anniversary. I wandered about literally under the hooves of the cavalry horses and got as close as I could to the senior officers who were supervising events in the square. On the day of the parade itself access to the centre of the town either by transport or on foot was prohibited and police cordons were set up. Vehicles and pedestrians were allowed in only with special passes issued for that one particular day. My father always supplied me with these passes. There were two types and I can remember exactly what they were like. The first was a small piece of green card on which was written: 'Comrade . . . is allowed to pass through the police cordon,' and bore the signature of the town Police Chief, First Lieutenant Kuznetsov. His son was one of my gang. The other kind was far more distinguished. It was on white card and said that '. . . had access to the guests' stand'. It bore the signature of the head of the Operational Branch of the Regional Administration of the NKVD, First Lieutenant of the State Security Service, Yakovlev. As a matter of fact there was no guests' stand. The guests stood on specially erected wooden platforms on the broad staircase of the Regional Party Committee building. These platforms flanked both sides of the only real stand which was for regional and municipal dignitaries. In front of the stand a long line of uniformed men in sky blue caps stood shoulder to shoulder. These were the Chekists of the operational branch. This was what always happened on the day of the parade and the first wartime anniversary was no exception.

The leaders' stand was packed. Apart from local leaders (including my father), the upper crust of the Ukrainian leadership, whose territory was already in German hands, was also present. In the very centre stood Khrushchev. The sharply defined squares of soldiers stood motionless in the square. In the far corner beneath a huge statue of Lenin, a general whom I had never seen before sat astride a horse, with a bared sabre in his hand. He bellowed forth the words of command, reared his horse up, moved forward, then into a gallop and, sitting with his sabre held vertically to his chin, galloped to the middle of the square to meet two horsemen who had appeared from the opposite end. My favourite march music sounded forth. The first horseman, a huge broad-shouldered man in a tall astrakhan papakha, sat masterfully astride a prancing horse. It was Marshal Timoshenko, at that time in charge of the whole south-western area. The second horseman was his adjutant. The marshal and the general met right in front of the stand and we heard the general's brief report. The march into battle sounded once again. Timoshenko galloped along the line of troops greeting them and congratulating them on the anniversary. He was answered with a thunderous 'Hurrah'. What a splendid sight it was! He then ascended the platform and made a brief speech. The guns roared out a salute, then came the strains of the *Internationale* followed by a triumphal march past of the troops. The infantry advanced with rifles at the ready, squadrons of cavalry swept past at a trot. Then came all kinds of heavy weapons, followed by swiftly moving tanks. The latter were extremely small in number that particular year, but, none the less, or so it seemed to me, an incomparably magnificent sight.

For several days I and some other members of the Auxiliary NKVD Group had been working in the Operational Checking Section of the Secret Political Branch in the main NKVD building. Each of us had a long typewritten list of names (including the first name patronymic, date of birth and sex of each individual). We had to search around an enormous quantity of folders standing on long rows of shelves for the files of each person on our list, and put them on one side on a separate table. Our work was directed by several uniformed Chekists. I knew that these were lists of inhabitants of the town whom the NKVD was instructing to leave at forty-eight hours' notice, and travel to towns in the east away from the fighting. I and other members of the group delivered notification to the houses of those listed. They were citizens who were considered unreliable and whose continued residence in the town was regarded as undesirable in view of the difficult situation on the various fronts. They all had to give a written undertaking to register at once with the NKVD as soon as they arrived at their new homes. Other unreliables were arrested and moved directly to a special station. There they were put on trains and taken to camps somewhere in Central Asia. As soon as they arrived at the station they were placed under the supervision of special transit teams of NKVD guards, who were responsible for delivering them to the camps. Members of our auxiliary groups were not used on this kind of operation. Operational Chekists and soldiers of the internal forces of the NKVD carried out the arrests and conducted the individuals concerned to the station.

Meanwhile the removal of equipment from factories in the town was also going on quickly. This affected factories such as Aviation Factory No. 18, Aero-Engine Factory No. 16, the Kirov Synthetic Rubber Factory (S.R.-2), the Comintern Machine Tool Plant and a number of others. It wasn't just the machine tools and instruments which were dispatched. With them went both skilled workers and machine operators. Their families were frequently left behind as there was no room for them on the overloaded trains. There was a shortage of both waggons and platform space. All this equipment and personnel were being dispatched beyond the Urals to Siberia and Central Asia.

At this period my father used to disappear for whole days at a time, snatching some sleep when he could in his office. He was made a member of the Regional Defence Committee, part of the most powerful body in the State in time of war. In Moscow all authority over what was happening in the country was transferred to the State

Defence Committee, whose chairman was Stalin himself. Despite my being in a hive of activity, I was bored and lonely. This was something which I had never before experienced. Hardly any of my close friends were left in the town. Yoska was somewhere beyond the Urals and my grey-eyed Nonna and her family had been evacuated with the factory where her father worked. In the absence of Yoska and Nonna I discovered in myself a feeling which was quite new to me. I now know that the name for it is nostalgia.

My grandfather had been ailing for a long time and had begun to spend a lot of his time in his own room or even in bed. Of course, he was getting on in years and into the bargain the doctors had found something or other. He was advised to go into hospital, but he refused point blank; in the same way he turned down my father's suggestion that he move further away from the front. My former nanny would have gone with him. But one day at the end of May 1942 I came home from the university during the daytime and at once realised that something quite exceptional had happened. Probably for the first time for as long as I could remember I found my father in the house. My mother and my nanny were in tears and Father too had a very strange look on his face. Grandfather lay on the table already washed and clad in his old long-skirted coat of English cloth. He held his favourite little icon in his waxen hands which lay folded on his chest.

It was the oddest of funerals. The coffin was borne to the grave by my father and his 'personal' State Security Service lieutenant, who was wearing full Chekist uniform. There were one or two other people, including our ex-horse-guard caretaker with his bristling moustache, who had donned his best suit specially for the occasion. The little old priest from the church by the river walked behind the coffin waving a censer. I had no tears to shed when Grandfather was lowered into his grave as the priest intoned, 'Eternal memory . . . eternal memory!' I simply felt a spasm in my throat and a kind of hot stinging sensation in my eyelids. As I turned quickly away I caught sight of my father standing to attention and the Chekist lieutenant with his hand held up stiffly to the peak of his cap. It was often said in my family that I was my grandfather all over again.

I didn't seem to be getting very far in the preparatory group at the university. It's obvious that in the upheaval of those alarm-filled days, when all kinds of rumours were rife, no one was in the mood for study. I used to attend lectures for a change and a bit of a chat. There I met a number of students who had recently returned from the western parts of the country. They had been recruited and sent there by the Komsomol to build defences and had spent their time digging anti-tank ditches and trenches. These had been useless after the Germans had come. The students had had to make their way back through occupied territory and one day had run into a group of Germans.

'Well,' I said, my interest at once awakened, 'what happened?'

The Germans had turned out to be cheerful, clean-shaven fellows with their shirt-sleeves rolled up and automatic rifles dangling from their necks, who had merely asked the students jokingly whether or not they were Komsomols (they had had the sense to say that they weren't). The Germans had sent them on their way unharmed, promising that they would come to our town. Two or three of the students understood and spoke German fairly well.

'All the same,' they said to me, 'you keep this to yourself!'

They knew whose son I was, and one of them was in fact the son of the Deputy Rector of the university, who was a friend of my father. Their story contained elements which were not confidential nor particularly cheerful. They had passed a camp containing many thousands of captured Red Army men. It stood in an open area surrounded by barbed wire and was guarded by men armed with automatic rifles and machine guns. The local inhabitants, who had given the students food, told them that the prisoners not only got nothing to eat but were even kept without water and as a result were dying off like flies.

On several occasions the group I belonged to, which was now called an NKVD Demolition Battalion, was driven outside the town in lorries in order to catch deserters and people trying to evade military service. We were issued with old 7.6 mm rifles, a number of rounds of ammunition, a couple of hand-grenades and gas-masks. I had already been taught how to handle all this equipment while I was at school. In the upper classes we had been taught a special subject which was called military drill and the teacher had been a military instructor (a reserve officer). I wasn't a bad shot and had been awarded the badge of 'Voroshilov marksman'. We caught and brought into the town about eight unshaven peasants, some of whom were wearing bits of military uniform. It was said that in our region alone about twenty-five thousand such people were in hiding. I don't know whether or not this was actually the case.

Late in the evening of the 28th June the German Air Force staged its first full-scale air raid on our town. Until then there had been only occasional flights by isolated aeroplanes, which had dropped a few small bombs, largely on the outskirts. In fact one of the bombs had fallen in the centre of the town in the Young Pioneers' Park. Several people had been killed and wounded. The evening and night of the 28th June turned out to be the beginning of the end of my home town. Planes flew over in waves, literally laying a carpet of bombs over huge areas. I spent the night in a basement with others who lived in our block of flats. It was a good basement, dry, clean and fairly solid. Whether or not it would withstand a direct hit from a heavy bomb was, I remember thinking, an altogether different question. All around frightened children were in tears and even the adults didn't seem any too cheerful. There were hardly any men, as most of them were either at work like my father or doing duty as civilian anti-aircraft defence wardens. As a matter of fact, the word defence seemed quite irrelevant as the Germans were behaving as if they were taking part in a fly past. There was hardly any anti-aircraft fire from our side. As I had heard from my father, the town had very few anti-aircraft guns and not many more fighter planes.

I began to feel an acute sense of shame that I, a healthy young fellow, was sitting there with the old men, women and children. At the same time I was gripped by a feeling of anger. I got up, and went upstairs and out into the main entrance. I opened the outside door. It was a glorious summer night, full of the scent of lime blossom and freshness. I took a look around. All I could see were flames and smoke. From the sky came a kind of sickeningly insistent whine which was getting nearer and nearer. It was the noise of an aeroplane, which turned into a terrifying howl. Quite close by, from the direction of the theatre, came the sound of a tremendous thud followed by an explosion and a huge burst of flame. . . . Some incredible force descended on me like a wave and hurled me back against the door. Then came another wild howl and another thud, this time slightly further away. So it continued for three hours or more. After that came the whining 'all-clear' of the siren, followed by fire-engine and ambulance bells. It seemed pointless, as there were so few of them and fires were everywhere. The scent of the lime trees had long disappeared, to be replaced by a smell of burning and another smell which I did not recognise. Then my father came. We were on our own, as my mother had for some time been staying with distant relatives in a town on the Volga.

From that night onwards one event followed another at a hectic pace, just like the frames of a cine film. In the morning our NKVD Demolition Battalion was ordered to report to barracks. The barracks were the deserted premises of the teacher-training college. The window-panes had been blown out by the bombing and some straw mattresses for us to sleep on had been hastily dumped on the floor. One of our boys had been put on sentry duty by the door. Everybody had plenty to do. Some were assigned to government and NKVD buildings for the urgent task of loading archives. Files of papers and steel boxes with wax seals were packed into large vans looking like boxes on wheels. They had the words 'Bread' and 'Meat' written on their sides and were sometimes even painted with pictures of loaves of bread and links of sausages. Inside them by the doors were Chekists with hand-grenades on their belts and armed with automatic rifles. Any remaining papers which were not secret were soaked with petrol and burned in the courtyard. There were so many fires in the town that one more would pass unnoticed. By this time the Germans were bombing in the daytime too. Other members of our battalion were drawn into operational NKVD subversive groups. They rushed about the town in cars, activating the mechanisms of the mines which had been laid earlier. Certain houses whose basements contained explosive charges were blown up by these groups there and then. Apparently the time had arrived.

I had one more fleeting meeting with my father. He told me quietly that the Germans had broken through the front and were expected in the town at any moment. I also learnt that the whole regional and municipal leadership was leaving (some had already left) for a small town in the far eastern corner of our region.

'You'd better try and find your own way there, too,' my father told me.

That was impossible. I did not intend to desert and felt unable to leave my battalion. My father realised this but nevertheless advised me to remember the name of the town and said that he would himself be there. Having first got my company officer's permission, I dashed home to change my clothes. The house was still intact, but the door had been blown out by bomb blast. There were cracks in the ceilings of our flat and dust, dirt and broken glass were everywhere. I pulled on a pair of dark blue (officer's) riding breeches, a field green (Commissar's) shirt and a pair of light canvas boots. I took my rifle in my hands, threw a gas-mask over my shoulder and attached a couple of hand-grenades to a broad belt of my father's. I glanced into my grandfather's empty room and took a last look at my ancient Royal Enfield bicycle which was standing in the corridor. I stopped by the gates to shake our ex-horse-guard caretaker firmly by the hand. His moustache drooped dolefully as he gazed with regret at the havoc and destruction wrought on the property which he had always kept in such good order. I dashed off to the college-turned-barracks, only just having time to leap aboard a lorry crowded with lads from my battalion.

The lorry was soon tearing along the road, not in an easterly direction, as I had expected, but towards the north-west. On the way I learnt that our battalion, with the help of other units, was supposed to drive back and then contain some German troops who had been dropped by parachute. By doing this we were supposed to ensure the safe departure from the town of the last motorised convoys carrying valuable state property. Our own order to withdraw we were to receive later by NKVD field communications. If these came at night they would be accompanied by the sending up of a special combination of coloured Very flares. We settled ourselves in trenches previously prepared by the civilian population.

'Well, there's one thing that's sure,' I thought to myself, 'we've got enough trenches to go around.' (As a matter of fact everybody in the town without other responsibilities had been mobilised to dig them.) High above us in the sky a German reconnaisance plane, known as a 'frame', was snooping about. Apart from that, for the time being everything was quiet. We ate some bread and sausage and had a smoke.

Behind me lay my home town from where I could hear the continuous sound of dull explosions. Clouds of smoke and fire hung over it. The stillness round about was disturbed by the noise of an approaching vehicle. Two officers leapt from it and ran up to our company commander. I heard the voice of the first of them say, 'What the bloody hell do you think you're doing? Having a party? Get moving quickly. . . . Go towards the racecourse, the Germans are concentrating in a ravine behind that wood. . . . The other companies are already on their way.'

Off we ran, spread out in a broad chain. We were soon in open ground with something whistling round us and throwing up little clouds of dust. I remembered the whistling sound from the military drill lessons at school. Bullets!

'On your faces,' yelled the section officer, who was running by my side, 'make for the wood in short spurts!'

There was a sound of something blowing up, then a whining howl as something flew over our heads.

'Mortars,' my neighbour said. 'Now we're for it.'

An explosion came from behind, then a whistling sound. Someone yelled in pain (I presume), trying to stifle the cry. Then another burst of fire. A young lad, running in the opposite direction collided with me. On the right someone bawled, 'Get a medical orderly.' I didn't know whether to run forward or back where I'd come from. Before I'd had time to think I heard a sharp authoritative voice from behind: 'Grenades ready. Make for the wood!' I saw that it was the same officer who had sworn at our company commander. He had spotted me too or, to be more accurate, he had spotted the mixture of officer's and commissar's clothing I was wearing. 'Get your section moving!' he ordered me. Where was our section officer then? the thought flashed through my mind. In a wild voice I bellowed, 'Follow me!'

Somehow I got to the wood. The others managed to throw their grenades, but I didn't. When I was already in the bushes I was pulled up short by the feeling of having something sharp, like needles, plunged into my left leg. It was just as if I had stepped into a burning camp-fire. I let the bushes take my weight and slid slowly down on to the ground. I did not lose consciousness. I remember someone binding my leg tightly at the knee with a tourniquet. Somehow or other, along with other wounded, I was dragged to a lorry. It was only when we had crossed the river and reached the field medical post that I had the first bandage put on. They made no effort to remove small shrapnel splinters, saying that that could be done when I arrived at my destination. This in fact was a long way off.

We travelled at first by remote roads through the forests (those same forests which had once delighted Peter the Great). People had stopped using the main roads which ran through open country, as German planes were already making sorties along them. I was then taken by hospital train to the little town of Morshansk, which is famous for its extremely strong makhorka,[1] and was now full of military hospitals, in one of which I landed. There doctors removed all the splinters from my leg, after first splashing on to it some foul-smelling liquid which was supposed to serve as an anaesthetic.

'You got off quite lightly. In a couple of weeks you'll be dancing again,' a middle-aged doctor remarked.

Life in the military hospital was solid boredom, with no distractions whatsoever. At that stage there wasn't even a library. When I was no longer troubled by pain from my leg I began to wander about the hospital limping slightly, on the look-out for entertainment. Alas, I found none. The medical personnel were largely elderly ladies who

[1] A coarse Russian tobacco produced from the stalks of the tobacco plant.

had been hastily dressed up in military uniform. They all seemed exhausted and overwhelmed. Of course, there was more than enough work to go round. The hospital was bursting at the seams. Some of the wounded were even sleeping in threes on two beds that had been moved together. Bandages were changed by a fairly young nurse whose face and 'property' were quite reasonable. As she was putting on the bandages she would enquire sweetly whether or not it hurt. My mind being elsewhere I muttered quite automatically, 'At first it hurts, then it's nice.'

'How can something like this be nice?' she remarked with genuine surprise.

'Well, of course, if it hadn't been for the wound I would never have met you.' But that was as far as it went. She had no time for things like that.

While I was in hospital, I wrote to my father in the town he had mentioned to me at our last meeting. I simply addressed it to Comrade Romanov, Regional Defence Committee. I gave the address of the hospital, or rather its field post number (they had no addresses as these were regarded as military secrets). For some time there was no answer. When the scabs on my wounds (or, to be more accurate cuts) had dried and begun to heal, I was put into a team of convalescents attached to the hospital. Life was dull here too. We convalescents were sent to the kitchens to peel potatoes for the hospital, which, of course, I had no idea how to do. The rest of the time we played cards and chess, which I did know how to do, as my father had taught me when I was still in the junior classes at school. The hospital barber introduced a little variety and excitement. Actually, it wasn't he who did this because he had disappeared into thin air, but his disappearance gave rise to certain events. It transpired that he had been the resident officer of German intelligence in that area.

Whether this was true I can't say, but the whole affair created a huge commotion. A group of counter-intelligence officers from the Special Branch of the NKVD descended upon us. They and the hospital's Special Branch representative summoned many of the wounded for questioning. They were attempting to collect more information about the disappearing barber, who as a matter of fact was never found. The wounded were divided in their opinions. Some said that the barber would have been as much use for spying as a prick for knocking in nails. Others asserted that he maintained radio contact with Berlin itself.

One day the officer in charge of the convalescent team sent for me.

It turned out that papers had arrived ordering me to report for duty at the Molotov Gunnery School in Gorky (MGSG). It was not difficult to work out that this was my father's handiwork.

'But why on earth has he had me posted to the artillery,' I thought indignantly. 'What kind of a gunner does he think I'll make, let alone anti-aircraft gunner? Now if it were the anti-tank artillery where one could talk about "blasting the tanks from point-blank range" it wouldn't be quite so bad. I bet everybody in the anti-aircraft forces wears spectacles. I shall be a complete laughing stock.'

This is what I said to the officer in charge of the convalescent team. But it was his turn to be indignant.

'Where the hell do you think you are? In a brothel? You get a posting issued by the Main Artillery Administration of the Red Army to one of our best schools and you, if you please, aren't happy about it. You're completely undisciplined. Tomorrow you go, and that's all there is to it.'

In the office of the Gorky Town Commandant I learnt the address of the school and dejectedly wandered off there. I had to spend a brief period in quarantine and pass two reception commissions: one medical and the other to check my credentials. The medical side presented no problems, as my leg had healed. When I appeared before the credentials commission I had to stand at a long table, give a curriculum vitae and answer the various questions of members of the commission. There were five or six officers, including the head of the school and his deputy. None of them held a rank lower than major. Everything went very smoothly for me and I felt sure that I was helped both by my father's position and by the recommendation of the Main Artillery Administration (one was connected with the other). An artillery major who was sitting at the end of the table listened with interest to the answers concerning my service in the NKVD battalion, though, of course, I was not able to go into details. I saw that he was making certain notes on a pad which lay in front of him, but was not himself asking any questions. At that time I paid no particular attention to that major, which is a great pity.

I was accepted for the school and assigned first to an artillery *divizion* (equal to a battalion in Soviet artillery), then to a battery and finally to a section. The next morning (too early in my opinion) I heard the sound of a bugle. 'Rise and shine,' shouted the duty sergeant, and ripped the blankets off everyone who like myself appeared to be fond of his bed. We kept to a very strict time-table with a very limited time for each job. The battery sergeant-major eyed his watch and with a slightly ironic smirk watched me trying to pull my left boot on to my right foot. 'Ready for PT. Shirts off. At the double,' he shouted. Cursing furiously to myself, I tore off my shirt, which had been so difficulty to get on. Then came breakfast (to my mind there wasn't enough of it), political studies and then either classroom work or instruction on the artillery range. So it went on day after day. I began to wonder what kind of a good turn my father thought he had done me. One consolation was that in view of the war the period of training had been reduced from two years to one. Even so, it was far and away enough for me. The other cadets were decent lads. One made acquaintances and later became friends. I got a letter from my father saying how pleased he was that I was at that particular school and hoping that I was making good progress.

There was very little to amuse one in the school. We weren't often allowed to go in to the town and I, who even at school had not cared for mathematics, had to work very hard indeed. Books were my only pleasure. The school had a good library and the librarian, who was the wife of the colonel in charge of the school, was an attractive woman of ample proportions (rather too ample for my taste). Even so, and I recalled an utterance of Yoska's, 'Whatever God sends'. It was, of course, a strictly one-sided platonic relationship. Moreover there was that absurd incident with Alexei Tolstoy's novel *Bread*. It was a well-illustrated book. Someone who had read it had appended to the illustrations various vulgar details and poses. I had already realised by then that a book is a thing of value which no self-respecting person will deface. My name was, however, on the list of those who had borrowed the book. We were summoned one by one to the Battery's Deputy Political Officer. He pointed his finger at the defaced illustration and asked me who had done it.

'But that's a real gift!' I cried. 'Now if I had a gift like that I wouldn't be in this school.' The Deputy Political Officer was not particularly bright, so I burbled on in the same inspired vein. 'Yes, somebody with a gift like that. What he could do for the State! . . .' Even today I have no idea exactly what he could have done for the State, but at least I was able to get away unscathed.

Rumours ran round the school that soon a special team of cadets would be sent into the forest to prepare supplies of firewood for the winter. In peacetime, of course, this could never have happened. Now there was a war on anything could happen. People said that all the novices and new arrivals in the school, i.e. people like myself, would land up in this team. That was all I needed. I'm very fond of the forest, but wielding an axe or a saw mars my enjoyment. However, fate herself saved me from the forest. She came to the lesson in the form of a messenger from school HQ.

As we made our way to the headquarters together he told me that I had been called to see Major Krylov.

'Krylov, who's he then?' I asked, my interest aroused.

'Well, he's from that er . . . that . . . from Smerch,'[1] said the messenger, pronouncing this word which was new to me, rather uncertainly.

I went in and reported to the major.

'Well,' said the man in the artillery major's uniform with a grin, 'strictly speaking, I'm not a major at all. It's just a rank I use. I'm the representative of a branch of counter-intelligence called Smersh. But you should know your way round our organisation!'

'Yes, Comrade First Lieutenant of the State Security Service.'

'Excellent, excellent.' He then continued with mild reproach that with my particular experience I should have thought it necessary to request a re-transfer to an NKVD unit. 'It doesn't matter, however,' he said, 'everything's been arranged and decided. You are to leave immediately for one of our schools. I congratulate you on the trust you have inspired and believe that you will justify it. Here are your travel documents.'

It didn't even enter my head to argue or object. In the first place such a change suited me well enough at that time. I was like a fish out of water in the artillery. And secondly my bitter experience of arguing with authority in the convalescent team had been very salutary. But the main thing was that I realised that there was rather an important difference between a convalescent team and the NKVD.

[1] This mistake is not without irony, as in Russian *smerch* means a tornado or whirlwind.

2

THINGS JUST COULDN'T HAVE turned out better. I had a travel warrant in my pocket which said that I, Cadet Romanov, had been withdrawn from the school and handed over to 'us', in accordance with the instructions he had been given. At the very top of the warrant it said 'NKVD of the USSR' and, just below, 'Main Administration of the State Security'. Of course, this would be far more interesting than preparing firewood or attending classes in gunnery. After all, I had a certain amount of useful experience, since I had already served in an NKVD demolition battalion. We used to lay charges of dynamite in the basements of houses, take part in rounding up subversive elements, get involved in exchanges of gunfire. And I also had a wound to my credit. But what would my father think of my being transferred to the NKVD? He had insisted that I enter a gunnery school after I came out of hospital—an anti-aircraft gunnery school, in fact, so as to become an officer in that particular branch of the armed forces. 'After all,' he had said, 'you'll have a better chance of staying alive there than anywhere and you're all I've got.' Later, when we said goodbye, my father took me on one side and whispered hurriedly: 'Never tell anyone that you've had anything to do with the NKVD or that you've served in a demolition battalion and, above all, son, always tell people that your father is just an ordinary teacher.' After looking round he added in an even quieter voice, 'Anything can happen. In a short time things may change completely, then you must tell "them" all of this. Do you follow me?' my father asked.

My poor father was afraid for me, of course. He thought I might fall into German hands and so had sent me deep into the home front, to Gorky. What on earth would he say now when he found out that I was coming back towards Moscow, to enter a special State Security Service school? A man in the uniform of a major in the artillery, who introduced himself as First Lieutenant of the State Security Service Krylov, said, as he handed me my orders to go to Moscow, 'You were hankering after the front. Well, you're now going to the most important and difficult sector!' It would be great to get into field intelligence. I might even be parachuted behind the German lines. Wonderful. I was just nineteen. The Germans had surrounded Leningrad, fighting was going on in the approaches to Stalingrad and they weren't all that far from Moscow either . . . they were penetrating deeper and deeper into my country.

Between ten and eleven kilometres north-east of Moscow there is a station called Losinoostrovskaya near the town of Babushkin. Just beside the main highway, in the forest, there is a group of houses, an open clearing and beyond it storehouses and garages. Even before the war all this already belonged to the NKVD. It now housed the special school of the State Security Service.

My induction into this school did not take long. My 'personal file', with all the forms I had filled in, about 240 questions in all, together with my signed declaration that I would not publicise any secrets of the NKVD system I might learn, arrived at the school before I did. First I went to the bath house and then had my uniform issued—there were riding breeches and a tunic, both well cut, as for an officer, but with the field-green colour facings of a private soldier, and leather substitute boots. Headgear was a peaked cap with an army star on it, nothing in any way linking me with the NKVD. It was a little odd that the greatcoat also looked like an officer's. Well, all sorts of things happen in wartime and who would bother to sort it all out anyway?

This school, like any normal school for army infantry officers, was divided up into companies. The sergeant-major in charge of my company was a small, strongly built Ukrainian, a career soldier from the NKVD internal troops who had volunteered for extra service. He didn't like the look of me at all. 'You look like an old gelding. Seeing you in riding breeches reminds me of a dog in pantaloons—and in that peaked cap you look like a turkey with a hat on!' He made lots of other remarks which did nothing for my self-esteem. 'Who on earth's been filling your head with that nonsense?' he grumbled. 'Well, never mind,' he said, at the end of our first talk, 'after a month in my hands you'll be a real fully fledged Chekist.' I thought of my battery sergeant-major in Gorky—the kindest and gentlest of men, an angel in comparison with this sergeant-major.

Then came a summons to the chief of the school. At the table sat a tall man with the tired face of an intellectual, not in the least like a soldier. On the field-green colour facings of his tunic there were three red metal bars.

'Comrade Captain of the State Security, Cadet Romanov reporting his arrival and readiness for further duties.' The talk was like an interrogation. The head of the school wanted to know all about me, although he had in front of him both the papers I had filled in in my home town when I joined the demolition battalion and those I had completed in Gorky in order to enter the school itself. He wanted to know who my parents were and my other relations, the details of my school career, which were my favourite subjects and the ones I didn't like, had I taken an interest in drama, how was my wounded leg, which sports did I take part in? The questions came in a steady flow. When I'd given an account of the trip my late grandfather made to England I had to explain why I preferred Mark Twain to Bernard Kellerman.

Quite unexpectedly, we came to my difficulties in German grammar. 'There's no need to be modest,' said the captain, 'although modesty does you credit.' When it comes to damn German grammar I'd nothing to be modest about. But it was all my own fault; I was to blame for the way I fooled around in German lessons.

'Here's where I reap my reward,' I thought. My poor knowledge of German could prevent my being dropped behind the German lines. That poor German teacher in my ten-year school! What a fight she had trying to pass her knowledge on to me! And as for my own contribution—I recalled my *tour de force*, after which Elizaveta Mikhailovna had washed her hands of me. That straight-laced old maid put her whole heart into her teaching. Once, when I was in the ninth form, my best friend, Yoska, and I had spent the whole evening at the ice rink instead of doing any homework. The first lesson next morning was German. Elizaveta Mikhailovna began to question our class on the previous evening's homework. When she got to Yoska he nudged me and whispered, 'Go ahead, I saved your skin last time.' I put up my hand. 'Yes, Romanov, what do you want?' the teacher asked. 'Elizaveta Mikhailovna, what's a pederast? I'm not quite sure,' I barked out at the top of my voice so that the whole class could hear. The teacher's face became very red. 'Ask the doctor,' she replied. The class reacted very quickly, with giggles from the girls and guffaws from the boys. Yoska squealed like a stuck pig: 'I can't stand any more,' he simpered. 'I'm a decent, honest girl and I'm not used to such language. I feel ill. Bring me some water, please!' There was no more lesson after that. No, Comrade Captain of the State Security Service, there's no question of my being modest, my German is really nothing to write home about.

The captain consoled me by saying that I could be useful and become a good officer of the State Security Service even without a knowledge of German. 'I'll sign your access permit,' he said.

The system of access permits is complex and has many forms. One needs a permit for access to work in laboratories where secret work is being done, to factories working on military contracts, archives containing secret material and so forth. 'This document I have signed,' he went on, 'states that A. I. Romanov through the nature of his work has access to decrees, orders and instructions of state and party bodies (organs), scholastic and other materials, belonging in accordance with decision of the CCACP(b) and the CPC of the USSR[1] dated so and so to such and such categories, in order to acquaint himself with their contents.' There followed figures and letters, whose meaning was at that time incomprehensible to me. In the top right-hand corner of the sheet there was a note: 'Access permit requested by Captain of the State Security, Shafirov'. In the left-hand corner it said 'Approved' Head of the Main Administration of the State Security, Commissar of State Security first rank, Merkulov. The chief of the school handed me yet another piece of paper. 'Read this very carefully and sign it,' he said. It was a resolution of the Politbureau, top secret and on no account to be released, relating to the classification of secret documents and the responsibilities of persons handling them.

I can't recall all the points of this resolution, which was printed on extremely thin paper like cigarette paper. But the gist of it was as follows: If I am handed a secret document, I must sign for it in a special book, giving date and time of day, in the presence of the person responsible for the safekeeping of such documents. I must not allow this document to be out of my sight even for a moment, must not put it in my pocket, on a table or in my brief-case, must not make a copy of it or write down any extracts from it, nor discuss its contents with anyone at all. After reading it, or, as they used to say in the NKVD, absorbing it, I had to hand it back personally to the man who had issued it. He was then obliged, in my presence, to make an entry in the same special book to the effect that on such and such a date, at such and such a time, he had accepted the document from me. He then had to sign this entry and stamp it with an official stamp. At the end of the Politbureau resolution it was stated that any indivi-

[1] Central Committee of the All-Union Communist Party (Bolshevist) as it was then. The Council of People's Commissars of the Union of Soviet Socialist Republics.

dual guilty of the slightest infringement of these rules would be liable to the most severe punishment, including the death penalty. Then came the signatures of Stalin and Molotov. Beneath these names I wrote, 'Contents noted by me', followed by my own signature and the date. The chief of the school put the paper in my personal file, closed it and placed the folder in a large steel cabinet. The key disappeared into his pocket. For a brief moment I remembered the artillery range in Gorky and even the topography lessons with longing and regret. 'That is all,' said the State Security Service captain. 'You may go. I wish you success.'

During my first night in the NKVD school in Babushkin I spent a lot of time thinking about the papers I had signed that evening, particularly about the last one which had Stalin's signature on it. All the events of my life hitherto, my service in the NKVD demolition battalion and the paper I had signed undertaking not to divulge any battalion secrets, now seemed like a joke or a children's game. One thing at least was clear: I should have to keep a very close watch on myself and keep my mouth tightly shut all the time, everywhere and in all kinds of company. If I didn't, I could expect short shrift from the authorities.

'How does one tell what is secret and what isn't? How best keep a secret so as not to get into trouble?' exclaimed our instructor at a special subject lesson on the following day. He went straight on to answer his own question. 'I trust that you all read our newspapers, magazines and books regularly. Well, everything that's printed there is for the masses and for general consumption, and it isn't secret. All that you will learn in the course of your studies and your service, none of which you will ever find in any of our magazines or books, is totally secret. Consequently, in your dealings with the masses, you must always, in any speeches, conversations, talks, confine yourself to exactly what is in the press—in our newspapers and journals. This is the only way,' our instructor concluded, 'that you can safeguard yourself from all kinds of unpleasantness.' This was my first encounter with this instructor—the man who taught us special subject No. 1 —dealing with the rights and obligations of the State Security bodies of the Soviet Union. The instructor was a middle-aged man, or so he then seemed to me, with greying fair hair, and he was known as 'Lord' among the cadets. He had come by this nickname because of his impeccably straight parting, and also because his suits were magnificently pressed the whole year round. From the very first lesson I was terrified about 'Lord'. For many of his remarks he could easily have been prosecuted at least on the basis of a series of sections of article 58[1] of the Criminal Code for counter-revolutionary agitation and propaganda.

'Lord' upset all our time-honoured ideas about the Soviet press, for which he hadn't the slightest respect, and about the Party and the government, which I had always thought never concealed from the people even the very worst items of news. I gradually got used to this kind of conversation and became convinced that neither 'Lord' nor the other teachers were trying to be provocative but were simply communicating facts to us which would be essential in the work we would have to do.

In many respects the school's daily time-table reminded me of the one in the Gorky gunnery school. Much to my annoyance, here too a bugler sounded the reveille, here too a sergeant-major chased us out for a physical training session for which, winter or summer and whatever the temperature, we had to strip to the waist. In many other respects the NKVD school was vastly different from the army school. The first time I had breakfast I could not believe my eyes when I saw the huge plates of bread, ready sliced, on the tables. Each cadet took as much bread as he could eat and there was no hint of any rationing! Bread had been strictly rationed both in the army hospital and in the gunnery school. I can't claim that I went hungry in either of these places, for on the whole we weren't fed too badly, but I was always dreaming of food, particularly in Gorky. My friends from among the cadets consoled both themselves and me by quoting a remark of Voroshilov's: 'A cadet is made up of bone, sinew and muscle.' The quotation didn't seem to help much.

In the NKVD school I soon stopped thinking of food. In hospital we were given People's Commissariat of Defence ration No. 10 and in the anti-aircraft artillery No. 9 (a special ration for cadets). Here in the NKVD we received special internal rations which had neither name nor number.

After the first breakfast I disgraced myself somewhat. Seeing the unbelievable abundance of the dining-room, I threw myself upon the food and gorged until I was fit to burst. The first lesson after breakfast was political affairs. The huge quantity of food had made me drowsy and as I listened to the monotonous voice of the platoon commander, who was taking the period, I began to doze off. Nothing dreadful happened, but I was politely roused by my neighbour saying, 'Wake up, he's almost finished.'

[1] Article 58 of the Criminal Code of the RSFSR (as it was then).

During the whole of my time at the NKVD school I don't recall a single occasion when the political affairs period lasted for more than ten or fifteen minutes. They used to read out to us the Soviet Information Bureau communiqué concerning actions in the various theatres of the war, after which first the *partorg*,[1] then the *komsorg*,[1] announced forthcoming Party and Komsomol meetings. At these meetings either new candidate members of the Party were received from the Komsomol or candidate-members of the Party were received into full membership. We all already belonged either to the Komsomol or to the Party, and indeed people without such affiliations are not considered for work in the field of State Security. Moreover, in the NKVD school political affairs had no special importance. Even in the ten-year school far more time was devoted to the subject. At the beginning of the course I was amazed by this discovery, but I gradually realised that it was no malicious omission on the part of an individual, but a well-conceived practical plan. Really, what was the point of wasting time, which was short anyway, on long talks about successes in the fields of the collective farms or the factories, or even about the splendour of Marxism-Leninism, when in all the special subject lessons we were taught hard facts about the essential nature of both the Soviet State and communism, about difficulties and mistakes and plans for the future, in any case without any dull, long-winded routine propaganda.

At a lesson in special subject No. 1 the instructor 'Lord' was listening hard to how a cadet answered a question which he had just put to him. The cadet, who, like myself, had arrived at the school not long before, wast alking about the official links between State Security bodies and the regional party committees. His speech was peppered with such expressions as 'Thanks to the wise leadership of our father and teacher the great Stalin,' or, 'Our field HQ is Stalin's Central Committee'. As usual, long-suffering 'Lord' began by drumming with his fingers on the table, then he started to put in remarks like 'Make it brief', 'Stick to the point' and finally 'This isn't a collective farm meeting'.

After the end of the lesson, when the instructor had left the room, the platoon commander made us all stay behind and turning to this particular cadet said, 'Now tell me whom do you think is the bigger fool, yourself or our instructor?'

'I can't see the point of this question,' said the cadet, his eyes goggling.

[1] *Partorg* and *komsorg*; the Party organiser and Komsomol organiser who headed the school and company committees.

'I'll explain,' the commander went on. 'Of course, it's a very good thing that you are absolutely devoted to Comrade Stalin and that you trust in the leadership of our Party, but if that weren't the case you wouldn't have been sent to this school in the first place. Do you really think that our instructor, a tried and tested Chekist, trusts in Stalin and our Party any less than you do? To answer as you did, even if we discount the valuable time you wasted, means that you regard him as an utter fool. Who are you grovelling before? Before your own brother Chekists. We need deeds not words. All we want from you for the time being is that you should study well. Do you understand now?'

'Understood, Comrade Second Lieutenant of the State Security,' answered the cadet, by now as red as a beetroot.

The vast majority of our cadets were sensible people, not badly educated and well read. There were a lot of young people of my own age, but there were also some who were already over twenty-five. In my company, as well as Russians, there were a lot of Ukrainians, Byelorussians, several Jews, a Latvian who spoke fluent German and three or four inhabitants of Central Asia—I think they were either Uzbeks or Kazakhs. I later found out that Hitler, and Himmler especially, valued these nationalities very highly. They recruited from them the 'National Committees' and the Moslem units within the SS, in the hope of breaking the Soviet Union up into a series of separate states. I know that one of my fellow cadets, an Uzbek, contrived to get into one of these committees in Berlin. For his 'service' he was awarded the Order of the Military Red Banner.[1]

Special subject No. 2, namely 'The organisation and activities of foreign intelligence services', was taught by a short, nondescript, youngish man, who held the high rank of a major in the State Security Service (equal to the rank of major-general in the army). Among ourselves, we cadets referred to him as 'Tapeworm', because he was very quiet and seemed to glide about the place noiselessly. Special subject No. 2 was split into two parts: the special services of Germany and her allies, and the special services of other countries. In the second part we studied only England, the United States of America and France. Before my arrival at the school there had been a few changes made in its academic programme. Previously its main aim had been the training of State Security Service officers for underground work on those Soviet territories which had been seized by the Germans and in Germany itself.

[1] A high Soviet military decoration. There also exists a comparable civil decoration called the Order of the Red Banner of Labour.

It was thought that the Germans would get at least as far as the Volga along the whole length of the front and possibly even further. Tens of thousands of Chekists, as I learned later, were supposed to penetrate all sectors of the German military and police administration; some as elders appointed by the Germans in rural areas, burgomeisters, policemen, interpreters; others as volunteers for the German army; others again into the camps of Soviet prisoners of war and *ostarbeiters*. They all had similar jobs. They were supposed to eliminate, if possible with German hands, but if all else failed with their own, any Soviet people who really had gone over to the Germans and were serving them faithfully; to sabotage and paralyse German activity, both at the front and behind the lines, and also to form groups of partisans; to provoke the Germans to commit still greater atrocities against the civilian population and conversely, at the same time, increase the number of partisans. These jobs still held good during my training, but they were already then oriented towards a movement to the west rather than to the east. It was already becoming clear that the Germans were no longer capable of mass attacks on a wide front.

As before, the German special services (intelligence and counter-intelligence) took up most of the time during the periods of special subject No. 2. England and the United States were allotted more time during my second year at the school of the State Security Service. 'Tapeworm' had undoubtedly visited all of these countries. He was quite at home talking about England and Germany. During the lessons he constantly flavoured his discourse with typical English and German proverbs, aphorisms and jokes, providing an immediate translation into Russian.

He considered that the single-mindedness of its ends—world domination and annihiliation of all dissent—was one of the strongest and most admirable features of the German service. 'That's good,' he said. 'Short and succinct, just like we are!' I was no longer put out by such a blasphemous comparison between Hitler's and our own Soviet regimé. 'The total absence of any liberal-democratic ethics,' 'Tapeworm' continued, 'is also a good thing and one of the Germans' strong points.' He then went on to talk about the weaknesses of the German special services. He criticised their total racial arrogance, their depressing stupidity, their self-satisfaction, their absurd concern with punctuality and their inability to improvise. He told us that German counter-intelligence was quite effective when dealing with Germans or the agents of another capitalist country.

It was during these lessons I learned that even before the war the

Germans had tried to copy the methods of our State Security bodies.
They had built an official system of political police into all spheres of
the German state, into the economy, education and even into religion,
in the same way that we had. However, as our instructor went on, it
hadn't really done them much good, nor could one expect that it
would, since although Hitler and many of his Party colleagues were
undoubtedly revolutionaries, they could not altogether free themselves from capitalist tenets and prejudices—they lacked the necessary
imagination and ability. From among Germany's allies our instructor
always paid particular attention to the Hungarian special services,
especially the Hungarian counter-intelligence service *Kemelharito*.
'They don't work at all badly,' he said. 'They have a useful combination of experience going back a long way, and a sense of purpose.
But,' he emphasised, 'the Hungarians cause themselves a great deal
of harm by the narrowness of their world view; healthy single-
mindedness degenerates into backwoods nationalism. They can't
abide either the Roumanians or the Slovaks. They loathe us, not only
because we are communists, but because we are Russians. In a word,
they sink in a welter of trivialities.'

During lessons in special subject No. 2 a great number of charts
showing detailed schemes of the organisation of the German and
other security services, with illustrations of the different kinds of
shoulder boards and colour facings they all wore, were hung on the
classroom walls. The instructor would run his pointer over these
charts, explaining the meaning of all the various markings and suggest-
ing that we commit them to memory. The markings of Roumanian
and Hungarian officers struck me as particularly handsome and impressive. Something happened, however, which cut my admiration
short. Our school was paid frequent visits by high-ranking officers,
sometimes wearing civilian clothes, sometimes in uniform. In their
presence our instructors stood respectfully to attention. Our guests
took an interest in everything, our successes (or failures) in our
studies, academic planning and many other things. I didn't, of course,
know any of their names then. Occasionally there would be a respectful whisper from some 'know-all' among the cadets: 'That's Fedotov,[1]' or some other name. During one lesson, when we were right
in the middle of learning all about Roumanian insignia, three men
entered the classroom. 'Tapeworm' leaped up as if he had had an
electric shock, bellowed 'Attention!' at us, and stepped smartly up to

[1] Commissar of State Security, 2nd rank. Subsequently a lieutenant-
general and head of the Secret Political Administration of State Security.

the first man who had entered the room. He began his report 'Comrade Commissar General of State Security'. The only man who had that title was Beria—Stalin's closest friend, a candidate member of the Politbureau, a member of the State Committee for Defence, and the People's Commissar for Internal Affairs. He was wearing a dark suit and his hair, which was receding on the forehead and the temples, was combed back. His eyes, behind the sparkling glass of his pince-nez, were attentive and rather sad. An inappropriate thought that he reminded me of someone I knew crept into my mind as I stood there at attention among the other cadets. Later that evening I realised with horror that Beria reminded me of a real childhood friend of mine, a Jewish paediatrician called Kapelson. He was also a bit like the misguided Trotskyist intellectual from a popular film called *The Great Citizen*. He greeted us, 'How do you do, Chekist cadets,' to which we answered, 'We wish you well, Comrade Commissar General.' Beria looked round the classroom alertly, pausing at the charts on the walls. 'What's this, a veteran's evening of reminiscences,' he said, nodding at the wall charts. He then continued, turning to the chief of our school, 'Do you really need all these?' Pointing in our direction, he added, 'And see that they get a bit more fresh air.' That was the end of this particular visit.

Beside Beria had been standing a man with an athletic figure and a splendid head of thick dark hair flecked with grey. On his colour facings there were four rhombuses and a small star. This was Merkulov, my future boss, first People's Commissar and then Minister. At this stage he was Beria's first deputy in the NKVD and head of the main administration of State Security. Throughout the whole visit he hadn't uttered a single word. The only man to match his silence was the school's chief, who was accompanying the important visitors.

This visit had two results which affected me directly. The first was that the wall charts with the handsome Roumanian and Hungarian insignia disappeared from the walls of our classroom. The German ones stayed and I learned them off pat. I can even remember them today. The second thing was that more time was found for our evening walks. The existence of the latter, despite their pleasant title, doesn't in any sense mean that we had a quiet stroll swapping jokes, or even a little female company before lights out. A sergeant-major presided over our evening walks, the very same who at our first meeting had promised to turn me from an old gelding into a fully fledged Chekist. Having formed us up, the sergeant-major drove us for long marches over the fields near Moscow, demanding a very high standard of marching. Even during very hard frosts overcoats were forbidden. 'Singing commence!' yelled the sergeant-major. The right-hand man in the front rank began to sing a song known only in NKVD circles, which was then taken up by the rest:

> The sentry has given the alarm, for the foe is at the gate.
> But we Chekists are ready for the fray, when Stalin leads us forth.
> Stalin our father and leader guides us with a wise hand
> To the place where people and party fight their last fight with the foe!

During lessons in special subject No. 2 we managed without the wall charts when we were studying the special services of Great Britain and the United States. We had illustrations of the military ranks of these countries in a reference book, together with the other teaching materials in a room with steel cabinets called the study. All this could be obtained there, from the officer on duty, if one signed for it and it had to be read on the spot. It was expressly forbidden to take anything out of the study.

The instructors of the basic subjects on the course were very busy people. They left the school immediately the lesson was over. I am sure that they had other duties. Perhaps these other duties were their main job or perhaps they just went to other identical schools and taught the same lessons there. Sometimes they would simply miss a lesson and be replaced by another instructor.

'Tapeworm' was often replaced in special subject No. 2 lessons by another instructor, who, because of his exceptional kindness, was loved by all the cadets. This instructor and another officer shared the teaching of 'operational work' which was special subject No. 3. He was stout, with quite a paunch and his large bald pate was fringed by a little ring of hair. His small nose was rather like a duck's beak and little sleepy eyes gleamed from behind his spectacles. If I hadn't known, I would never have believed that he had two high decorations for distinguished service and the Chekist's Badge of Merit. Friends of mine among the cadets said that this instructor had often been to England and the Far East to carry out extremely delicate operations. When he replaced 'Tapeworm' he used to read us lectures about the British special services. 'One can't discuss the British special services without knowing something about the character of England itself,' he said, having first sunk himself cosily into an armchair, folded his hands across his stomach and closed his eyes. 'You see, all the contrasts and contradictions of any capitalist country are mirrored in the workings of its intelligence service. However good such an intelligence service might be, no matter how strong or active it is, its members can never free themselves from the social, economic and educational traditions they have known all their lives and which go on holding them in a death grip. Only we, the Bolshevik-communists, tempered in the school of Lenin and Stalin, have discovered how to set men free from this harmful and dangerous chimera. Soviet Chekists are the finest representatives of this new, free type of man. This is why it is easier for us to work and get the results we need. I have given you this long preamble,' the instructor said, opening his eyes, 'because I was thinking particularly of England. There are as many traditions crammed into England as there is stuffing in a pickled pike. As for the British intelligence service, in my opinion it's the best in the capitalist world. As the saying goes, the best of a bad lot.'

He then proceeded to list the positive features of the British special services; their great practical experience on a world-wide scale, their sound financial backing, the high average educational level of their members, their ability to keep a cool head and their loyalty to the Crown and to the interests of their own class. But he thought their lack of technical and operational training was a weakness. 'Too much dilettantism,' he declared. Another weakness was the Englishman's belief that England was the greatest nation in the world. 'They are resting on the laurels of their former glory,' was his comment. He admitted, of course, that, unlike the idiot Germans, the British did not proclaim their superiority on every street corner, but tended rather to have a silent faith in it. 'That's probably even worse,' our teacher observed. 'Moreover, like the Germans, they don't understand, and don't seem capable of understanding, either our system or our true aims. The British ruling circles seem still to think that they are dealing with a Russian government like the old Czarist government. They still believe in the Russian threat to India and similar inanities. We'll not disabuse them. It's very useful to us now. All this, and the many traditions which I mentioned at the beginning of the lecture, hamper their intelligence personnel.' I remember thinking how much I would have liked my late grandfather, an ardent admirer of England and the British, to have been beside me during that lesson. Of course, he hadn't been an intelligence agent, but he had been a respectable, scrupulously honest man who had seen a great deal in his time. The main thing was that knowing him as I did, I could have wholly trusted his judgement. At this point I became absorbed with thoughts of my own and remembered nothing of what the instructor said right up to the end of the lesson.

The lesson on the American special services was taken by 'Tapeworm', who reappeared in the school after a long interval. 'I must say,' he began, 'that when we discuss the American intelligence service we should mentally put the term "intelligence service" in inverted commas, because, in my humble opinion, this term cannot by any stretch of the imagination be used seriously to describe what exists in the USA. This means not only by our standards but by British standards too for that matter. Of course, they have organisations capable of running to earth and catching groups of gangsters who are fighting among themselves, or of putting a bullet through the balls of some pocket-sized Mexican or Cuban dictator, whereas I have in mind real political intelligence. Let us not, however, criticise the Americans too severely because they haven't yet managed to set up a respectable intelligence service but rather try to assess America's potential from the point of view of setting up such an organisation. In her favour she has the absence of narrow self-satisfaction and smugness, in so far as all the nations we find in the United States, if we discount the Negroes and the Red Indians, are on an equal footing.

'Another good thing from their point of view, if only they can lay their hands on some good teachers, is the fact that young Americans are very keen to learn and receptive to anything new. But they have no political experience at all, and their whole view of politics as a cheap fairground weakens them considerably. They have no unifying ideology, and each individual American's ideal seems to be to make as much money as he can for himself.' Our instructor observed in passing that this held good for the whole of the capitalist world, but unfortunately in his view for the Americans, the pursuit of money in the USA was particularly stark and hideous. 'But that,' he concluded, 'is the guarantee of the ultimate downfall of the capitalist world, since the never-ending pursuit of money turns man into a dull, stupid animal capable of neither serious thought nor political struggle, especially in dealing with a political system like ours. Remember all this, as we shall have to deal with America after the collapse of the old capitalist countries.'

Throughout the whole period of my studies in the NKVD school I never once heard our teachers refer to the British or the Americans as allies. In the press, for mass consumption, in our leaders' public speeches, they were referred to as 'our valiant western allies' or 'the Anglo-American allies', in army circles 'our allies', in better-informed circles, with ironic mockery, 'our worthy allies'. The Chekists themselves just called them 'the English and the Americans' or simply 'the western capitalists' as they called the Germans either 'Germans' or 'German fascists'. I ought to add that this was said without any hatred towards the British, the American, or for that matter the German nation. A Chekist's hatred was directed exclusively against the social systems to which these nations belonged. This was fully in keeping with the instruction I received in the State Security Service school. In the lessons on the rights and duties of State Security bodies 'Lord' repeated over and over again that our basic task was to fight to eliminate anything which came into being or was in existence and which was contrary to the will of our Party. 'Everything,' 'Lord' said on one occasion, without a trace of a smile, 'belongs to this category; from the Boy Scouts, all political parties, the British Empire, the Roman Catholic Church, the American trades unions to a Russian religious sect called the Shakers and their like.'

A cadet raised his hand and said, 'I have a question.'

'Very well,' said 'Lord'.

'Where do the foreign communist parties fit in?'

'That's very straightforward,' 'Lord' replied. 'If they come into being through our Party's good offices, then long may they live, but of course, we have to have certain permanent contacts with them for purposes of control and giving instructions. If such a party appears spontaneously, then we attempt to subject it to the will of our Party. If this proves impossible, then we fight it. There are various ways of fighting; schisms, arranging to compromise the elements in it which don't suit us. In the last resort, we can use physical means. After all, these parties don't exist in a vacuum, but in some country or other. Well, we can usually arrange that the government of the country in question will take the steps we feel should be taken.'

'Lord' explained that when he spoke of fighting he was not urging us physically to exterminate either Boy Scouts, let's say, or even all priests of the Roman Catholic Church. On the contrary, we were even ready to help them in their work by guiding them along a path that suited us. If this proved to be too difficult, there was no reason for being discouraged. There were plenty of other ways! As I learned later, there were indeed plenty of other ways all involving the exploitation of human weaknesses; stupidity, greed, failure to grasp the real situation, thirst for respect or the outward appearance of power.

The spring of 1943 brought much news and many changes. The Germans were finding it quite impossible to get over Stalingrad and generally appeared to be failing, although even before this no one in the NKVD system had doubted that we would win. All our teachers and with them the higher ranks of the State Security Service had constantly proclaimed both during lessons and at special lectures that the only possible outcome of the war was victory for us. All these explanations sounded very convincing. The Germans, so we were told, could have achieved enormous successes on our territory, but it was our good fortune that their leaders had turned out to be dozy half-wits, with a total and utter ignorance and lack of understanding of both political and national problems within the framework of the Soviet Union. All that was left for us to do, was to thank God (i.e. all there would have been to do, had He existed) and pray him to send the Germans on their way with all speed to total rout.

At a meeting of 6th November 1942 Chernyshov,[1] the head of Smersh's[2] counter-intelligence, had said, 'Let the Germans take Stalingrad, even ten such Stalingrads! What of it? Their lines are over-extended, and behind them we shall organise mass terrorism and partisan warfare. We shall have our men in every link of the German police administration chain, so as to sap its strength from within. The Germans and their occupying garrisons will be as much use as shit in a hole in the ice. We'll wipe them out gradually and the few that are left will be glad to crawl off on their backsides to their damn Vaterland. But they won't even be safe from us there. Our Party, led by Stalin, guarantees that. We are the vanguard of that Party, the children of Felix,[3] that man of iron, and we Soviet Chekists dedicate ourselves to it!'

All this was said at a meeting to celebrate the 25th anniversary of the October Revolution by a man responsible for the security of all the many millions of the Soviet armed forces. Had any ordinary Soviet citizen made such a speech just five yards away from our private NKVD club, where Chernyshov was speaking, or anywhere else for that matter, he would have been seized by Chekists and shot as a panic monger for active anti-Soviet propaganda. At that time, the whole of the Soviet press and radio was proclaiming, 'We shall not yield to the insidious enemy the city which bears our leader's

[1] A colonel-general of the State Security Service, the first head of Smersh, but soon succeeded by Colonel-General Abakumov.
[2] Smersh (Death to Spies) military counter-intelligence of the NKGB, details in other chapters.
[3] Felix Edmundovich Dzerzhinsky, creator and first head of the Soviet secret police.

sacred name.' The fate of Stalingrad had hung by a thread at that time, but now the Germans were beginning to slide back westwards.

There was also news within the NKVD system itself. The NKVD had once again been divided into two people's commissariats, one for internal affairs and the other for state security. Our school became part of the NKGB, where Merkulov was the new People's Commissar. Beria remained People's Commissar for Internal Affairs and, in addition, had control over the NKGB in so far as he was deputy chairman of the Council of People's Commissars (i.e. Stalin's deputy) in the fields of internal affairs and state security.

Another item of news was that shoulder boards became part of the uniform both in the army and in our forces. It was really rather a pity that my own shoulder boards were 'plain', without stripes along their length or officers' stars, but I was still only a cadet. My girl friend, a twenty-two-year-old doctor from a military hospital in the Moscow area, gloated over me, pointing to her own single stripe and three stars. She was a first lieutenant of the medical corps. During our rare meetings in her tiny room in the hospital she would poke fun at me by saying, 'Comrade Cadet, you've got above your station. Well, never mind,' she reconciled herself, as she lay beside me. 'I'll screw up my eyes and imagine that you are a colonel.'

'In that case,' I said, 'you'd better slip smartly into the lieutenant-colonel's place.'

What a girl she was, with her greenish eyes and slightly tip-tilted nose. But alas we had precious little time for such splendid activities in the school.

In peacetime the course in advanced State Security Service schools lasts from three to five years. Our school was a wartime hybrid. We had to cover a course reduced in time, but increased in scope, in the space of two years. Some of us would graduate early. It was wartime and the demand for State Security Service personnel was immense. 'Never mind,' the cadets used to say, 'we'll get through this school first and then we really will take the girls out.' Others said that something was put into the food to make us less interested in sex. Perhaps, but it didn't seem to have much effect on me.

The course programme really was packed to capacity. In addition to the five special subjects[1] we also covered a shortened infantry

[1] These were as follows: 1. Organisation and activities of our State Security bodies; 2. Organisation and activities of foreign special services; 3. Operational work; 4. Law of the Soviet state, military statutes, the criminal code and special statutes for internal troops of the NKVD; 5. Operational equipment.

training school course. All graduates of our school had to be prepared, if need be, to take command of any unit, either army or
partisan, up to and including a battalion. We also had to pass a
driving test for a private car. Not many people in the Soviet Union
had a driving licence and there were very few cars. I thought with
gratitude of my father, and of his chauffeur even more so, who had
both often allowed me to sit at the wheel of the official cars; first an
Emochka[1] and later a Zis.[2] They had given me this modest skill even
before I entered the school.

Cadets who graduated from the school early were usually people
rather older than I was, who had had some experience of real operational work before coming to the school, although there were exceptions. There were, for example, two cadets, a Russian and a Latvian,
who both spoke excellent German. They were suddenly withdrawn
from classes and put into a small group of six or seven men assembled
from the other companies. Various instructors with special qualifications, including, as I later discovered, both a parachute specialist and
an expert in coding, worked with them for two or three weeks. This
group left to go under the command of the operational reserve of the
fourth (intelligence-sabotage) administration of the NKGB. Everyone in this group was given the rank of lieutenant. The other group
which graduated early included about ten men, one of whom was a
Jewish cadet. 'Surely they aren't going to drop him behind the
German lines,' I thought in amazement. In point of fact, after a short
period of extra training the group was attached to GUKR[3] of Smersh
NKGB (military counter-intelligence). I very well remember one
particular member of just such another group, which went to the
fourth administration of the NKGB. The cadets in these groups
continued to share our quarters even when they were undergoing
special tuition. This particular cadet, whose bed was close to mine,
suddenly stopped shaving and began to grow a small beard. The
official attitude to shaving in the school was rather strict. Anyone who
had anything to shave had to shave it every day. In this particular
case our indefatigable sergeant-major pointedly failed to notice a
flagrant breach of the rules. One evening, during the period of free
time before lights out, each one of us was busy with his own affairs. I

---

[1] 'Emochka', a Soviet saloon car 'MI' made at the Molotov (then) car factory
in Gorky.
[2] 'Zis', a Soviet limousine, 'Zis 101', was made specially for high Soviet
officials at the Stalin (now Likhachev) car factory in Moscow.
[3] Main administration of counter-intelligence.

was totally absorbed with my favourite pastime, which was to lie on the bed and gaze at the ceiling, thinking of a pair of greenish eyes and a slightly tip-tilted nose. The cadet growing the beard wandered to and fro between the beds mumbling something to himself. I caught the odd word here and there: 'Mother of God . . . Rejoice O Virgin . . . Thy will be done . . . and deliver us from evil . . .' There was not a shadow of doubt that the cadet was saying prayers. I had learned very early on never to be surprised at anything that happened in the NKVD school, but saying prayers was a real turn-up for the book. Prayers indeed! Was he round the bend! Eventually, I could contain myself no longer. 'What are you up to?' I said.

'Well, you see,' the cadet answered, 'it's my "legend". It's religious and my "roof" is too.'

In our operational jargon 'legend' is the false biography that the NKGB gives you, and your 'roof' is the part the man with a 'legend' plays openly when he is sent to a new place, often into enemy territory.

The bearded cadet went on with his muttering, but was interrupted by our company joker who said, 'You're fucking useless, mate. You're like a collective farm book-keeper counting piglets. You want to put some life into it. Now listen to me,' he offered. He bellowed forth in the deep bass of a deacon, loud enough to fill the whole barracks. 'Lo and behold, the dogs ate the priest . . . The archdeacon's fucking cost him a sheepskin coat and a penknife . . . let us pray!'

The bearded cadet listened to this prayer for a moment and then began to curse. 'What good's that kind of advice to me? I've got to conduct church services, marry and bury people. What'll happen there if I remember your words and say them by mistake,' Before he left, like all the others, the bearded cadet became a lieutenant in the State Security Service.

Our school made up a battalion with four companies in it, in all about 700 cadets. As certain cadets used to say with pride, because of the importance of the school, its head possessed the same disciplineary powers as the head of a regional administration of the State Security Service. I later found out that this was in fact quite true and he literally held the power of life and death over each of us. During my period at the school there was not a single such extreme case, although there were breaches of discipline. Two cadets got slightly drunk and started a fight with some anti-aircraft artillery officers of the Moscow defence district. The chief of the school and the school representative of GUKR Smersh had a long talk with them. This was a bad omen for the wrongdoers. Both these cadets were expelled from the school and transferred to the jurisdiction of Colonel-General Nedosekin—a fate that scared all of us stiff. Nedosekin was a deputy of Beria in the NKVD and was the head of the Main Administration of Corrective Labour Camps, abbreviated in Russian to GULAG. Of course, the cadets who were expelled did not go to the camps as prisoners. They and others like them were usually sent into the Third Administration of GULAG which provided the staff responsible for state security in the labour camps. Instead of the career of an intelligence or counter-intelligence agent of the NKGB, the best they could hope for would be to serve in the third section of some labour camp in the Urals, or at worst to do the same thing in the region of eternal snow and polar night. 'Amongst the polar bears', as we used to say. Such cases were, however, very rare and the standard of discipline in the school was extremely high.

The Soviet forces were moving westward on a very wide front with ever-increasing speed. I began to be afraid that the war would end without my having taken part in it, so I put in a report to the chief of the school requesting early transfer to the front. 'If necessary', I wrote, 'I am prepared to go with any rank', showing thereby that I simply wanted to fight. I genuinely did want to fight and into the bargain I was fed up to the back teeth with the school. As far as rank was concerned, I was terribly anxious to strut about with a couple of shiny new stars and a light blue stripe on my broad shoulder boards. My girl friend, the doctor, had already got her fourth star and became a captain, although admittedly it was only in the medical corps and the shoulder boards were rather narrow.

I was eventually summoned to the chief of the school. The same tired-looking intellectual, but now he wore the shoulder boards of a colonel. 'So you've started sending me reports too, have you,' he began. 'I suppose you think you're the only one who's reached for his pen? You say you're not even bothered about a commission. All right, I'll take you at your word.'

'But, Comrade Colonel . . .' I said. He was no longer listening, however, and waved me away. 'Very well, right about turn!' When I reached the door, hearing his chuckle I paused. 'As soon as they start recruiting, I promise you'll be one of the first to go, because of your excellent knowledge of German grammar.' Some ten days later the duty sergeant came into the classroom during a lesson: 'Okunev, Romanov, report to the school office!' This was it.

3

Hello Murka, hello my dear . . .

From an underworld song

SIX OR EIGHT CADETS had already gathered in the corridor of the school HQ outside the chief's office. We had all been sent for, and we were called in one by one. My turn was a long time in coming. I racked my brains to guess what it was all about. We were obviously being posted, but where? We all searched greedily for the answer to this question in the faces of the cadets as they came out of the chief's study. They either fended us off with a dreary wave of the hand, or quickly whispered: 'To Abakumov.' Smersh wasn't exactly what I wanted, but was quite a catch!

Finally I was called in. There were three colonels in the room. The chief sat at his desk, the school's permanent Smersh operational representative was sitting on the sofa. I reported to the chief of the school who nodded towards the third colonel sitting slumped in an armchair beside him. This colonel looked like a gipsy—his hair was black and long and he seemed cheerful and energetic. I learned later that he was one of the deputies of the head of the First Adminstration of the Main Administration of Counter-Intelligence (GUKR), Smersh. He handled the whole interview. There were the same old questions about my family, about myself, my studies, etc. Eventually, the colonel enquired whether I had a good grasp of Special Subject No. 4 (the laws, statutes, criminal law and the like). My heart sank. This wasn't much use for operational work at the front.

'We're short of time,' the colonel said. 'You are being posted from the school after an urgent requisition; I hope that you will justify our trust.'

He stood up, the chief of the school stood up too and the Smersh representative rose from the sofa, wheezing as he did so.

'Order of the People's Commissar of the USSR for State Security,' the 'gipsy' colonel read out, 'that A. I. Romanov be commissioned with the rank of lieutenant.'

Then came the number of the order and the date. The colonel handed me a pair of shining new shoulder boards divided down their length by a single pale blue stripe, with a small star on each side of it.

'Congratulations,' he said, shaking my hand.

'I serve the Soviet Union,' I answered. I made an about turn with elegant precision and, clutching the shoulder boards in my hand, left the room.

Next door, I received more detailed instructions. Tomorrow (as quick as that!) I was to collect my papers and receive further instructions from the personnel department of the reserve of the Main Administration of Counter-Intelligence (GUKR) Smersh (not far from Kuznetsky Most in Moscow). The word 'tomorrow' meant one of two things. Perhaps the matter was really urgent, which could be a good sign. On the other hand, I wasn't even being kept on at the school for the usual extra training, i.e. studies with special instructors. That could be a bad sign and might mean that the work wouldn't be particularly interesting or important. I wasted no time in putting on the lieutenant's shoulder boards, only to bid them goodbye on the very next day when I was issued with a fresh pair, but this time battle-dress shoulder boards of an infantry lieutenant. I had to say goodbye also to the proud thought that a lieutenant in the State Security Service was equivalent to a captain in the army. The bloody war had changed all that.

In the morning I was one of the first people to arrive at a large stone building not far from the Bolshoi Theatre. A middle-aged major issued me with a brand-new identity card, a small, pale blue booklet with the letters NKGB-USSR stamped on the front cover. I was delighted that the booklet was pale blue and not red! To the initiated this meant that I belonged to the Main Administration. Inside, under the main heading NKGB-USSR, it said, in slightly smaller letters, Main Administration of Counter-Intelligence, Smersh. Underneath was my full name and place of work, namely the First Administration. This was bad for reasons which I will explain later. I was described as an Operational Representative, which was standard procedure. There was also my photograph (without a cap), an official stamp and the signature of the deputy head of the Administration. On the other page was the serial number of the gun that had been issued to me. (It was a new TT.[1]) The remaining spaces had

[1] TT. An automatic pistol—'Tokarev-Tulsky'.

not been filled in. What I heard from the major hit me like a bolt out of the blue. I was being posted to a special operational group which was already working in some military transit camps not far from a railway station called Tatishchevo in Saratov Region. There I would be attached to an experienced member of Smersh to undergo a period of training. This was instead of the supplementary training cadets usually underwent before passing out from the school. I was given twenty-four hours' leave in Moscow for personal matters before taking up my posting. After all, it was wartime, so there were no real grounds for complaint.

'Of course, you know the general instructions,' the major said in a tone which was half statement and half question. I had still not recovered from the shock of my posting and, contrary to all the statutes, I did not speak, but simply nodded. I collected my travel warrant and my orders. I had already found out certain general details in the school at Babushkin. They needed no further explanation. On the basis of a secret resolution of the USSR State Committee for Defence (chairman Stalin, deputy chairman Beria), for the duration of the war the status of the State Security bodies was substantially altered. I read the resolution carefully and signed it to acknowledge that I had done so. It amounted more or less to the following. All serving personnel of the State Security bodies were to begin using the same system of ranks as obtained in the USSR armed forces. We were no longer allowed to use our usual ranks and it was also forbidden to address senior personnel by their old ranks. This was not all. NKGB personnel, and in certain cases NKVD forces,[1] were forbidden to wear their own special uniforms and had to wear ordinary army uniforms instead. This was a camouflage measure to make it impossible to distinguish them from the rest of the armed forces. These changes had a particularly important effect on Smersh. Every single member of Smersh personnel began to wear ordinary military uniform.

I must say that at that time all these details were the least of my worries. I had been posted to Saratov Region, just about as far away from the front as one could get! This meant total ignominy and disgrace. Was it for this that I had passed out of one of the best State Security Service schools? After all, any old half-trained officer could cope with that kind of work. He needn't even be a Chekist. An ordinary policeman could manage. Various thoughts ran through my mind: What should I say to my girl friend? Why had this happened?

[1] See Chapter 5, page 141.

It all seemed very unjust I had, after all, made a reasonable job of my studies.

I turned up at the hospital with a funereal countenance. She was on duty, but without much trouble she was able to arrange for a replacement. Her colleagues were only too happy to help. The reason was understandable and valid—a friend had finished his training and was leaving for the front. I ground my teeth when I heard this excuse being offered. 'A fine front I'm going to!' I thought, lowering my eyes.

We had a whole evening and a whole night at our disposal. As I walked along beside her I admired the greenish eyes I knew so well, the slightly tip-tilted nose and other features which were set off to such advantage by the dark green uniform with its silver shoulder boards. She's probably put on those silk stockings and black high-heeled shoes in honour of my departure. I began to feel a bit more like my old self. I booked a room in an hotel for officers. That was a devil of a job. Moscow was bursting with higher-ranked officers, but my new identity card seemed to possess magic powers when it was pushed under the nose of the reception clerk. At that time, of course, I had only the vaguest notions of its power. There was no one and nothing to disturb us. I even managed to forget bloody Tatishchevo and the First Administration of Smersh. We said a friendly farewell, without any illusions about the future.

I had first met her at a party in Moscow at the flat of one of my fellow cadets, who was the son of a high Party official. I had immediately tried to make a conquest, and hadn't given her a moment's peace. Even after my victory it was a long time before the feeling of pleasant surprise left me. I had managed to get my hands on a pretty girl who, into the bargain, was a year or two older than I. I am endlessly grateful to her for her wit, her company and her friendship. There is no doubt in my mind that after my departure a new boy friend came on the scene. She had takers on all sides, who were in many respects rather more impressive 'comrades' than I. The war made significant changes to relations between men and women. One learned to live very much for the present.

The Main Administration of Counter-Intelligence, Smersh, was created in the late summer of 1942, on the basis of an organisation which was already in existence called the Main Administration of Special Branches of the State Security Service. People who were in the know said that the name Smersh was an acronym made up by

Stalin himself, from the two words *Smert' Shpionam* (Death to spies). I find this easy to believe, as Stalin always took a close personal interest in such details as shoulder boards, ranks and abbreviated titles. Because there was a war going on, and because between fifteen and seventeen million adult Soviet citizens were serving in the various branches of the armed forces, Smersh became a key area of the State Security Service. Initially, the previous head of the Special Branches, Chernyshov (Commissar of State Security of the third rank, as he was then styled) stayed on as head of Smersh. Later, because of Smersh's crucial role, he was replaced by a man who became at the same time First Deputy People's Commissar for State Security, Colonel-General (according to the new nomenclature) Abakumov. In the following paragraphs I shall describe the structure of these various administrations, which was bureaucratic and complex.

Like any other main administration of the NKGB, Smersh had a number of basic operational administrations which made up the Main Administration in Moscow and certain auxiliary servicing administrations.

Present-day Soviet publications, when they go into the subject at all, state that Smersh was subordinated from 1943 to the People's Commissariat of Defence. It was indeed subordinated, but only to the People's Commissar of Defence himself, whose name happened to be Joseph Stalin.

The First Administration, of which I had such a low opinion, was engaged only on grass-roots work in all the detachments,[1] units,[2] formations[3] and amalgamations[4] of the Soviet armed forces. In every one of them there were branches and sections of this administration. Regular Chekists worked there as operational representatives (there were three grades of these; junior operational representative, operational representative and senior operational representative). They were to be found in all detachments from battalions and independent companies upwards. Their job was to prevent, or in the last resort to root out any elements in the army hostile to Soviet power. They kept an eye on everything and everybody, from commanders of fronts and

[1] Detachments—anything up to and including a battalion.
[2] Units—anything from a battalion up to and including a division.
[3] Formations—anything from an independent division up to and including army corps.
[4] Amalgamations—anything from an independent corps and subordinate units to a front* (or military region).
* Front—a formation in the Soviet armed forces including usually four to five armies.

marshals to the most humble soldier in a transport convoy. They also controlled all the political bodies in the armed forces. No one was above suspicion. A permanent network of informers was secretly recruited and maintained throughout the army. Activities like keeping tabs on one's own officers and men, listening to reports from informers and compiling regular dispatches for one's superiors did not attract me at all. What bearing had that on either intelligence or the war?

The Second Administration of Smersh controlled the operations. It was responsible for collecting intelligence and dropping agents in areas immediately behind the enemy lines. It also co-operated with special units of NKVD forces to ensure that our rear was properly guarded. It did the work of the NKGB on Soviet territory immediately after its liberation (before the regular NKGB staff arrived). It answered for the personal security of the front's high-ranking personnel and for attacks on everybody and everything which represented a threat to Soviet power. (This included our own military personnel, civilians near the front, and real enemy agents.) These detachments of troops, permanently assigned to Smersh and made up of specially selected soldiers, were also under the jurisdiction of the Operational Administration. On average there was a company of such troops to each army, or a battalion to each front. Where necessary their numbers were increased. They were also known as Smersh Military Police. Their duties included guarding arrested persons and carrying out death sentences. As far as intelligence gathering was concerned Smersh's Operational Administration was helped greatly by the intelligence branches of NKVD Frontier Troops, which were already in existence in peacetime. Almost all their members, who had worked in areas near the western frontier, were absorbed into the Operational Administration.

The Third Administration of Smersh was its secret administration. Its branches and sections were to be found in all detachments, beginning at corps level. This administration had the job of gathering and summarising the information which was constantly coming in from the other Departments of Smersh. It also received all orders and information from the top brass of Smersh. The chief of Smersh received the most important instructions directly from the Supreme Commander of the Armed Forces, from Stalin himself. All these matters were digested by the Third Administration and disseminated, by various methods, throughout all Smersh Administrations. This Administration would dispatch its own operational groups (or individual representatives) to the various fronts, to military regions in areas behind the lines and to the fleets. I knew a great deal more than most Chekists solely because I later served in the Third Administration.

The Fourth Administration of Smersh was the Investigation Administration. Its branches and sections were to be found in all units at corps level and above. Its representatives were called Junior Investigators, Investigators and Senior Investigators. There also existed a category known as Investigators of Specially Important Cases, but as a rule they were to be found only within the Main Administration of Smersh in Moscow. In a crisis groups of investigators from the Fourth Administration travelled to wherever they were needed. This Administration conducted the cases of all persons arrested on suspicion of anti-Soviet activity. At every front, in every military region, in all fleets and armies, there were places where prisoners could be remanded in custody. Sometimes an actual undamaged prison building was used, sometimes houses, huts or even dugouts. The Fourth Administration 'processed' all cases for investigation before they were handed over to the Fifth Administration.

The Fifth Administration of Smersh was the tribunals. Neither more nor less than the judicial *troikas*.[1] They were to be found in every army or larger formation. They were made up of a President with legal training and who was a senior officer. The other members of the *troika* were not always jurists but were, of course, always regular officers of Smersh. The sentences pronounced by these tribunals were final and not subject to appeal. At all the court hearings of the Fifth Administration the secretary of the tribunal, a junior officer of Smersh, was always present to take notes. Sometimes this would be a woman. There were also women in the Fourth (Investigation) Administration, where they worked as Investigators. To do this work they had to have been commissioned as Smersh officers. This held good for all employees of the five administrations I have mentioned. Everybody who worked in them had the rank of an officer, including all the clerks, secretaries and typists.

The remaining Smersh administrations were auxiliary servicing administrations: Personnel, (which was an important one), Administration and upkeep of facilities, Finance, Supply and Transport. In all these administrations there were Party and Komsomol organisations and their political organisers. However they did not interfere in the operational activities of Smersh—they had no such right—and

[1] *Troika*—a carriage drawn by a team of three horses side by side. Used here figuratively because there were three members of the tribunal.

in general played only a minor part. Smersh's technical communications, for example V.Ch (high frequency—government communications for constant contact with Moscow), were maintained by special personnel from the NKVD 'communications forces'.[1] There was also a special staff of secret couriers. Smersh had its own doctors and nurses, its own restaurants, arsenals and stores of other operational equipment.

The confounded wartime train, half passenger, half goods, carried me slowly towards the Volga, stopping frequently, sometimes out in the open country, sometimes in the forest, without any apparent reason. The majority of the passengers were military personnel. During the war journeys were difficult for the civilian population, involving many bans and restrictions. I was soon bored to tears with this kind of travelling. I got off and joined the train of some tank unit, which was travelling to the rear to pick up new equipment. This was a bit more entertaining and I soon reached the station of Tatishchevo. The well-known Tatishchevo Military Transit Formation Camps were my destination. I call them well known because hundreds of thousands of soldiers and officers were sent to the front from the Reserve Formation Units which were permanently based near there. The camps were huge towns of hutments, or, more often, just dugouts, each holding about five hundred men and standing right in the middle of the steppe, which was dotted here and there with copses and occasional clumps of bushes. Even the grass had been trampled down over many kilometres.

I found the base of the Smersh Special Operational Group in a large, fairly clean hut. My direct superior was a thickset, middle-aged captain, whose face was pitted with the traces of smallpox. He was a Chekist regular, who had come into Smersh from an NKGB administration in central Russia. He ended our talk by saying, 'If anything is not clear always ask me about it, or else it'll be worse for you later.' I was very careful to follow his advice. After all, this was my first real job. At that time a lot of things weren't clear to me. This captain was my official mentor to whom I had been attached so that I should acquire practical 'know-how'. The captain took off his belt, unbuttoned his holster and, after checking his pistol, slipped it into the right-hand pocket of his riding breeches.

'After all,' he said 'they're not in the armed forces yet. Is that clear?'

[1] For NKVD Communications Forces, see Chapter 5, page 139.

Of course it was quite clear. In the NKGB school I had studied the Statutes of the NKVD Internal Forces. In them it said that ranks of the NKGB or NKVD, particularly if alone, were forbidden to display weapons openly among prisoners. They might cut off the holster with the pistol in it, or snatch it away from you, then there would be no escaping trouble. Just imagine trying to sort out, who it was who snatched your pistol and trying to find it among hundreds or even thousands of prisoners. You could end up in front of a tribunal for a silly mistake like that. Or worse. So I followed the captain's example, removed my holster and put my pistol in the right-hand pocket of my trousers.

We came out of the hut and went into the quarantine zone. The people living there were criminals who had come to Tatishchevo from prisons and labour camps in various parts of the USSR and had not yet been screened. They had come for final screening, conscription into the armed forces, training and dispatch on active service. The final screening was our responsibility. Of course, before they left the prisons and camps the local branches and sections of the Third Administration in GULAG[1] of the NKVD and the local NKGB bodies had screened them carefully. But the final responsibility for their suitability and reliability was ours. For the time being I was no more than a trainee officer, but even so . . . I knew that what was going on was by no means an innovation. Already by 1941 large numbers of criminal (and only criminal) prisoners, had been sent straight into action on the front line after only a brief period of training. Many of them proved to be excellent soldiers, intelligence material, parachute troops and so on. They were awarded medals, decorations, some even became Heroes of the Soviet Union.[2] In the summer of 1942 Stalin issued a special order (No. 227) concerning the formation of penal companies and battalions. Instead of serving sentences in labour camps and prisons for sundry crimes, prisoners were now sent under guard to the front, often after only the briefest military training. For example, instead of serving eight years in a labour camp a man could be sentenced to two months in a penal battalion, or, instead of ten years—three months, etc. All this had purely academic, abstract significance. It was a lucky man who managed to survive five days or a week in a penal battalion at the

[1] GULAG—Glavnoye Upravleniye Lagerei—Main Administration of Camps.
[2] Hero of the Soviet Union—The highest decoration. It comprises the Order of Lenin and the 'Gold Star' medal.

front. Battalions like these were usually sent to the most dangerous places—on reconnaissance missions under conditions of battle, to break through the enemy lines or storm heavily fortified German positions. Moreover, they often had to attempt these missions without any covering fire whatever. Men were sent into these penal battalions until 'first blood', i.e. until they received their first wound. Then those who came through alive were sent to hospital and had all their sins forgiven them in the form of a subsequent posting to an ordinary unit of the armed forces. As is well known, the dead are in need of neither medical treatment nor forgiveness.

Many western specialists consider that under the same order of 1942, blocking detachments were created to combat desertion or disorderly withdrawal from the fighting line. This is incorrect. The blocking detachments were organised a year earlier in 1941.[1] These detachments subsequently became the travelling companions of the penal battalions, being usually deployed immediately to their rear.

The ex-prisoners whom I now had to deal with were in no danger of being put into penal battalions. After we had screened them, they were posted to ordinary reserve regiments, trained and then drafted in companies near the front. There were two reasons for this innovation. In the first place the losses in penal battalions at the front were far too high. And secondly there was far too much valuable military material in these battalions. However, penal battalions remained in existence too, right up to the end of the war, although their numbers declined.

When we entered the quarantine zone, which was no more than a cluster of dugouts surrounded by barbed wire with a sentry by the gates, I noticed a group of people some distance from us. They looked like a typical group of senior Party or State officials. They were dressed in smart, semi-military clothing—gleaming boots, riding breeches of green or dark blue cloth, commissars' field shirts and tunics. Their faces were pale and rather puffy, but there was nothing odd about this as during the war our leaders went short of both fresh air and sleep. Amongst them I noticed one or two in foreign military uniforms. I assumed that it was some sort of important commission, which included representatives of our British and American allies. I automatically tucked in my field shirt and straightened my cap, which I always wore at a rather rakish angle. I took a squint at the captain. He was still walking unconcernedly beside me and hadn't even removed his hands from his riding breeches. Walking straight

[1] See Chapter 5, page 141.

up to the group he addressed a greeting to them. His choice of words would have been the envy of any docker.

'Well, I can see that you buggers have already managed to swipe all the *shmutki* (togs, gear) you need, but don't forget there'll be a *shmon* (search) tonight. I'll bloody well be there myself and if I find a single non-regulation *prokhar* (boot) or a *slyunka* (knife) I'll have all your bloody balls off. Get changed at once.'

The captain borrowed all these incomprehensible words from Soviet criminal jargon, which he appeared to know very well. After his remarks the 'senior Party officials' and 'Anglo-American allies' rapidly scattered to their dugouts. Berating myself for my stupid mistake, I asked the captain, 'How on earth did they manage to deck themselves out like that, Comrade Captain?'

'Oh,' he said, with an airy wave of his hand, 'they're just a bunch of bandits. They've been through a whole lot of transit stations, prisons and camps. And, of course, places like that attract all sorts— our own, German prisoners, Roumanians, Italians—well, they just skinned them. You still don't know our clientele,' the captain said to me then. 'We'll be sorry before we're through with them.'

His words turned out to be prophetic. They made *us* sorry—and the militia, and the Soviet civilian population, and also people from East European countries which we later occupied.

We were allotted a room in the only wooden hut in the zone. A sentry with a machine gun stood at the door. The room was full of cupboards which were crammed with the personal files of our prisoners. There was also a table and three or four stools. The remainder of the day was spent in sorting out and preparing cases and compiling lists. Not all of these people were professional rogues, although there was no shortage of these. Amongst them there were also rapists, some who had worked as lone wolves and others who had hunted in packs, petty thieves, bribe-takers, embezzlers of state funds and even counter-feiters. Each case had two clearance certificates fastened to it, one of which was from the NKGB bodies at their place of imprisonment and stated 'Accused of no political offence'. The second was a medical certificate which said 'Physically and mentally fit for military service'. In actual fact, as the following days convinced me, there were no very abnormal people among them, though if one had dug a little more deeply, who knows what one would have found? We didn't do any digging. There was a catastrophic shortage of both time and Smersh personnel. All the members of our group worked from twelve to fourteen hours every day. Our main job was to investigate and check that no political prisoner had slipped out into relative freedom as an ordinary criminal.

All sorts of silly thoughts came into my head in those days. The only places in the Soviet Union where slogans and portraits of the leaders were not supposed to be hung were, and still are, lunatic asylums. In other institutions for normal people slogans such as this were very popular: 'We shall fulfil the five-year plan in four years'; or among pilots, 'Long live our leading pilot—the great Stalin!', the railwaymen just substituted 'best engine driver' for 'leading pilot' and so on. I remember a joke about Stalin inspecting a Moscow lunatic asylum. In preparation for his arrival all the inmates were urgently trained to shout 'Hail to the great Stalin'. On the day of the visit, as he passed through the rooms, Stalin noticed a single silent person. 'Why do you not call out a greeting to me with the rest?' he asked. 'I'm not a patient, I'm one of the guards,' the man answered.

Throughout my whole time in Tatishchevo I spotted only one or two people, who after a short conversation struck even me as having something seriously wrong with them. They were, as we say in Russian, plainly 'without a Czar in their head'. My captain undoubtedly noticed this too, because he remarked mockingly about one of them, 'We really ought to send him to the seaside, to Artek[1] in the Crimea, but the trouble is there's a war on there too . . . we'd better send him to the front—he's as fit as a fiddle anyway.' The men who came to Tatishchevo were summoned one by one by a soldier armed with a machine gun. There were two of them, one who stood by our door and the other who patrolled up and down the corridor. A third guard stood by the outside door and pairs of soldiers constantly patrolled the zone itself. The men living in the zone were not allowed to approach them. The men who survived our screening were removed from the zone and transferred to normal army conditions.

The captain sat at the table and I to one side. Glancing now and then into the 'personal file', he fired questions at the candidate, who sat on a stool some way away from the table. The captain was a past master of interrogation and in particular of cross-questioning. As soon as he sensed a weak spot or lack of confidence in the answers of the person he was talking to, he would latch on to it. He did not do this in an obviously crude way, but with gradual insistence, now leaving the subject and then again returning to it at the most unexpected points in the interrogation. In this way, he made several criminals

[1] Artek (Crimea)—A model camp for Young Pioneers, at that time named after Molotov.

reveal additional crimes which had been carefully hidden from other investigators. However these crimes were purely criminal offences; somebody else they had 'filled in' or goods they had 'knocked off' from some warehouse or other. The captain would plaster this kind of candidate with a generous layer of the vilest invective for previously concealing the truth, and once convinced of his political reliability, let him depart in peace, making no mention of the matter in the 'personal file'.

The overwhelming majority of cases were depressingly monotonous. The only thing that was different was the face on the other side of our table. So far as I remember, neither we nor any of the other pairs of Smersh officers (we all worked in pairs) rejected a significant number of candidates. Apparently our Chekist colleagues in the places where the candidates came from earned their bread (and butter). There was only one candidate in our zone who let them down seriously. He got into a quarrel with a group from a neighbouring dugout and in the heat of the argument spilled the guts of one of his opponents with a flick knife, which he had somehow or other contrived to hide. He was sent straight to the prison in Saratov, where fresh proceedings were taken against him. There were a few similar cases of violence but they involved only a small percentage of the total number of candidates.

My routine was once disrupted by a brilliant forger of official documents. He was a very pleasant and urbane man with a large bald patch, which he covered with hair from the side of his head on the principle of 'mutual credit'. He wore a pair of professorial spectacles. For a long time he had enjoyed great success, until, as he stated, 'Citizen[1] Officer, damn his eyes' had clobbered him. He had decided to set himself up as an employee of the CID. With skilfully forged search warrants, he conducted 'searches for and confiscation of stolen socialist property' in flats which he had previously marked out. Cleverly, he did this in the presence of a witness, as the law required. This was usually the caretaker of the apartment house. He compiled a neat inventory of the confiscated property—as a rule gold and silver —and left a stamped and signed copy for the victim himself, 'I'd got it to a fine art, Citizen Officer,' he told us with modest professional

---

[1] Citizen Officer—in the Soviet Union a prisoner loses the right to use the word *Tovarishch* (Comrade) as a form of address and must call all representatives of the authorities Citizen Major, Citizen Warden, etc. Incidentally, the accidental use of the word Citizen as a form of address in Soviet society is a way in which one can often recognise an ex-convict.

pride. Greed had been his undoing. Having conducted a number of searches in one town he had in mind one more flat, which afforded good prospects. But someone tipped off the real agents of the CID, who descended on the flat. Our nice, agreeable companion got nabbed and went to a labour camp with a substantial sentence, which the CID gave him as a parting gift. From this whole case, the most interesting thing that I remember was the fact that not a single one of the victims of our candidate's searches dared to report what had happened to the police. 'They'd all got skeletons in their cupboards, they were all thieves who had robbed our state,' he informed us sadly. And apropos himself he added the words of the Jewish joke, 'Comrade Wolf knows who to eat.'

In the brief amount of spare time I had at night there was absolutely no way of amusing myself. The nearest villages were too far away from the camps and there were no books whatever. Even I, who had some modest experience with army medical personnel of the fairer sex, was unable to find anything suitable in the camp sick bay. The few girl doctors and nurses they had there were, as I discovered, pretty well soiled. It's not surprising that, with such a large number of men around, all sorts and sizes had had a go at them.

Songs were the only distraction. I happened to come out of the hut where we slept around midnight one night for a stroll and a smoke. Regardless of the fact that it was ages after lights out, in the criminal zone there was still plenty happening. A splendid lyrical tenor, no worse than Lemeshev,[1] was singing a sad, lingering song: 'Come to the *bahn* and I will be there . . .' I listened, forgetting everything else. Then a triumphant choir of many voices broke in: 'Oh yes, oh yes, I was there at the *bahn*, I ate and drank well and had pricks up my arse.' I suddenly came back to earth with a bump, my pensive mood vanished, after all the singers were from the underworld. Afterwards, on other evenings, they had an accordion and a guitar, which they'd doubtless stolen from somewhere. They had probably been swiped from the 'Lenin Room' of some club or other. But nobody raised a hand to retrieve what had been stolen. They played and sang too well for us to want to do that. Our Smersh officers used often to go and listen, standing in the bushes by the fence. I've never anywhere heard singing like theirs. The song I particularly remember from their extensive repertoire was the famous thieves' song, 'Up with the Bow', with an interminable number of verses. There was even one verse

[1] Sergei Lemeshev—famous Soviet tenor, soloist of the Bolshoi Theatre, People's Artist of the USSR.

which described how a thief arrived in heaven without a penny in his pocket. 'Here I am without a penny, I'll search God's pockets for some money . . . I shan't take all He's got . . .' There were songs about international politics too, which mentioned the Japanese Emperor, the German Führer, the Italian Duce and leading foreign diplomats, although the expressions used to describe them were often far from diplomatic. The criminals never mentioned our leaders. They had too much sense for that, for they knew that the slightest dig at Stalin or others would mean their prospective career at the front would immediately vanish into a long prison sentence as a 'political'. I remember too a wonderful Jewish song: 'There's a hell of a noise at Schneerson's house'. The song told with a degree of sophisticated detail of the wedding of Schneerson's son, Solomon. All of us who listened to these songs laughed till we cried and my usually morose captain was no exception. I am sure that even a corpse would have been hard put to it not to laugh at some of those songs.

The story of the expert forger ended rather unusually. My captain took a serious interest in him. He sent for a sergeant from the camp office and ordered him to bring some documents with him. I think they were requisition forms for foodstuffs and uniforms. The captain then invited the specialist to forge the signatures on these forms. Feeling that his professional reputation was at stake, he studied the signatures attentively for some minutes, looking at them first from one side and then from the other. Then he took a clean piece of paper and a fountain pen and made a series of deft movements with his hand. I'm sure that none of us could have distinguished which signatures were false and which were genuine.

'What about the stamp?' the captain asked.

'Of course, of course, why not? Even here in these, er, rather primitive conditions . . . I shall need a piece of raw potato or turnip,' he said.

It was all he needed. He spent rather more time working on the piece of raw potato with a tiny penknife. The stamps were no less magnificent than the signatures and quite indistinguishable from the originals. But the expert himself said rather disdainfully that it was the best he could manage in such primitive conditions. The captain, however, was vastly impressed. After allowing him to go, he told me that the lieutenant-colonel, who was chief of our operational group, should be informed. The captain convinced the lieutenant-colonel, and a coded message was sent to GUKR Smersh in Moscow. A few days later we sent the specialist to Moscow. He was put at the disposal of the Operational Technical Branch of the Operational Administration for further screening and possible use professionally. This is more or less what was said in reply to our coded message. Of course I don't know what happened next, but people with these kinds of abilities made valuable members of the intelligence-sabotage groups and operational-sabotage groups of Smersh and other administrations of the NKGB which were dropped behind the German lines.

While he was doing the screening the captain didn't forget the other duty of a representative of the First Administration either: the recruiting of secret workers; *seksoty*, or informers. There was a special method for doing this which had been worked out over the years. It could be tailored to the personality of the person being recruited.

'Do you realise,' the captain asked one candidate, 'where you've landed up and who we are?'

The candidate, a youthful criminal, nodded his head and bleated 'NKVD'.

'We're not from the bloody NKVD,' the captain explained. 'We're from Smersh. Have you heard of that? No? Well, we can tell the NKVD where to fuck off and we shall do the same to you if need be and not waste much time about it. Got that?'

The criminal, impressed by the new and hitherto unknown word (Smersh) and by the fact that the captain could 'tell the NKVD to fuck off', nodded his head. The captain went on to say that, according to his information, there was in the camp, in the very same dugout where the criminal himself lived, an anti-Soviet group which was literally about to go into action. He added that, of course, he was already well aware of who the members of this group were, but he would like to obtain more information about them. The story ended simply. The criminal memorised a code name, a surname other than his own, which was given to him (he himself chose it). This was the established practice. All stool-pigeons sign their reports with code names like this. His 'file' with the code name and his own surname would be passed on to the Smersh representative in the unit to which he was posted. There and then he signed an undertaking that he would 'collaborate and not divulge anything'. If we were dealing with 'noble criminals', i.e. bribe-takers, embezzlers and people who had been sentenced for wrongful use of their professional position, the captain avoided using vulgar expressions. With such people another aspect of the situation was stressed; 'Smersh,' the captain said with relish, 'means death—death to spies, never forget that.' One had the impression from their faces that they had no intention of forgetting.

By the way, when the captain was so colourfully describing to the criminals certain physical advantages that Smersh had over the NKVD he was not exaggerating or boasting at all. There actually were representatives of Smersh in all NKVD detachments and institutions, just as there were in the armed forces.

In sending vast numbers of criminals into the Soviet Army, Smersh was aware that any criminal, particularly if he was isolated or alone, could desert to the Germans. Of course, there were in our forces quite substantial staffs of political workers, who were conducting propaganda designed to avoid this. But no one could give us a guarantee that something like this would never happen. There was no need for such a gurantee. We knew of more weighty facts, and it was on them that we relied, rather than on our anti-fascist propaganda. For years certain people with very strong anti-Soviet sentiments had been in German hands. People like the Deputy Commander of the Volkhov Front,[1] the former head of the Red Army Personnel Administration and Moscow City Commandant,[2] a series of corps and army commanders and a large number of eminent intellectuals, largely professors and engineers. The Germans had turned out to be incapable of using a single one of them intelligently. What chance had some wretched criminal of squeezing any advantage out of the Germans? Moreover this was a two-edged sword. Any criminal of ours who found himself in western European conditions could set himself up professionally in such a way, that not only the Germans, who knew nothing of the scope of criminal activities in the Soviet Union, but even the devil himself would have felt rather queasy.

After a week or so the captain suggested that I might try my own hand at conducting an initial 'sounding-out' interview. He sat down at the side and I moved into the centre. I made a complete hash of my first attempt. Without thinking, I put a most stupid question to this particular candidate: 'Are you prepared to defend and fight for Soviet power?' I at once realised the idiocy of the question, but it was already too late. The candidate, a great, strapping fellow, began suddenly to whine and wail in a shrill, womanish voice: 'Please, guv, I'd do anything for the darling, sir, well, sir, what I wouldn't do for the Soviet power . . . If I tell a lie, sir, just you bundle me straight back into jug, sir . . .'

'All right,' the captain broke off this touching flood of emotion. 'Belt up!', and explained that there was not a chance of his being sent

[1] Lieutenant-General Andrei Vlasov.
[2] Lieutenant-General Mikhail Lukin.

back to prison. 'That's all, but,' the captain elaborated, 'if you try any tricks we'll sort you out without the help of either a trial or a prison. This time it'll just be a bullet in your forehead or the back of your neck.'

I remembered this conversation for a long time and made no more mistakes like that. The captain's promise was repeated to many of our criminal candidates to lend more weight to his orders.

Some weeks later, I can't remember now how long it was, the chief of our operational group got a coded message from Moscow. I and young officer trainees like me were to be recalled, with detailed reports on our work, into the reserve of GUKR Smersh. I later got a hint that my captain had given me quite a good reference. The work of screening and selecting criminals at Tatishchevo was coming to an end. There were few left, and no new arrivals for the present.

Back in Moscow I discovered to my chagrin that my doctor girl friend, together with most of the medical personnel of her hospital, had been posted to a field hospital somewhere in the area of the Second Baltic Front. Such little free time as I had, I killed by going to the cinema and to a jazz concert. I also visited some distant relatives of ours. I was pleased with my new posting to the Smersh Operational Reserve of the First Ukrainian Front. This was splendid, just what I wanted. Another useful thing was the fact that my journey to the Front would take me quite close to my home town. After all, I wasn't so stupid as not to be able to wangle myself at least a two-day visit there.

I arrived in the town sitting beside the driver in the cabin of an army lorry, which happened to be travelling the same road. When I was still on the outskirts I saw that something enormous and irrevocable had happened. I knew from my father's letters and from communiques from the front that my home town had been on the front line for a long time. I expected a certain amount of tangible destruction, but what I now saw went beyond my worst nightmares. The town as such no longer existed. There were heaps of ugly ruins, skeletons of houses, deep craters overgrown with grass—and nothing more. There was a wretched town of miserable dugouts with smoke coming out of their iron chimneys. It was nearly winter and people had to find somewhere to live. The few isolated houses, which had somehow escaped destruction, could be counted on one's fingers. For almost nine months the front had run through my home town. The Germans, who had seized the greater part of the town which stood on the right bank of the river, had been unable to effect a crossing. I suppose that worse things do happen, but not very often. All that was left of our house were my memories and a deep hole. I already knew that my father was not in the town. He was directing the work of reconstructing certain important factories in Kharkov region. Because of his bad heart he had not been accepted for political work in the army. My mother was still with the same relatives far away from the front line, but after all I still had a large number of friends in the town.

I found out the new address of Yoska's parents at the railway offices. Their old house had been destroyed. They themselves had already come back from where they had been evacuated. Uncle Abram looked much older and very drawn. He looked at me, nodded his head and made a seemingly helpless gesture with his hands. Yoska's mother, 'Crazy Rosa', was sobbing quietly in the background. Yoska himself looked down from a photograph on the wall . . . Yoska—Yosif Abramovich Brauder—a first lieutenant in an Armoured Brigade of Guards, twice decorated in the field, killed in action near a small Belorussian hamlet. His platoon was leading an attack on the flank of some German position. His tank was hit by a shell. It did not immediately catch fire, but no one was able to escape from it. It often happens that when a tank is hit by a shell, the crew lose consciousness, or perhaps the hatches were jammed. . . . Then the petrol tanks had caught fire and the supplies of shells had begun to explode. I discovered all this much later through Smersh channels. I have never devoted more zeal to any operation. Why did I try to find out? What could I change by it? I don't know, but I just felt I had to do it. I stood there on that day looking at Yoska's photograph. The words came into my mind. 'Comrade Policewoman, could you tell us how to get to Revolution Avenue?' I was on the verge of tears, as in my early childhood.

In the streets one saw the occasional poorly clad passer-by. People said that at night owls hooted and hares and foxes ran about there. I noticed a queue of people with saucepans and cooking pots standing by a hut, which appeared to have been knocked together very hurriedly. They seemed to be selling something there. I ran my eye aimlessly along the queue . . . and spotted a familiar face. It was my German teacher. Her dress was old and shabby, her face had a yellow tinge to it, but there was no mistaking that it was her.

'Elizaveta Mikhailovna,' I called to her as I approached. She recognised me too and looked respectfully at my well-cut uniform and my infantry lieutenant's shoulder boards. 'Why don't you come with me,' I said insistently. 'Let's go and have some lunch. I'm just passing through and I haven't had a bite to eat all day.'

Noticing the expression on my face, for I had still not recovered from the news of Yoska's death, she hesitatingly agreed. I took her, almost mechanically, to some canteen in a large, clean basement. It turned out to be for senior municipal workers. I cordially invited Elizaveta Mikhailovna to sit down at a table covered with a sheet of clean oil cloth. Some fellow, dressed like a commissar, was watching what I was doing with ironic surprise. I deduced unerringly that this was the manager of the canteen. Even before the war many sellers of beer, wine and fizzy drinks, shop and canteen managers, had dressed like this, to lend themselves authority, as it were. However, his irony and surprise were very much to the point. What business had some kid of an infantry lieutenant and a middle-aged, poorly dressed woman to be in his canteen, which was only for a select minority. I began to boil with furious rage—for Yoska's sake, for the sake of my home town, for poor, worn-out Elizaveta Mikhailovna's sake, for a thousand and one other reasons. What would I have given to have punched that fellow once or twice in the teeth! (Which as I discovered later turned out to be gold.) However, things got no further than this purely Christian yearning or desire. I was, after all, an officer of Smersh and had to keep a tight rein on myself.

I walked up to the manager and flashed my identity card under his nose, carelessly throwing in for good measure 'Main Administration'. The manager's attitude changed as if at the wave of a magic wand. He smiled broadly, and it was at this point that I glimpsed his gleaming gold teeth, bowed, and himself led us to a table.

'Please sit down, you and your mamma will be more cosy here.'

My 'mamma', Elizaveta Mikhailovna, was clearly astonished by what was happening. Bewilderment was written all over her face as to why that lout and scrounger, her former pupil Romanov, should be accorded such deference. The lunch was brought, thick borsch with an appetising smell, and then I think there were meat balls with a sauce and something else. She attacked the food with an intensity that she made a poor job of concealing. I couldn't have felt less like eating.

Over lunch I discovered that her life was, to put it mildly, pretty appalling. My teacher had been unable to be evacuated from the town because of a partially paralysed elder sister, with whom she lived. While the Germans were in the town, so as not to die of hunger herself, and also to feed her invalid sister, she found work as an interpreter in some warehouse of the municipal administration. When our people returned she discovered that she would be given neither work nor ration books, and what was even worse, was often summoned to the district police for interrogations. It transpired that she was being interrogated by some non-uniformed officer. The rest of the story was clear to me without further explanations. Elizaveta Mikhailovna had fallen automatically into the category of 'collaborators with the German occupying forces'. The fact that the warehouse where she had worked was not a military warehouse was immaterial. She would presently be arrested and deported to special camps somewhere in Central Asia. The fact that she hadn't yet been arrested simply meant that there were an awful lot of people in her position. So far, the only people who had been arrested were the real 'collaborators with the enemy'. I came to a decision quickly, perhaps too quickly. I said to her triumphantly: 'I swear to you by the untarnished honour of 10B, our great class, that nothing untoward will happen to you.' She smiled at me uncertainly. She had too much on her mind to pay attention to silly jokes.

I summoned the manager of the canteen and told him that as I had to travel into the country I wanted to take something to eat on the way. He nodded and returned with a sizable bundle. I probed it with my fingers and discovered that he'd even included a bottle of vodka. I paid for the whole lot, including the lunches, with some trivial sum. That's the way it always was for senior officials, admittedly only for senior officials, and that's the way it still is. What a fine fellow that gold-toothed man was. I was sure that by the end of the war he'd have even more gold teeth than he had then. I put the bundle into Elizaveta Mikhailovna's string bag, but she absolutely refused to take any money from me whatever, although she was obviously very touched by my offer. I myself was choking with fury, both at what had happened to her and my own behaviour. There I had been, skulking about hundreds of miles behind the lines with a bunch of criminals, while Yoska had died in his tank, my home town had been razed to the ground and my teacher, who had been so plagued by my oafishness, was on the point of being arrested. Even the fact that I had been wounded in action, and had the appropriate red stripe[1] above the right-hand pocket of my tunic to prove it, was no justification whatsoever.

A short while later I was sitting in a tiny snack bar with an old classmate of mine called Styopka. We had in front of us glasses of red wine of the sort known as 'communion wine'. Styopka was an operational representative of our regional NKGB Administration. He

[1] The official badge for a wound in the Soviet Army is a red stripe for a slight wound and a gold stripe for a serious wound.

too was a lieutenant who had been commissioned after completing a crash course. He was in mufti.

'It's safer that way,' he explained. 'I do a lot of travelling about the villages. It only needs some bugger to clonk you on the head and that's your lot. You bleeders in Smersh are well out of it. And you! In the Main Administration!'

Styopka went on nagging in this vein. We'd never been close friends, but I'd dug him out and, almost holding a knife at his throat, demanded that he should do something to help our former teacher.

'That's not at all easy,' mumbled Styopka.

'Of course it's not easy,' I said.

I suggested to him rather maliciously that if he were really such a nobody and, into the bargain, such a bastard, then I'd go to Perov myself. Perov was one of the heads of the Municipal NKGB. I had been a friend of his daughter's and had often visited their house.

'Of course,' Styopka said, 'everybody knows about you and Lyudka Perova.'

Actually, things hadn't gone much beyond hugging and kissing, since at that time Nonna had appeared on the horizon, but it was something to work on. Eventually Styopka agreed.

'It's so simple,' I persuaded him. 'You're a Chekist, after all. The official case against Elizaveta Mikhailovna hasn't even started. You must have some pals in the right places. Get her included in the lists of people who've been screened and let the police know, so that she can be issued with a passport and ration books and be left in peace. She's got nothing to eat, you know.'

'All right,' said Styopka, 'I'll fix it.'

I felt a bit better now, but not much. I wanted to clear out of the place, which had begun to remind me of a cemetery.

'Things'll be better at the front,' I thought.

Before I left I took a last stroll through the streets and ruins, saying goodbye to the town, as it were. I walked by the Regional Party Committee building. It had been damaged, but not too badly. The mines and explosive charges that my colleagues from the NKVD Demolition Battalion had laid before they left the town had been rendered harmless by the Germans before they exploded. Benefitting from their bitter experiences in Kiev and other cities, they had rushed straight to government buildings in search of mines and explosives. The huge black statue of Lenin, which had formerly stood in front of this building, had vanished. All that was left was the pedestal. During the Occupation the Germans had hung some poor Jew from

Lenin's outstretched arm to amuse themselves. Ilych (Lenin), in accordance with the architect's intentions, stood with his hand pointing the way towards the bright future of communism. Local jokers, however, affirmed that in actual fact he was counting the crows and jackdaws flying about in the square. It had always been a somewhat unfortunate monument. Shortly after it was unveiled it was indirectly responsible for the arrest of a *kolkhoz* woman, who had come to the town to sell some milk. Near the square was a tram-stop. The woman had got off the tram and in the bustle somebody knocked the large clay jug of milk out of her hand. The jug was broken. The *kolkhoz* woman began to curse loudly. Up came a policeman.

'What's the matter?' he asked.

'It's him,' the woman answered. 'I was looking at that there tyrant, he wasn't there before.'

She pointed at the monument to Lenin. They took the woman away to the NKVD and soon moved the tram-stop a little further away.

Actually it was nothing to do with the tram-stop. There was a similar incident in Moscow concerning the monument to Minin[1] and Pozharsky[2] in the Red Square. In the 1930's, on the orders of the NKVD, this monument was turned round to face a different direction. There was a common joke about this. The standing Minin was meant to have said to the sitting Pozharsky, pointing to the Lenin Mausoleum:

> 'Prince, I don't like that filth at all,
> That's lying 'neath the Kremlin wall.'

The Germans, however, either couldn't or didn't have time to defuse the majority of charges placed in buildings by Chekist demolition squads. The NKVD Administration building had been blown up, as had the police, the Town Garrison headquarters and many others. Moreover, repeated bombing raids, both by the Germans and ourselves, and an artillery duel, which lasted nine months, finished the job off. My home town no longer existed. The work of rebuilding moved slowly, although many thousands of German prisoners and citizens of the town worked on it.

I took a train for the city of Kursk. From there I had to travel to Kiev and beyond, into the western Ukraine. In that area, somewhere near Lvov, was the Smersh Operational Reserve of the First Ukrainian (previously Voronezh) Front.

[1] Minin, Kuzma—a butcher from Nizhni-Novgorod (Gorky).
[2] Pozharsky, Prince Dmitri—he and Minin organised national mobilisation against the Polish intervention in 1611.

4

'The bold intelligence company
has now become my family . . .'

From a Soviet song

THERE WAS NO CHANCE of my being able to stop off in Kiev. I
had made one illicit stop in my home town and couldn't extend my
journey any further without inviting trouble. Once I was beyond
Lvov I could definitely feel the disturbed atmosphere of the front.
Lvov had in fact been liberated by our forces only at the end of
July 1944. I called in at the Smersh Administration of the First
Ukrainian Front, chiefly to have a good meal and a bath. I had been
warned by a patrol of rearguard forces (NKVD troops) that military
personnel travelling alone were strongly advised not to stop in
villages and hamlets.

The civilian population had been deported from the hamlet where
the administration was stationed. There were road blocks everywhere. Patrols armed with sub-machine guns stood with weapons
at the ready on sentry duty. There were also armoured vehicle
transporters with heavy-calibre machine guns mounted on them.

Having ascertained the precise location of the Operational Reserve
base, I managed to get a lift in a jeep which was travelling in that
direction. The reserve had occupied some sort of Catholic monastery,
standing in a hollow at the edge of a wood. Generally speaking, there
was no shortage of crucifixes and icons in this area. One often came
across them at cross-roads in the open country with flowers, sometimes withered, but sometimes fresh ones too, placed in front of
them. A broad belt of forest by the monastery itself had been specially
felled. The Germans, who were afraid of partisans, had taken what
measures they could to prevent anyone from creeping out of the
forest and up to the monastery unnoticed. This situation suited
Smersh equally well. The chief of the Reserve, a lieutenant-colonel,
ordered me to report to the Second Operational Section. He said

that this was a temporary measure since that section was short of staff. The section chief, a young-looking major, came from almost the same part of the country as I did. The room in which I had to live was a narrow monastic cell with a stone floor, and a tiny crucifix in a niche in the corner beside my bed.

The Second Section, along with others, was then engaged on working with the partisans. The front line had moved up ahead, and many partisan detachments were emerging from the forests. They had either to be disbanded and have their members reposted after screening, or again, only after being screened, they might be sent behind the German lines for a further period. In addition to them, we had to deal with a never-ending stream of Chekist and partisan operational groups, as well as individual intelligence agents. They came to us both from immediately behind the German lines and from further away, from Poland and from Germany. We were also sending out fresh personnel to all these places. We had to accept and process the information brought by our incoming agents, so that it could be used on the spot by Smersh itself and so that any strategic information, which had been abstracted from it, could be sent to Front HQ. All the most important information was sent to GUKR Smersh in Moscow. Outgoing personnel, who had to cross the German lines, had to be given a final briefing and if necessary supplied with guides.

The partisan movement on German-occupied territory had come into being in 1941, right at the beginning of the war. Initially, however, things had gone far from smoothly. The nation as a whole hadn't had the slightest desire either to fight for or to assist Soviet power. The Chekist secret agents, who had been specially left behind on enemy-occupied territory, had a very rough time of it. It was common practice for the local population to kill them or to hand them over to the Germans. Chekists who were dropped by parachute, or who crossed the front line secretly, shared the same fate. Of course, I can't quote the exact number of people who perished in this way, but it was quite substantial. Later, things began to look up. The Germans showed their true colours. It became clear that they were conquerors and not the liberators for whom the people had taken them. A vast number of Soviet prisoners, who had voluntarily gone over to the Germans, died in camps as a result of hunger and inhumane treatment. The invaders began to massacre the Jewish population, including small children and old people. They started the forced mass deportation of the population, young men and girls in particular, to slave-labour camps in Germany. The Germans did not even disband the collective farms, which people hated so much. All these points were taken into account and exploited by the leaders of the State Security Service. A host of partisan groups and detachments sprang up. Often they came into being spontaneously. People who were unwilling to put up with German oppression and insults began to arm themselves and go into the forests. Small detachments of this type began gradually to unite with one another and grow into a powerful force. The leadership of the NKVD (and later the NKGB) took a most active part in all these activities. Chekist representatives were dropped in the forests behind the German lines. Drops were also made of arms, ammunition, medical supplies and personnel. Secret airfields and aerodromes were built and permanent radio contact was established with the partisans. The leaders of partisan detachments were gradually replaced, if necessary, by people who were to the taste of the Soviet authorities, often by professional Chekists masquerading under some sort of cover. The partisan leaders whose faces did not fit and who were not one hundred per cent pro-Soviet were removed by time-honoured NKGB methods. Some way was found to compromise them. They were accused of treachery, or of working for the Germans, of robbing the civilian population, or of moral depravity, etc. Sometimes they were simply killed by person or persons unknown. More occasionally they were invited to Moscow to receive some honour, or for an important 'top-level' conference.

The NKGB was also active in another sphere on German-occupied territory. There remained behind in every village, small town and city from which our forces had retreated, the so-called undercover leadership of the Party and often of the Komsomol as well. This leadership was usually made up of active members of the Party or Komsomol organisations, including, for example, district and municipal Party Committee Secretaries, and chiefs of MTS[1] political branches, collective farm political organisers, etc. The whole operation of leaving these undercover workers behind and keeping in contact with them as often as possible was effected by the NKGB. As a rule, the undercover men went to ground in specially designated hideouts for an initial period. These hideouts were in false roofs, basements, or specially built concealed dugouts in gardens of houses whose owners remained loyal to Soviet power. Sometimes they were

[1] MTS—Machine Tractor Stations. An organisation from which collective farmers hired their plant. They were later disbanded by Khrushchev.

discovered by the Germans or their helpers from among the local population. The result for the inhabitants was either the hangman's noose or the firing squad, but this didn't happen all that frequently. When the initial period was over, the undercover men emerged into the light of day, having altered their external appearance as best they could. They grew beards and moustaches, dyed their hair, donned spectacles and acquired limps. They avoided basing themselves in places where they were well known. Many of them weren't local people anyway.

All their papers were in perfect order and each had a cover story, which had been concocted by the NKGB. They often pretended to be people who had suffered at the hands of Soviet power. Some complained of repressions, while others said that they were 'un-persons', or committed religious believers. Others claimed that they had escaped from a Soviet prison or labour camp. In consultation with the NKGB they chose a safe 'roof' for themselves. Some went to work in the police force, which the Germans organised. Certain of them who worked as policemen and investigators did very well in the service and became district police chiefs. Others worked as secretaries, interpreters, village elders and sometimes even as muni-cipal burgomasters in the local government bodies set up by the Germans. They ingratiated themselves with the Germans in every way, even surpassing the latter in their cruelty towards the local population. They unearthed all manner of 'communists' and 'Yids', and squeezed all kinds of taxes and foodstuffs for the occupying forces out of the peasantry. The Germans trusted them implicitly and greatly admired their work. Another group became involved in private commerce, which was permitted by the Germans, and opened all kinds of shops, setting themselves up as watch repairers, shoe repairers, tailors and, in some cases, restaurateurs. Some of them kept brothels. There were even some priests among them, like my colleague in the State Security Service school. This was a good 'roof', as the Germans never meddled in the affairs of the Church. Yet another group of undercover workers had no obvious overt function. They were the NKGB link men. They collected informa-tion from other secret agents for transmission further up the pipeline. They also received fresh instructions and tasks 'from above', to be passed on to their own group of contacts. People who belonged to this category found themselves playing the most improbable parts—wandering holy men, medicant cripples and even village idiots.

By the time I arrived at the front, the whole huge clandestine partisan machine was running very smoothly, the control system worked and there was a fairly high standard of discipline. I was put to work straight away. At first, because I was a novice, I was occupied entirely with paperwork. I checked lists of partisans who had come out of the forests, sorting them out and deciding on the basis of age and physical fitness, who should be put on non-military work, who should be sent into the army and who would be of further use as an agent behind the German lines. I had almost no contact at all with living human beings. This kind of work almost drove me up the wall, but Chekist discipline made it impossible either to protest or to complain. I already understood that one had to devote all one's strength and all one's resources to fulfilling the orders one was given. And this wasn't just empty words. Everyone who surrounded me worked in this way, from the lieutenant-colonel, who was branch chief, to the young, green lieutenants like myself, who had just been posted from GUKR Smersh. We used to spend fourteen hours a day on the job.

Life had its more pleasant sides. I became very friendly with a first lieutenant called Kolya, who was about my age. He had arrived there two months before I did. He consoled me by saying that the paperwork would be only temporary and had been caused by an unprecedented influx of partisans. The armies had just completed an advance, which had liberated large new areas of Soviet territory. Preparations were being made for a fresh leap forward, towards Poland and Germany. Snatching a bit of spare time when we could, Kolya and I used to jump into a jeep and go and visit a demolition squad made up of local Komsomols from NKVD demolition battalions and auxiliary police groups. In addition to our pistols we had PPSh.[1] sub-machine guns hanging round our necks. This was part of standing orders in those areas. We also had a couple of hand-grenades on the floor of the jeep.

Our consuming interest was not the demolition battalions as such but the young girls who served in them, for here they had girls in them too. I complained to Kolya about my prolonged, enforced abstinence, due to unsuitable conditions in Tatishchevo. He sympathised, stating that it was indeed time for me to break my fast. I got my 'breakfast' after two or three evenings with the local young people, who were for the most part Komsomol activists. I spent the greater part of the night in somebody's hayloft on the fresh, sweet-smelling hay. I had for company a cheerful Ukrainian Komsomol

[1] PPSh. (*Pistolet-Pulemyot Shpagina*)—Shpagin machine pistol.

girl, with a large bosom, a slim waist and a complete inability to resist tickling. We were both happy, but as before there wasn't time to meet often. To my mind we had far too much work to do. Moreover, our bosses in Smersh frowned upon encounters of this kind, or for that matter any non-professional encounters with the local population, even with local people who were active communists. Our bosses maintained that the task of screening the local population's political reliability was far from complete and one ought to be particularly cautious and vigilant, so as not to get into trouble or even endanger one's life. As I discovered later, this kind of attitude was by no means unfounded.

The activities of the clandestine partisan movement were controlled from Moscow, which was where its general HQ was situated. There was also a position called 'Commander-in-Chief of the Partisan Movement', occupied by Marshal Voroshilov. I was well aware, however, that Voroshilov himself allotted very little time to this particular job, if any at all. He was actually nothing more than a figurehead, who was used in this way because he was quite a popular personality in the Soviet Union. The real reins of the partisan movement were all in the hands of the NKGB or, to be more precise, in the hands of Colonel-General Bel'chenko, a professional Chekist from the top brass of the State Security Service. He was known officially at that time as the Deputy Chief of General HQ of the Partisan Movement. The other bodies which exerted a direct influence on the control of this movement were the Fourth (Intelligence-Sabotage) Administration of the NKGB, headed by Lieutenant-General Sudoplatov, the Second (Main Intelligence) Administration of the General Staff of the Soviet Army, headed by Colonel-General Kuznetsov, where matters relating to military intelligence was concerned, and of course our own GUKR Smersh under Colonel General Abakumov. GUKR Smersh was represented at the First Ukrainian Front by the head of the Front's Smersh Administration, Lieutenant-General Korolyov. In addition to these, the People's Commissar of State Security for the Ukraine, Lieutenant-General Strokach, also had a hand in the control of partisans and undercover workers. It is easy to see that there were more than enough bosses to go round.

The victor's crown for power and influence, however, undoubtedly belonged to Abakumov. Over and above everything else he was also the First Deputy of the People's Commissar of the USSR for State Security. In consequence, so far as all matters concerning partisans or undercover agents were concerned, the final word was with us officers of Smersh, which had its own representatives in all partisan formations. Partisan detachments were made up of companies, battalions and brigades. In all detachments above and including independent battalions, there was a post called 'Deputy Detachment Commander for Intelligence Matters', i.e. a quite unexceptional post in the military hierarchy. However, lurking behind this title, known only to a small circle of initiated persons, was the permanent Smersh representative. He had in his hands all the detachment's means of communication and all its intelligence and counter-intelligence work. Moreover, what was more important, he was in no sense subordinate to the detachment commander and in no way dependent on him. This meant that even if the detachment commander himself was a professional Chekist, the Smersh representative was still the most powerful man in the detachment. Higher up the ladder, in the larger headquarters of partisan formations, Smersh was represented by intelligence sections, staffed by its own regular officers. Only a few people knew that they were in fact Smersh officers, as these officers were protected by reliable 'roofs' and cover stories. After all, as the whole world knows, the Soviet partisan movement had its roots in the people themselves and came into being spontaneously, in response to the will of the masses.

Attached to the headquarters of a Front, in the given instance the HQ of the First Ukrainian Front, there were permanent partisan representatives and operational communication groups. The same overall picture held good in these bodies too, however, and the real master was in fact Smersh. This whole system had been created for a very good reason. The partisan detachments frequently participated in full-scale fighting against the Germans, usually striking at their rear at the same time as our regular forces were attacking on the front line. This was not, however, their main value. The partisans collected and transmitted to the field HQ of the Front an enormous quantity of military information, and kept under constant surveillance all the important German garrisons, aerodromes and lines of communication.

There existed various methods of collecting and transmitting information from behind the enemy lines. The local population was questioned. Identification marks of vehicles and tanks were noted, and the shoulder boards of German units were studied. The movement of trains and columns of troops on the roads were also recorded. If there was no radio contact or regular couriers, dead-letter boxes were resorted to. Hollows in certain trees or tree-stumps, or graves in cemeteries, could be used for this purpose. A bouquet of flowers, or curtains of a special colour at the windows of certain flats or houses, could also serve as signs. All these places were regularly visited at frequent intervals by undercover partisan communications personnel. A valuable way of obtaining information which was urgently required was the capturing of a 'tongue', i.e. the kidnapping of individual German officers and men. For this purpose special operational snatching groups existed, under the command of professional Chekists. Each partisan brigade had such a group, comprising fifty to fifty-five men, or sometimes there were smaller ones with twenty-five to thirty members. The work of these groups was to stage ambushes and raids on senior German officers, who in many cases were carrying important papers. An example that comes to mind was the snatching of General Ilgen from the town of Rovno. Chekist snatching groups were active not only on German-occupied Soviet territory. General Shatlosh, who was the Minister of Defence of the German puppet regime in Slovakia, was snatched in the Banskaya Bystritsa District of Czechoslovakia and handed over to Smersh. He and General Turants, the commander of the Slovakian land forces, were snatched by a group of Chekists not far from a local aerodrome. After interrogation at the Smersh Administration of the Front the important guests were sent by air to Moscow, to Abakumov's Administration.

I shall never forget the day when I was first included in an operational group flying to a raiding detachment based on Polish territory. My new friend Kolya, the first lieutenant, flew with me. The raiding detachments were yet another variety of partisan activity. They moved about behind the enemy lines, constantly changing their base camps. Their routes had been precisely worked out in the Smersh Administration of the Front. They often carried out missions which had been planned from GUKR Smersh itself. The type of missions they fulfilled were the destruction of German police and military garrisons and of rear supply bases of ammunition, fuel, spare parts and foodstuffs, the cutting of German telephone communication lines, and all kinds of other acts of sabotage and terrorism. Raiding detachments located behind the enemy lines sent out their own operational groups and also individual agents.

There were two types of groups, the intelligence-sabotage group and the operational-sabotage group. The first type had specific jobs concerning the collection of intelligence data on the basis of a net-

work of agents. For them acts of sabotage were of secondary importance. The second carried out missions to destroy prearranged enemy
installations, such as bridges, aerodromes and buildings, and also to
murder certain individual Germans or persons of any nationality
who happened to be working for them. The victims of this type of
group, or individual agent, included the Chief Justice of the Ukraine,
Funk, and two assistants of the German Commissar General of the
Ukraine. We didn't manage to reach Gauleiter Koch himself,
despite repeated attempts. He must have been a very sensible man,
as well guarded as Stalin himself.

The raiding detachment to which we were flying was based behind
the German lines in Poland. We flew across the front line at the
strictly prescribed altitude for this kind of flight. We began to lose
height, and could see the seemingly limitless forests of Poland,
dotted here and there with gleaming lakes. We swung round above
a broad glade in the forest. I suddenly saw two intersecting blue
lines of tracer-bullets. Somebody was firing from rocket pistols, not
upwards however, but horizontally, to show us where we should
land. The aeroplane was soon surrounded by partisans, most of
whom were wearing full Soviet military uniform, complete with
decorations and badges of rank. The remainder were dressed in
varied garb, but all wore the obligatory partisan badge, an oblong
red ribbon, stitched to their headgear. The commander of the
detachment was a Chekist colonel from the Main Administration of
Smersh, who also was in full army uniform, infantry uniform as it
happened. The chief of the group I had arrived with, which had
about six or seven people in it, reported our safe arrival. We went
into a large underground shelter, which was the colonel's headquarters. Apart from ourselves, the Deputy Detachment Commander
for Intelligence, himself a Chekist, was also present. As we were all
from the same outfit, there was no need for secrets. The colonel, of
course, knew the time and purpose of our arrival. He was in constant
communication, not only with the Smersh Administration of the
Front but with GUKR Smersh in Moscow too.

During one of my evenings with the detachment I was able to
observe how these communications worked. At that time Moscow
used often to broadcast concerts for soldiers at the front. They would
have a jazz orchestra playing songs which were popular at that time,
an accordion playing, cymbals clanging and a drummer beating out
the rhythm. A Chekist communications man sitting beside me had
his eye attentively fixed on the watch on his wrist. The beat of a

drum came through once again. The communications man picked up a fountain pen and began to write down on a piece of paper short lines of dots and dashes. I listened carefully, and through the jazz music I could catch the quick tapping of a morse key, every now and then interrupted by a pause, dash-dot-dash-dot-dash dot dot. . . . The voice of the woman singer died away. The drummer came in again and then once more the morse key pushed its way through. This continued for several minutes. Of course the transmission was being made in a prearranged secret code. Even if any outsider had happened to hear this broadcast it is most unlikely that he could have understood it.

We had also brought the colonel fresh instructions and a list of new missions. We had brought them of course inside our heads, in case the aeroplane had been shot down by German fighters, or if we had had to make a forced landing on enemy territory. For the same reason we had left all personal papers connecting us in any way with Smersh, at Front Headquarters. This same went for our Party and Komsomol cards, letters from our families and so forth. The detachment to which I had flown sometimes operated in the area of the Polish-German frontier and had set up firm lines of communication with Polish non-communist resistance detachments, leaving a network of its own intelligence agents, each with a completely watertight 'roof' in many Polish towns and villages. Small groups and individual operational agents were being sent out from the detachment all the time. On a quiet road an anti-tank grenade had been thrown at a German SS armoured car. The driver and the other passengers had either been killed by the explosion or finished off afterwards. A slightly wounded SS *Hauptsturmfuhrer* (captain) had been brought back to detachment base, complete with maps and papers. He lay in a dugout, under the eye of our partisan doctor. He later accompanied us when we flew back to Smersh Administration of the Front. The chief of a German anti-partisan school, a *Volks-deutsch* from the western Ukraine, had had his throat cut while he was in bed with his mistress. Polish underground workers assisted in finding out where he lived. These were but two of many such operations. The most important thing was, however, the mass of military information that had been collected about concentrations and movements of German troops. The greater part of it had already been radioed to Moscow and sent to Front HQ by special courier. We conscientiously memorised all the other details.

It was while I was with this detachment that I was present at an execution for the first time in my life. An operational snatching group had brought two German police guards to the detachment. Along with others they had been accompanying a group of Polish prisoners to some destination, I can't remember which. Our people staged an ambush, in which some of the police were killed, and the others took to their heels. Some of the liberated Poles wanted to join our detachment. Their offer was politely declined, but they were supplied with arms, food and a large sum of German Occupation money, of which there was an enormous quantity in the detachment. It was forbidden to take Poles, or for that matter any other outsiders, back to detachment base, as this was top secret. When the police were interrogated, it became clear that they were very uninteresting individuals. There was no prospect of extracting valuable intelligence data from them, so there was no point in taking them back behind our lines. All detachment personnel who were free from other duties were formed up in the forest. We officers stood together in a group at the side. Opposite us was a freshly dug hole. In front of the hole stood the policemen. One was a Russian ex-POW and the other a western Ukrainian. In front of them stood about five partisans, armed with sub-machine guns. The colonel pronounced sentence: 'In the name of the Soviet Union . . . as a punishment for treason . . . and for collaboration with the vilest enemy of our motherland and of the whole Slav race . . .' then followed their names, 'are sentenced to death by the firing squad.' He snapped quickly to the marksmen, 'Carry out the sentence!' 'At the fascist slime,' shouted the officer in charge of the firing squad, 'fire!' There was a short burst of firing, followed by a second. One of the prisoners fell straight away and disappeared into the hole. The second slid with apparent reluctance down on to the ground, and lay with his legs twitching. One of the squad ran up and kicked him into the hole.

In my first battle, near my home town, I'd seen men dead and dying from wounds, but this was something quite different. I must say that those two made a good job of dying. There was no begging for mercy. They wore no bandage over their eyes and silently stared death straight in the face. I afterwards tried to avoid being present at such scenes, but this was not always possible. In Poland too, in an area already occupied by our forces, I witnessed the execution of one of our officers, who had raped a young Polish girl in her parents' home. The order of sentence in this case was widely publicised, both to our forces and to the local population. Later, in Budapest, I was present when a group of leaders of the Hungarian pro-fascist party

'Crossed Arrows', was hanged. All these scenes left me with an impression that can in no way be described as pleasant.

Following the instructions that the colonel had just received, the detachment once again set off on a long journey, but this time in a different direction, towards the German frontier. As I discovered, one of the many jobs that the detachment had to do was to select routes suitable for tanks, convenient river crossings and even to collect hydro-meteorological data. All this was very useful for the subsequent advances of our Front. Just as was the case on our own territory, Chekist partisans also collected detailed information about persons who had collaborated with the Germans. Long lists were compiled of all the collaborators, or just plain sympathisers, often accompanied by their photographs and exact descriptions of their physical appearance. All this was handed on to the Smersh Administration of the Front and passed to the Operational Records Section of the Operational Branch. During the advance groups of Chekists from this branch moved with the troops and when villages and towns were occupied they went at once to the appropriate addresses. In Poland, however, our agents did not only gather information about people who worked for the Germans. Data was obtained for the operational files on all the Polish political parties, on the Polish People's Army (*Armia Krayova*) and on individual personalities in the civic, commercial, scientific and religious life of Poland. Smersh devoted no less attention to all these subjects than to the people who had collaborated with the German occupying authorities. Little by little, a network of agents supplying information was set up among the local population. This meant that cadres of secret informers were recruited, and the members of these cadres were by no means all Polish communists.

Our Smersh Administration had several such long-distance raiding detachments. I remember the detachment of Colonel Medvedev, active in the western Ukraine and Poland, and of Colonel Belov, active in Czechoslovakia and particularly in Slovakia. Another, similar detachment, which was directly subordinate to Abakumov in Moscow, brought to light very valuable information about the firing and testing grounds of V1 and V2 rockets, somewhere in the district of Brno. The officers of all these detachments were drawn entirely from regular officers of the State Security Service. NCOs and privates were selected from interior and frontier troops of the NKVD. They had all done four- to six-month crash courses in training schools for partisan warfare and intelligence gathering.

On our return from the detachment to the 'mainland', unpleasant news awaited us at the Smersh Administration. There had been a sharp rise in the activities of anti-Soviet partisans behind our own lines. There were many more cases of groups of our soldiers, or individual officers and men, being fired on and killed. All this had begun as soon as our forces had entered the western Ukraine, flaring up and dying down again, only to reappear in the most unexpected places. The main protagonists were the OUN (Organisation of Ukrainian Nationalists) and also the UPA (Ukrainian Insurgent Army). At the beginning of 1941 they had been active with the full support and assistance of the Germans. Then there had been a parting of the ways. The Germans did not intend, as many leaders of the OUN and a section of the population of the western Ukraine believed, to create a free, independent Ukraine. When the Ukrainian nationalists chanced their arm and declared a free Ukraine in Lvov the Germans broke them up by force and arrested many of the Ukrainian leaders.

At this point many of the nationalists began to go into the forests and take up arms. There were more than enough guns to go round, what with German arms and Soviet weapons that had been left by our retreating forces. Detachments of partisans came into being. They fought the Germans, but when the Soviet army came on the scene they began to fight that too. The nationalists had their own security service system, an intelligence service which wasn't at all bad, hidden stores of weapons, ammunition and foodstuffs. They made themselves quite at home in the forest thickets and impenetrable swamps, and in fact many of them were literally at home. Their main asset was, however, that with a small number of exceptions the local population assisted them. Some were forced to give such assistance, since the security service of the nationalist partisans undertook merciless reprisals against any who betrayed their movement or even wished to remain neutral. Another section of the population helped them out of conviction, because they really loathed Soviet power and everything it stood for.

The nationalist partisans wore no special uniform and often, after carrying out some mission or operation, split up peacefully to their homes, hid their weapons and got quietly on with the most unwarlike agrarian tasks, so continuing until the next operation. Fighting them was consequently far from easy. They were in the habit of knifing or shooting local representatives of Soviet power who had been appointed in the areas liberated from the Germans. Individuals about to take up such posts considered their death warrants already signed. NKGB bodies were seldom able to provide adequate protection. There was a war going on and every Chekist was worth his weight in gold. It would have been impossible to open branches of the NKGB in every remote western Ukrainian hamlet. Mobile emergency operational teams of Chekists and militia often arrived on the scene of the crime when the show was over, that is to say when all that was left of the Soviet officials and activists were bits and pieces. Before embarking on an operation, the nationalist partisans usually cut the telephone wires which linked remote villages with the district centres. This kind of activity did not inflict vast losses on our forces and a series of protective and precautionary measures were taken; but these were not always enough.

For a long time I was a close friend of a Chekist lieutenant from the Rearguard Administration of the First Ukrainian Front. Before he took up this position he had worked in a special purpose operational guard group, attached to the Smersh Operational Section of the Military Council of that Front. The following personnel belong to the Military Council of a Front: Front Commander, Front Political Organiser (i.e. First Member of the Military Council), Chief of Staff and the chiefs of the various arms of the services belonging to the Front. The incident my friend told me about occurred at the end of February 1944. The Commander of our Front at that time was General of the Army Nikolai Vatutin, and the First Member of the Military Council was Lieutenant-General Nikita Khrushchev.

The Front Commander wished to acquaint himself personally with a new deployment of the units of one of his armies. The party was travelling through a typical area of western Ukrainian countryside. The roads ran through fields, and more often than not in that area, woodland, passing through the occasional village. An armoured vehicle transporter was travelling in front with a heavy-calibre machine gun mounted on the roof of the driver's cab. Behind its armour-plated sides, which came up to waist height, sat about eight soldiers armed with sub-machine guns. In the cab with the driver was an officer. Behind the transporter came the Front Commander's car. General Vatutin was sitting beside the driver and in the rear seat sat his adjutant, a colonel, and a soldier armed with a sub-machine gun. Next came the car of the First Member of the Military Council. Lieutenant-General Khrushchev was sitting beside the driver and in the back was his personal bodyguard, to which he was due as a member of the Politbureau, and a soldier with a sub-machine gun. One further vehicle was behind them, a sort of pick-up or small truck. Sitting in that, with another five or six soldiers, was the man who told me the story.

They drove into a village, which was no more than a single long street of houses, with domestic outbuildings, gardens and plots of vegetables. When it reached the end of the street, before leaving the village, the leading transporter put on speed and separated itself slightly from the other vehicles. As the officer in charge later explained, he very understandably wished to get a look at what was happening outside the village. At this point there came a burst of firing. The lieutenant told me that the shots seemed to come from every direction, from behind the houses, out of lofts and out of gardens. The adjutant was hit straight away, and, so far as I can remember, killed outright. My informant, being at the back, had a good view of what was going on in front. The transporter turned round with all speed and roared back toward the Front Commander's car. The soldiers leapt to the ground and opened fire in all directions. The Front Commander left his dead, or dying, adjutant in the care of the soldier in the back seat. He himself leapt to the ground, grabbed a pistol, and joined the soldiers who were shooting. By this time the machine gun on the transporter had opened fire too. In the rear portion of the column, that's to say right under the nose of the lieutenant who was telling me the tale, events had taken a different turn. The Chekist who was driving Khrushchev's car quickly turned his vehicle to one side in an attempt to turn right round and leave the inhospitable village. The First Member of the Military Council lay across the back seat like a pig's carcass. The lieutenant, who was a Ukrainian, said as much, *Yak kaban* (like a boar). Khrushchev's bodyguard and the soldier in the car spread-eagled themselves on top of him, protecting him with their own bodies. All this flashed before the lieutenant's eyes. 'It's a good job,' he said, 'that nobody threw any hand-grenades!' The lieutenant's pick-up, with the other soldiers on board, turned round and roared off after Khrushchev's car, as indeed it was bidden to do in such situations by the military statutes. During the firing, Vatutin, the Front Commander, was wounded in the thigh. I was told, by the way, that the firing soon stopped and peace and quiet reigned once again in the village. That soon changed when the Smersh operational groups and NKVD forces arrived.

Vatutin was taken with all speed to a hospital in Kiev, which I think was on Artyom Street. Stalin, who valued Vatutin very highly, had the very best doctors sent to look after him. It proved impossible to save the Front Commander's life. He died after one and a half months in hospital. The First Member of the Military Council of the First Ukrainian Front survived him by more than twenty-seven years.[1] Khrushchev's bodyguard was certainly still alive until Khrushchev himself was ousted from power. He remained at his master's side throughout all those stormy years. I can't remember his name, but I well remember his face, which I saw many times. It stood up to the ravages of time. It was a typical round Russian or Ukrainian face, with a bulbous nose and cheerful, friendly eyes. All the foreign correspondents in Moscow saw him as often as they saw Khrushchev. The inhabitants of all the countries that Khrushchev visited saw him too. His photograph appeared hundreds of times in all the newspapers of the world. It even got into the Soviet papers. He and Khrushchev were like Siamese twins. He was a colonel in the State Security Service and quite a decent, friendly chap.

After Vatutin's death Marshal Zhukov became Commander of the Front for a short time, but by the time I arrived there, Marshal Konev was already in command. General of the Army Vatutin still remained very popular among the officers and men. He was even well liked among officials of Smersh. I myself never met him, but I am quite certain of two things. He took part in liberating my home town from the Germans, and had he lived he would most certainly have become a Marshal of the Soviet Union.

I came across Khrushchev several times, not counting the occasion when I saw him on the platform at the military parade in my home town. I have, however, a particularly clear memory of one of those meetings, which was somewhat unusual. It took place at a rather important river crossing in the Ukraine. A serious traffic jam had formed at this crossing, in which a whole lot of vehicles were involved. As it was still light and German aircraft were very much in evidence, the traffic jam at the crossing created a potentially very dangerous situation. The privates and NCOs who were driving the vehicles, which were mainly lorries, had collected into a group and were cursing one another and trying to find out who was to blame for what had happened. They didn't pay the slightest attention to the threats and entreaties of the crossing commandant, some flustered officer from the Engineers. Another officer from Smersh and I were standing not far away. We weren't in a particular hurry to get anywhere, but the thought of possible bombing by the Germans made

[1] Khruschev died in September 1971.

us feel less cosy than we might otherwise have been. A small, stocky man in military uniform, but without shoulder boards, ambled up to the drivers with an unhurried, rolling gait.

'Now let's have a look,' he began. 'What's all this shouting and bawling about?'

Our army drivers are a pretty wild lot and not usually at a loss for words.

'Who the hell do you think you are?'

'Where's this walrus' prick popped up from?'

I remembered the last remark well, because I'd always been interested in walruses! They remind me of Maxim Gorky and vice versa. And here they were again, at a remote river crossing in wartime. Evidently the stocky man's silent bodyguard and companion heard the words too. With a resolute expression on his face he was about to step over to the drivers when the stocky man stopped him and said, 'Don't bother, don't bother.' He then went across himself and joined the group of drivers.

'Calm down, comrades! My name's Khrushchev. We've got to get this jam moving immediately!'

The traffic got moving fairly quickly and we went on our way. Khrushchev vanished, and in fact fairly soon vanished altogether from the First Ukrainian Front. He remained behind in the newly liberated Ukraine. Lieutenant-General Krainyukov took his place as First Member of the Military Council of the Front.

Many of the slogans of the Ukrainian nationalists annoyed and bewildered me and my friends. I read many of their slogans and appeals to the people, which were passed on to us in Smersh. Although, according to the book, everything like this had to be passed on to us, I have no doubt that officers and men also read such papers quite freely, before handing them over. One often saw these slogans stuck to telegraph poles in the fields and woods, or to the walls of outbuildings. Sometimes they were even fastened to long poles and set up by the roadside. 'Long live the free and independent Ukraine!' On occasions, however, the content was different. 'Hammer the Russian bears, the Yids and the Poles—the sworn enemies of the Ukrainian nation!' I, and for that matter most of the rest of our officers and men from all units, found it difficult to understand and approve this kind of appeal. All the many nationalities of the Soviet Union had suffered and endured the upheavals of Soviet life: hunger, the purges, the war, together. In addition, an enormous number of people from all the various nationalities in our country, in particular

Russians and Ukrainians, had intermarried and formed ties with one another. Even Hitler himself would have been hard put to it to decide exactly whom he should 'hammer'.

Apparently the greater part of the Ukrainian nationalist leaders, who were western Ukrainians from Galicia, did not understand this. After all, Galicia had never been a part of Russia. Before the Revolution it belonged to Austro-Hungary, and between the wars it was a part of Poland. Even worse, many of the leaders of the Ukrainian Nationalists in the west have not even grasped this today, so many years after the event. This is one of the reasons why their movement was not able to win the mass support and response of our people. Of course, there were other reasons, such as the overwhelming superiority of strength and experience being on our side, but their ideas too contributed to their undoing. A pure, good, just idea, which is intelligently directed at the people, will always find a way into their hearts.

The Nationalists' mines which were concealed in roads, houses and elsewhere were far more damaging to us than were their slogans. On a windy, cold day, two other officers and I were rushing by jeep towards a Smersh Counter-Espionage Branch (OKR) which had thrust far ahead with our Front's Tank Army. On the road ahead of us we observed a group of soldiers and a Studebaker lorry lying on its side. As we braked to a halt we noticed the blood-spattered driver lying there in the slush. Someone was trying to put a bandage on his wound and a sergeant close by was wiping his blood-stained face with his hand. They had hit a mine in the road surface. We turned off the road to go round the spot. Suddenly there was a terrible crash and I seemed to be flying somewhere or other, self-propelled. Then came a void, empty of all thoughts and sensations.

When I came to, I was lying on my cape at the side of the road. There was no trace whatsoever of our jeep. I noticed a large hole in the road and beside it something which I couldn't make out. I wanted to get up, but the pain in the left-hand side of my body when I tried to made me scream. Some soldiers and officers whom I didn't know hurried over to me. I heard a voice saying something like, 'Ah ha! this one's alive and in one piece, but he looks as if he's just been to a dog's wedding—all his clothing's torn to bits' I hadn't actually been to a dog's wedding. It was just that our jeep had detonated a mine with one of its back wheels. Thank God it wasn't an anti-tank mine. All the same, the man who laid it had

used his brains. He had worked out that if someone set off the first
mine, which had been laid in the road, then the next vehicle would
make a detour, just as we did.

I had been very lucky. I had been sitting in the front seat, next
to the driver, and had simply been hurled out of the open jeep by
the explosion. The captain, who was driving, also got off lightly and
although his back was rather badly bruised, there was luckily no
damage to his spine. The lieutenant who had been sitting behind
was killed outright. All this I discovered much later. All that I
knew then was that I was on my way to the hospital in some army
lorry, and I had to lie on my right-hand side all the time. After that
I found myself in the field hospital of a Tank Corps of Guards. My
whole left side swelled up and turned all the colours of the rainbow,
from a malevolent black to lemon-yellow. After I'd had some injec-
tions the pain abated. I even began to walk about, 'like an old
degenerate', as the doctor who was treating me told me. It turned
out that my efforts to walk were somewhat premature. My old
wound, which I had sustained in my left leg in 1942, reopened. My
unlucky side! I did not know then that the balance would be somewhat redressed later and that I would be wounded in the right-hand
side of my face. The major in charge of my section of Smersh, who
came to visit me in hospital, said there was no point messing around
in a field hospital, and that he intended to have me sent to hospital
in Kiev. Of course, none of the local doctors dared to argue with
the representative of such an organisation.

'We've asked for the "Patriotic War",[1] whether or not it'll be confirmed I don't know, but you can be sure of a "Little Star",'[2] he added.

The Tank Corps soldiers reclothed me from head to foot. My old
uniform had quite literally been blown to shreds by the explosion.
Limping and dragging my leg, I reached the Kiev hospital on the
Brest-Litovsk Chaussee by the film studio. There was something of
a hold-up in the reception ward. The doctor who was supposed to
examine us was on call somewhere. When I say 'us', I mean a fifty-
year-old Ukrainian soldier with a light wound in his foot and a
shiny, new 'For valour' medal, and a young sergeant who had been
wounded in his side. The Ukrainian soldier was slightly drunk and
in an excellent mood. Till then, as he was only too happy to tell us,
everybody, including his own wife, had looked down on him, and
regarded him as a good-for-nothing.

[1] The Order of the Patriotic War (first and second class).
[2] Order of the Red Star—a more modest decoration.

'Now,' he said proudly, nodding towards his wounded leg, 'everything's going to be different.'

His wife had managed to get him in the transit hospital. Heaven knows how she found him! She had wept over him and left him a hefty piece of garlic sausage and a large flask of first-rate, home-distilled vodka.

'Just you try some, Comrade Lieutenant,' he said. 'It's as pure as the Virgin's tears and as strong as Soviet power.'

I didn't refuse his offer and neither did the sergeant.

All this time there was no sign of the doctor, so the flask of excellent vodka went round from hand to hand. The soldier, who by now was quite drunk, told me in confidence that he had actually served in Petlyura's[1] forces, which had done nothing to improve his standing, particularly with the village authorities.

'But now I invite you to be my guests,' he said, patting his shining new medal by way of explanation.

If he had known where I worked, then drunk or sober, he would have chattered a great deal less, although at that moment I couldn't have cared whether he'd worked for Himmler himself, or even been Hitler's uncle. The home-distilled vodka really was fiendishly strong. I too was carried away by the general merriment and we soon began to raise the dust in the reception ward and make a noise as if all hell had been let loose. The sergeant was dancing the *gopak* and the *kazachek*, while the soldier and I sat there clapping our hands and beating time with our uninjured legs. An elderly duty orderly glanced in at the door several times in an effort to quieten us down, but what chance had he of making an impression?

At the height of the party the hospital duty doctor walked quickly into the room. There was still no sign of the doctor for whom we were waiting. The duty doctor was a young woman of medium height, who was a first lieutenant in the Medical Corps. Her black, expressive eyes flashed with indignation. Her lower lip, which was slightly full, curled in disdain. I noticed too her lovely white skin and slim shapely legs. That was at a first superficial examination when I was tipsy into the bargain! The orderly handed her our hospital cards. Mine was on top. She ran her eyes across it, they were like two forest lakes, and then turned them towards my own rather unusual figure. I was wearing the smart uniform of a lieu-

[1] Petlyura, Simon (1877–1926). A Ukrainian nationalist leader and Commander-in-Chief of the Ukrainian National Armies from 1917 to 1920. Assassinated in Paris in 1926.

tenant of tank troops; a pair of very wide, full riding-breeches, the height of elegance at that time, a field shirt of steel grey cloth, a cap with a black velvet band with my hair sticking out rather untidily from beneath it at the back of my neck and new box-calf boots. It would be truer to say one box-calf boot, because I had a large felt boot on my injured foot.

This clothing had been issued to me from Tank Corps stores. The cloth was really magnificent. Many of the passengers on the train to Kiev had come up to me and sampled the cloth of my riding breeches and my field shirt with their fingers, nodding their heads and clicking their tongues approvingly. On my chest I had a red stripe signifying that I had been wounded in action. Above my left breast pocket hung the 'For valour' medal, which I had received for taking part in a raid on the base of a group of SS saboteurs in the mountains of Czechoslovakia. In addition I was wearing the 'Partisan of the Patriotic War' medal, second class, which was an unusual decoration for an officer in the tank forces to have. At my belt I had a shining new German 'Walther', which I had acquired from an SS officer. I remember thinking how nice it would have been if that delectable doctor had come up and fingered my clothing like the people in the train, but no, in a voice ringing with indignation she asked me how it was possible for an officer to have a binge with subordinates, and, what was even worse, how could this happen in the reception ward of a military hospital?

This fine speech only made me like her even more. After all, she had seen my hospital card, on which it was clearly stated that I was an officer of the Main Administration of Smersh, attached to such and such a unit, etc. Unlike most other people, however, she didn't seem to be in the least afraid. The hospital political officer, a pale, round-shouldered captain, came into the room. He gave me a very sour look and seemed to want to say something. The orderly quickly whispered a few words in his ear, nodding in my direction as he did so, whereupon the captain vented his wrath on the sergeant and the private, my drinking companions, who by this time had become somewhat subdued. At this point I could contain myself no longer.

'Just a minute, Captain, surely you can see that these men have just got back from the front line—they're still alive and glad about it. What if they have had a glass or two, at least they've had them while they were in hospital and not while they were on duty. Soviet power will be no worse off for that. And I don't want any thoughts of disciplinary action! I answer for their behaviour today and any explanations you require can come from me.'

The next morning, suffering from a hangover, which did nothing for my temper, I waited for the doctors to come on their rounds. The doctor who visited me was alas a pleasant, middle-aged lady and not the young doctor of yesterday. I was furious, and mostly with myself. Why on earth did I pitch into that political captain, and particularly when there were soldiers there? After all, he was quite right and the reception ward had in fact been turned into a complete shambles with my connivance. There was nothing the captain could say. What kind of an idiot, civilian or soldier, would get involved with Smersh? Even if he had taken it into his head to put in a complaint to my own bosses, which would have been extremely unlikely, then he himself would undoubtedly have got the backwash from it. I was already well aware that if there was one thing Chekists couldn't stand it was outsiders telling tales about their people.

This train of thought reminded me of a silly joke about the professor and his Chekist neighbour. The Chekist really got on the professor's nerves with his crude ways and habits. A point was reached where the professor could bear them no longer.

'Oh you,' he said to the Chekist, 'you probably don't even know who wrote *Evgeny Onegin*.'

The Chekist was offended, as he really didn't know the answer. He made arrangements for the professor to be arrested. A few days later the Chekist was walking around with a happy, seraphic expression on his face.

'Do you know,' he told everybody, 'that professor who lives next to me has finally confessed. *He* wrote *Evgeny Onegin*.'

It was partly this joke, but mainly the thought of yesterday's lady doctor, that led to an improvement in my mood.

Towards the evening of that day, the hospital Smersh operational representative, a first lieutenant of about my own age, dropped in to see me. As he was going through the cards of new admittances, he had caught sight of mine. It was no more than a social call, to swop some gossip. Isolated Smersh representatives in military institutions are usually very lonely and bored. I was delighted by this visit. Without wasting any time, I set about collecting information from my agent and planning the operational handling of the case. The subject of the case was yesterday's lady doctor. I found out that she was called . . . well, let's call her Rosa here, in honour of Yoska's mother, for they were both Jewish. She was twenty-five. I was twenty-one and a half, so that was all right. No current admirers, although not long before there had been a pilot in the hospital, a very handsome fellow and a Hero of the Soviet Union, who had been taking a very serious interest in her. I was far from handsome and I wasn't a Hero of the Soviet Union, or for that matter of any other union either. But why shouldn't I try my hardest? My colleague didn't know what had passed between her and the pilot, which didn't say much for his operational competence. He told me that she was a very decent young woman who wouldn't just bestow her favours on anyone. Unfortunately, she worked in a different section of the hospital, in a neighbouring building. This was enough information to be going on with.

The following Sunday there was a party for officers in the hospital club, followed by dancing to a record player. I put on full uniform, which I kept by me in the ward, and with a carpet slipper on my left foot in place of the felt boot I set off for the party. Rosa was dancing the 'Officers' Waltz' with some stripling from the medical staff, or at least I thought he was a stripling. My Smersh colleague was there too. When the music stopped he took me up to Rosa and said gallantly:

'Allow me to introduce my friend. He's just come from the front and has been recommended for a high military decoration.' This was a slight hint about the pilot Hero. 'I have had enough of listening to his stories about what he did there,' he went on.

'This rogue can spin quite a yarn,' I thought to myself. 'I must have been wrong when I decided he wasn't much of a Chekist.'

Unfortunately for me, however, Rosa had a merry twinkle in her eye.

'Well,' she said, 'I've not only heard more than enough about your friend, I've had some personal experience of some of the things he's been getting up to here in the hospital.'

I said nothing and tried to look as if I hadn't heard. I happened to notice the political captain passing by. I stood up stiffly to attention and greeted him punctiliously with a movement of my head, in much the same way as I might have greeted Stalin had he happened to be passing. The captain was pleasantly impressed and flattered. After all, it's a well-known fact that Chekists greet army men who are their senior in rank very carelessly and unwillingly. This goes even for army generals. Of course, I did all this simply for Rosa's benefit. I thought quickly about my next move. I tried asking her for the next dance.

'I beg your pardon,' she said, 'but perhaps you've not quite come round yet. When did you ever hear of a doctor dancing with a patient who has an injured leg.'

I explained to her that a single tango with her would have more medical value than twenty years under the treatment of the best doctors in the world. Rosa said that I really ought to have spent a week in bed.

'Yes, of course,' said I, clutching gladly at such a straw, 'particularly if . . .'

But her look stopped me short. I realised that this wasn't a hay-loft, and I wasn't dealing with a sweet little Party zealot from the country.

There were certain forms of amusement in the hospital. There was a library, but I somehow didn't feel like reading. There was also a record player and some records in the club and singing among the patients in various wards. I got used to going into one soldiers' ward. There were about twenty-five beds in that ward and sometimes there would be sixty or so people in it, all on account of the songs. We all used to sit jammed together on the beds. There were majors, captains and even a lieutenant-colonel of the Guards. The whole thing was run by a skinny little middle-aged Ukrainian soldier with a cataract on one eye which also had a pronounced cast in it. He had nothing of a voice, but he more than made up for this with his humour and his expertise. He used to get up in the centre of the ward and at a wave of his hand everybody, majors and all, began to 'make background music'. This meant that we repeated quickly and monotonously, but amicably, *'Dooyem, dooyem, dooyem . . .'*. Against this background, which didn't sound at all bad, the cross-eyed soldier first set the pitch, which he did by emitting a noise like the bleating of a goat. Once he was sure that all was in order, he began to sing.

Of course, most of the words were obscene. But we were listening to pure Ukrainian folk music superbly performed. He sang in Ukrainian and there were four characters in his songs: the village elder, the policeman, the verger and a certain woman. The setting was a vegetable garden near the priest's stile. Against a background of fifty or sixty strong Russian and Ukrainian voices repeating *'Dooyem, dooyem'*, this soldier performed the most delicate high-pitched runs, which he ended on an incredible high falsetto note. Most of the injured who could walk, came in crowds to these concerts, as one bold joker put it, 'Like people going to the Lenin

Mausoleum'. We used to stand or sit in a crowd in the corridors. The orderlies listened to these concerts and the doctors as well. Sometimes even the hospital's political officer listened to them. He understood perfectly well what was going on. It was wartime and all around were grief and loss and deprivation. This was a way in which exhausted, wounded men could unwind and relax spiritually, forgetting unpleasant realities, listening to this unpretentious singing, which despite its bawdiness, was completely inoffensive. An official concert in the club or over the radio had by no means the same value. . . .

The singing, however, caused a setback in my personal affairs. On one occasion I emerged from one of these concerts, flushed with elation, and bumped straight into Rosa, who was walking past. In answer to my respectful bow, she stuck out her full lower lip and said, 'I see, Lieutenant, that your tastes in entertainment have not altered,' and went on her way, with a slight wiggle of her splendid hips. I spat in disgust and wandered off to my ward. The man in the next bed to me was a middle-aged major, who served as an instructor in the political branch of one of the armies of our Front. He was sitting at the table playing patience. I found him very boring. He either played patience all the time or complained about his multifarious ailments, in particular about his chronic piles. Consequently, just as in the good old days, I lay on my bed and began to dream of . . .

From somewhere came the sound of jazz music. I got up and, paying no attention to the major's protests, opened the window. Just as I thought, the 'Officers' Waltz'. It was then just beginning to get popular. I like it even now. First the violin, then in came the accordion, then the saxophone took up the melody and the soft, but very expressive voice of a well-known band leader sang: 'The night is short, the clouds are asleep, and I feel your unfamiliar hand on my shoulder board'. To be quite honest, though, my friends and I used to change the words! The thought of Rosa was driving me mad. I said quite mechanically as I turned from the window, 'No, brother rabbits, this just won't do any more.'

'What's that you're saying?' said the major anxiously.

My instructor 'Lord' in the NKGB school used to say, 'For a Chekist there is no such thing as a situation from which there is no way out. There are always a number of ways, and one only needs to choose the right one competently.'

I found out the dates of Rosa's night duty in her section from the duty sister. Of course, I didn't mention Rosa's name, and asked about something quite different. After talking with the sister for a little longer about signs of approaching old age, I went back to my section, via a covered passage.

On the first evening that Rosa was on duty I turned up at the large consulting-room, where duty doctors usually sat. I was wearing pyjamas, a dressing-gown and hospital slippers, which is how wounded in military hospitals were usually dressed. I behaved very modestly, as Yoska would have said, 'Like a cardinal being received by the Pope'. We talked first about Odessa, then about literature. To be more precise, I did most of the talking. She simply sat at the table, leafing through some medical records. As soon as she made any attempt to send me back to my ward, I quickly changed the subject of the conversation to medicine. I got up and came closer to her. I said that she was agonisingly like Anna Karenina, particularly the ringlets of hair on the neck. I bent over and kissed her there.

'A physical-culture greeting!', Rosa exclaimed in indignation, and hit me fairly lightly on the cheek. 'A physical-culture greeting' is part of the official greeting between Soviet football teams before a game begins. The opposing team answers it by shouting 'A physical-culture hurrah!' This was how I answered Rosa too. Then, talking like a sporting commentator, I said quickly, 'After a lively and attractive game, both teams leave the field to get ready for the second half.'

She smirked, sat down and . . . did not drive me out of the consulting-room. I thought quickly what I should do next. But at this point the devil sent along the duty orderly because some patient's something or other had either risen or fallen catastrophically. I think it was his blood pressure. Rosa hurried off. I left too, cursing that patient and all his kin. The bloody reptiles, they picked their time to send their flaming blood pressure up and down.

The next time Rosa was on night duty, I began again. She seemed to be gradually getting used to me and to be putting up with my pressure like an illness in children that wasn't dangerous. I paid about four such visits. There was a shortage of doctors, and like the others she was often on duty. Things went no further than light kisses on the cheeks and anaemic hugs, for which I, of course, bore most of the responsibility.

On one particular evening, or night to be more exact, I imperceptibly, or so it seemed to me, turned the key in the door. Sitting on the arm of her chair I began to kiss her wherever I could, on the forehead, on the nose, on the chin and eventually I sank my lips into hers. I felt the palms of her hands pushing against my chest.

'Oh, you'll be the death of me,' said Rosa, 'you cheeky kid. Let me go!'

She got up from the chair. I put my arms round her and sat her down on the sofa, which was, after all, for the 'medical staff'. I began to kiss her on the neck and tried to unbutton her field shirt. Who on earth had invented that sort of uniform for girls? It had too many buttons on it. The resistance continued. In between kisses I said to her quickly:

'It's not my fault, Rosa, that you're such a pretty girl. After all, all this goes back to my early childhood, when I was a tiny, tiny child. My poor mother dropped me from the first floor. A crowd had gathered, a lot of people were in tears, the fire brigade came, somebody had called the police.' I exaggerated my way from floor to floor with the appropriate reactions from the crowd. '. . . she dropped me from the eighth floor. The crowd was shouting. The firemen were wiping tears from their eyes, the police were sobbing . . . and ever since that day, Rosa, I can't see a white skin, black eyes and crimson lips like yours without losing my head. I'm to be pitied . . .'

Rosa was clearly swept off her feet by my unbroken chatter with kisses. Unexpectedly she gripped my shoulders with both hands. She then began to gasp and groan very passionately. I glanced at the door for fear that someone in the corridor might hear her. What did it matter? This was a hospital, a place where groans were not uncommon.

When we got up Rosa shooed me away, saying that there was something she had to do in order not to get pregnant. I calmed her down and told her that there was no need to worry.

'You cheeky kid,' she said indignantly, 'you mean to tell me that you were banking on this when you came here?'

I had to say that I was.

'Don't think that I didn't see you lock that door,' said Rosa. 'And what do you think would have happened if I'd suddenly been called to a patient?'

I mumbled something about how she'd been ministering to the urgent needs of another patient. Standing there without her pants and with her stockings round her ankles, she began to laugh.

The duty sister in the corridor eyed me suspiciously as I strode past her with dignity. My neighbour the major was reading something. I looked over his shoulder and noticed that it was the poems of Konstantin Simonov. I was in an exalted, poetic mood myself. I assumed a pose suggestive of inspiration and began to declaim a parody of Simonov:

> 'No hero at the front avoids
> A bad attack of haemorrhoids!'

The major smiled sourly.

'What's the matter with you?' he said.

'I've been decorated,' I said. 'I've just had a top-priority message from Front HQ.'

Rosa refused categorically to repeat the scene on the sofa. I besought her, swearing that everything would be all right. My eyes ranged round the walls of the consulting-room for something to swear by. There wasn't even any portraits of our leaders on the wall. Just cupboards with glass door, full of medicines, a couple of enema tubes and some rolls of bandage.

'No,' she insisted, 'it's too risky here.'

I got dressed and went into town, to the Central Committee of the Communist Party of the Ukraine. I asked the duty official to tell me my father's exact address. I knew that he was somewhere in Kharkov, where he was one of the Party leaders in a special trust[1] which was re-establishing some top-priority factories vital to the war effort. It had become very difficult and uneconomic to transport equipment from the Urals, from Siberia and from Central Asia, to a front that was no longer on Soviet territory. After a telephone conversation with my father, in which we exchanged all our news, I obtained his agreement that I could use a room which was permanently reserved for him in the hotel belonging to the Central Committee of the Communist Party of the Ukraine. I said that I wanted to have a look at Kiev and go to a concert or two and so on, and told him that the hospital was a long way from the centre. I did indeed go to a concert or two, but I needed the room to spend the time pleasantly with Rosa whenever she could manage to get away.

There was nothing particularly outstanding or unusual about what happened between Rosa and me in the consulting room. All young injured soldiers, and for that matter not so young ones, officers in particular, took steps in the same direction. After all, they all experienced the same lack of female company. There was no leave in wartime. An injury and a period in hospital was the best chance one got. I know of an example concerning one particular wounded

[1] A conglomeration of factory and defence installations.

sergeant. He and a young nurse did the same thing as Rosa and I had done on the floor of the morgue, which happened to be empty at the time.

Rosa and I got to know one another better. As we walked along a street together we would talk about our families. Rosa came from a family of doctors. Her father was a doctor in a hospital at the rear. Her elder brother, who was also a doctor, had been called up into the army before the war. He had been stationed somewhere near Brest. There was no news or any trace of him whatsoever. His fate was clear to me without any further explanations. The name Brest was enough. The town had sustained the first German tank attack in June 1941. Large numbers of our troops had been taken prisoner. If her brother looked at all like her I could imagine what had happened, but I said nothing about this. Rosa used to talk sometimes of the mass murders of children and old people that the Germans had committed. She had visited Babi Yar, which was quite close to our hospital.

'It's up to you Chekists,' Rosa said, 'to find and punish the people responsible for all that.'

In respectable, medical language I explained to her what we would do to Hitler and the rest. There was no surprising me with Babi Yar and the like. I had already seen enough of such things in the western Ukraine and in Poland, albeit not on such a vast scale. I changed the subject.

Rosa was interested to know where I had learned so much about Jewish ways and sayings. I told her that I was myself a Jew and had even been inside a synagogue, although I gave no details of my visit. She didn't believe me, so I suggested that we slip into the nearest bushes so that I could prove my point. We were walking along Shevchenko Boulevard. It was cold and we were both in military uniform.

'You'll be the death of me, you cheeky kid,' said Rosa.

My medical treatment was working well. I was having regular paraffin treatment for my leg. I sensed that I would soon be back at the Front once more. Rosa realised this too. I was called to the Communications Section of the Administration of Counter-Intelligence Smersh of the First Ukrainian Front, which was attached to the Ukraine People's Commissariat for State Security. For the time being there were no coded messages concerning me either from GUKR or from Front Smersh HQ. The Ukrainian NKGB was a hive of teeming activity all twenty-four hours of the day. Mass purges of the population were being conducted in the areas which had been liberated from the Germans. Networks were being set up for operational work and registration throughout the whole population of the Ukraine. There was a tremendous shortage of Chekist personnel. Most of the best Chekists were either in Smersh or in other administrations directly concerned with the war. Crash courses had been set up by the NKGB for new intakes of Chekists. They were accepting many former partisan undercover workers.

Mobilisation was also being conducted by the Komsomol among students in institutes of higher education, among the injured and persons no longer fit for active service at the front. Eventually the coded message for me arrived: 'You are posted to the base of GUKR Smersh in the zone of the First Ukrainian Front.' I was then handed the decoration I had been promised. My boss, the major, and I were both mistaken in our guesses. I received the 'Order of the Patriotic War, First Class', not second class, as at best might have been expected. The explanation for this was not my heroism but simply that I had been wounded. Presumably this had pleased the top brass. Almost all Chekist officers in Smersh of my rank and position had, by the end of the war, received the 'Order of the Patriotic War, Second Class', the 'Order of the Red Star' and the medals appropriate to the campaigns of the Fronts with which they had served.

The time came to say goodbye to Rosa. It would have been nice to have had her arrested and sent to Smersh Front HQ, to amuse me there, and I hope herself too.

Rosa did not laugh as she stood by the train. She wept and murmured through her tears, 'You fool, you cheeky kid.' Sitting in the train, the thought came into my head that it wouldn't be at all bad if Rosa and I were to be together always. I consoled myself slightly by thinking that with hot tempers like ours we would have been constantly at each other's throats.

5

'The Berlin street leads us to victory'

From a song by Leonid Utyosov

THE TROOPS ON MY Front had just taken the town of Keltse, in Poland and were approaching Chenstokhov. All the roads in the area, and not only the roads, were packed with soldiers. It was not much more than two hundred kilometres to the German frontier. Our strategic target, in general terms, was Dresden. What a pity it wasn't Berlin, I thought, remembering my promise to Rosa about what we would do to Hitler. Luckily I had avoided being posted to our Front's First Branch of Smersh, which was demanding big new intakes of Chekists.

Before striking at Germany, the Front was given large reinforcements. Part of them came from the ranks of the partisans, since in the main the partisan movement no longer operated and the war had left Soviet territory altogether. Our isolated partisan detachments operated only in Czechoslovakia. The vast majority of young partisans came to swell the ranks of our regular forces. This of course happened only after Smersh had screened them carefully for political reliability.

In many new units and detachments in our Front, the Smersh establishment was considerably under strength. This was one of the threats to me personally. In all fairness, I knew that there wasn't much chance of my being banished to some battalion or other as representative, or being put into the Smersh section of a regiment. For a start I was on the books of the Main Administration of Smersh and secondly, and more important, I had graduated from one of the best State Security Service schools. I already knew in our particular Front there weren't all that many graduates with my qualifications. The kind of men who were eligible for work in battalions and regiments were those who had completed one of the State Security

Services many crash courses. That sort of work in front line units required no special knowledge of either military or political intelligence work. These were my conclusions, but nevertheless certain apprehensions remained.

I was eventually assigned to an operational group attached to the Smersh Administration of the Front. The group's basic job was to guarantee contact links with groups of agents and individuals who were carrying out missions behind the enemy lines, commissioned by the Main Administration of Smersh. Some of these had already been in Germany or on the territory of her allies for a long time. They had penetrated German strategic institutions and military units. Others had found places in punitive police bodies. A third group had stuck to civilian life and set themselves up in German industry, in transport, in the reconstruction of various installations which had been destroyed during bombing raids by the Anglo-American air forces. The remainder had been directed into political channels, i.e. they worked with various anti-Soviet committees and organisations, in the editorial offices of newspapers printed in Russian and the other languages of the Soviet Union, in *émigré* ecclesiastical and benevolent organisations. Others had jobs in the German Ministry of the Eastern Territories; Ostministerium, and in the Ministry of Propaganda.

All these people had other guardians in Moscow apart from the GUKR Smersh. The GRU[1] of the General Staff, headed by Colonel-General Kuznetzov, controlled the military side. The intelligence-sabotage administration of the NKGB under Lieutenant-General Sudoplatov had charge of the punitive-police and industrial sides. The political side in non-military spheres was handled by the Secret Political Administration of the NKGB under Lieutenant-General Fedotov. This administration usually worked with the Soviet civilian population. However, due to the war, a situation had arisen where millions of Soviet citizens found themselves outside Soviet territory. I am thinking here of prisoners of war, *ostarbeiters*, that is persons who had been deported by the Germans as forced labour, and a large number of others who had often fled in whole families with the Germans from the advancing Soviet army. We in Smersh also worked in constant contact with the Foreign Intelligence Administration of the NKGB under Lieutenant-General Pitovranov. This administration shared fewer common interests with us than the other bodies I have mentioned. Its sole concern was certain highly pro-

[1] GRU (*Glavnoye Razvedyvatyelnoye Upravleniye Generalnogo Shtaba*)—Main Intelligence Administration of the General Staff.

fessional agents in places far behind the enemy lines. It had, for example, its own people in the highest bodies of state in Germany and in the countries allied with her. At that time NKGB foreign intelligence had its hands more than full in other spheres. A huge number of its agents had for example 'discovered' America on a large scale for the first time. Nor did the other countries of the western alliance pass unnoticed. In the same way attention was given to the Far East and Japan, although the latter was officially regarded as a neutral country.

Our group was a real Noah's Ark. In it, apart from young officers from GUKR Smersh like myself, there were also experts on Germany and specialists on the countries under the Anglo-American umbrella. After all, the day when we would meet our western allies was no longer all that far off. German territory was slipping from the hands of the Third Reich at a headlong rate.

The major who was in charge of my group was from the same neck of the woods as Beria, an Abkhazian. He was small, slim, with a crafty expression on his face and mocking eyes. He worked like a man possessed. He dashed from one division or regiment to another everywhere 'wicket gates' were being arranged. A 'wicket gate' was a place where our agents could cross the front line. Aeroplanes were hardly ever used for these purposes by now. The distances to be covered were no longer a problem. Moreover, Germany was frequently being bombed by our western allies, the British and the Americans. There was no point in putting valuable agents and aeroplanes at risk. For some reason or other this major had taken a fancy to me and he often took me with him on his many trips. When we were travelling he never talked shop.

'Do you really think,' he said, with many gesticulations and a thick Caucasian accent, 'that I'm a machine who never needs any rest or relaxation?'

No such thought had ever entered my head. All this was, by the way, part of a long-standing habit of his when beginning any conversation, regardless of whom he was talking to. I myself heard the major talk to the chief of our Front's Smersh Administration, Lieutenant-General Korolyov, exactly like this. Admittedly he did use the polite second person plural form. There was a certain difference both in rank and age, to say nothing of other matters, between Korolyov and myself.

The major suited me fine. At work he taught me a lot. When we were on a trip together it was sheer enjoyment to listen to his genuine

Caucasian jokes. There was, however, in all his jokes a detail which disturbed me. After his jokes the major was always the first person to burst into maniacal laughter, throwing back his head and waving his arms about, usually when he happened to be sitting at the wheel of a jeep. On one occasion he all but drove straight into a column of T.34 tanks which was approaching from the opposite direction. On another occasion his laughter and his jeep were jointly responsible for frightening the horse of the Commander of the First Ukrainian Front. We were going along a narrow minor road on the German frontier when we met a group of mounted senior officers and generals coming slowly towards us. My major had just dashingly overtaken a platoon of infantry, which was marching in the same direction as us, and was about to overtake a second one. Seeing the mounted top brass, the infantry officers shouted to their soldiers: 'Stand to one side.' The major couldn't have cared less. He had just told me and our driver-sergeant, who was sitting in the back seat, the latest Caucasian joke, and was himself enjoying a loud laugh. We skipped past the mounted colonels and generals, almost touching them. Their horses snorted and squinted at our jeep. Some of the riders shouted something after us like 'Where the hell does he think he's going?' or still more trenchant observations. The next to the last officer in the group was a tall, middle-aged, fair-haired man. He had a broad Russian face and was wearing a field-green cap and overcoat and marshal's shoulder boards. It was Marshal Konev. The Marshal's large dark horse started and shied away from us. Konev shook his fist at us, and his adjutant, who was bringing up the rear, bawled out some indignant remark. It all happened as quickly as a scene in a film.

On the other hand, once the major arrived at some regiment or division, he was transformed in the twinkling of an eye. As soon as he had laid his hands on the agent who was about to cross, or had just crossed, the front line, we retired to the seclusion of a separate room or shelter. Then, with animation, he made one of the following remarks: 'Let's lick him into shape' or 'Let's suck him dry'. 'Let's lick him into shape' meant that we had to find out whether the agent knew all the details about how he was to cross the front, where he was to make his first secret rendezvous and whether he knew all the extra contingency plans of the operation, etc. Incoming personnel had to be 'sucked dry', that is to say, any useful information had to be got out of him during an initial period of questioning. Quite frankly, in the vast majority of cases of incoming personnel, there was no real need for these trips. The incoming agent would in any case have been sent to us, albeit after some slight delay. But the major was simply incapable of staying in one place, and he also liked to put everybody else's nose out of joint by always being first on the scene.

I found returning agents far more interesting. It was nowhere near so easy to get into conversation with outgoing personnel. One could hardly ask them about details of their missions. As for instructions about crossing the German lines, they were depressingly similar in all cases. They dealt in great detail with the exact position of the German lines, and also took into consideration a series of typical features from the life of a German soldier. These included the time at which sentries were relieved, the time at which patrols passed, German soldiers' mealtimes and even the time when they usually went to the lavatory. The Germans remained pedantically punctilious right up to the end of the war, thereby rendering our Security Service a great favour.

Soon the major began to commission me to conduct preliminary 'sucking dry' sessions of incoming agents, particularly when the agents came in in groups of two or three. These were largely communications couriers, who duplicated and supplemented clandestine radio contact (which by no means all resident agents had in any case). In addition, on that territory that remained in Hitler's hands there had been an increase in the use of radio signal detectors by the SD (*Sicherheits Dienst*). This was hardly surprising as all the specially qualified personnel who had been removed from jobs elsewhere in previously German-held territory had gravitated back towards the centre. I spent many hours in the company of our colleagues who had come from 'over there'. As soon as I had finished my business with them and passed on all the urgent information 'up the ladder', i.e. to the major. I bombarded them with questions.

It was clear that victory was just around the corner, although we had not yet reached Berlin. But there were a great many questions still to be answered. I found it difficult to believe much of what I heard, although I knew that these agents did not lie or exaggerate. This would have been a crime against the service in so far as they would have been passing on false information and attempting to deceive a Smersh officer.

I shall never forget how I burst out laughing when I first heard the words of 'Horst Wessel', the official hymn of the Nazi Party, in particular the words *Wenn juden Blut von unsern Messern Spritzt*!

How could they sing something like that? I wondered. After all, that tune was played at all major state functions. Within the Smersh organisation I had already seen many of these occasions on film. Vast crowds of people rose to their feet at the sound of this tune and shouted '*Sieg Heil! Sieg Heil!*' Many of them had tears in their eyes and it transpired that these words were the words they wept over. For a long time I was unable to take seriously many official German slogans, e.g. 'There's no place for the Yids and Commies even in Siberia' or 'Bash the Yid political officer, his face is begging for a brick', although one could not dispute the fact that they actually existed. In the NKGB they even had photographs of these slogans which had been taken, for example, in the Reich's Ostministerium of Minister Rosenberg. These photographs along with a large number of similar concoctions were sent to us across the front line. I spent a long time, not without cursing my inadequate knowledge of the language, looking at a large number of German magazines. The magazine *Untermensch*, which was brought out by Dr. Goebbels, Ministry of Propaganda, struck me as particularly disgusting. This magazine regularly published photographs of Russian prisoners of war. The Germans chose specially wretched wild-looking unshaven creatures with broad cheek-bones and Asiatic features. Making such a choice was no problem. After all, our chaps weren't fed and often weren't given anything to drink in the prisoner-of-war camps. The photographs bore inscriptions in large letters: 'Here are the Russian *Untermensch* who threaten our European culture'. Another magazine called *Der Sturmer* specialised in anti-Jewish material of the same type. These magazines also contained much obscenity, but of a crude, primitive variety. Before one could see anything funny in them one had to sit and scratch one's head for a long time. When they saw my obvious puzzlement our agents from 'over there' dismissed it with a wave of the hand and said, 'What's wrong with that, the Germans are complete idiots, that's why we're mashing them. Idiots always get mashed.'

Not much time had passed before I saw almost equally insulting Anglo-American publications, directed this time, however, at the *Russians*, never at the *Soviets*. But this all belongs to the future. For the time being I had to 'suck dry' Chekist agents coming in from Germany on the other side of the Front. I doubt whether I shall ever forget one particular agent. He had spent some considerable time in Germany and in territories occupied by the Reich. He was intelligent, an acute observer, and he had a good memory. At one time he had 'worked' in a German concentration camp in Poland, where he had had a job in the kitchen, helping to dish out the food. He had got into the concentration camp specially in order to carry out a mission for the Fourth Administration of the NKGB. It had been necessary to collect information on certain senior officers of our army, who were being held in the concentration camp. At the same time, he dispatched to the next world, with the help of German hands, a number of people of whom Soviet power did not approve and whom it regarded as potentially dangerous. He betrayed them to the camp Gestapo as 'extremely pro-communist elements'.

Later, after the war was over, he was in the PFK[1] of the NKGB whose work was to screen Soviet prisoners of war. They were liberated by the Anglo-American allies and subsequently handed over to us, in many cases against their will. It had been easy to arrange his escape from the German concentration camp as soon as his work was over, with the help of our own people in the camp administration. He had been included in a team of prisoners who worked outside the camp during the day and supplied with a rendezvous. It was from him that I first learned, for example, about 'physical exercise' in the camps. On the order of a German officer, who would strike a piece of rail with his riding crop, the prisoners who were standing on the parade ground were obliged to begin leaping like frogs or to walk about squatting on their haunches. The Germans enjoyed this kind of gymnastics, particularly when the front rows were occupied by old Jews or Polish priests. I imagined the elderly half-blind Rabbi from my home town trying to jump like a frog. This was the same Rabbi who had been one of the persons who had thrown Yoska and me out of the synagogue. The very thought sent shivers down my spine and I felt shame and revulsion, as if I myself had had some part in the setting up of camps like this.

Much later I encountered people from many nationalities who had spent time in our Soviet NKVD and MVD prison camps. I have also spoken to people who have been there quite recently. All these people saw and experienced many dreadful things in the Soviet camps, but not one of them had encountered such cynically calculated ridicule of human dignity as this frog jumping. Nor had they encountered such things as the 'friendly reception' accorded to new arrivals at the camp, which was very popular with the Germans. I would like to tell briefly the story of an NKGB resident whom I questioned in the

[1] *Proverochno-Fil'trovochnye Kommissii*—the vetting and screening commissions.

early spring of 1945. The new arrivals entered the camp compound in small groups. Members of the camp administration rushed energetically to meet them, all dressed in smart uniforms, clean-shaven and smelling of eau-de-cologne. 'In a word,' as the agent said, 'true representatives of European culture.' They bellowed cheerfully, '. . . Ah! Juden!' or 'Polen!' or 'Russian!', and immediately set about pummelling the new arrivals with rubber truncheons, without even showing any strong feelings.

Many of those NKGB and GRU agents who had dealings with me and other members of our operational group at that time were working for 'the liberation of the people of Russia', from the German side. From 1941–2 onwards the Germans had in their hands a large group of Soviet generals and senior officers, many scientists, journalists, artists, technicians and other 'thinking' Soviet citizens, who had either been taken prisoner or had voluntarily gone over to the enemy. The majority of them held fiercely anti-Soviet views. They had a burning desire to fight to liberate Russia from the Soviet regime and were ready, if need be, to lay down their lives for this cause. In many cases this was what they actually had to do. Right up to the end of the war the Germans were completely incapable of grasping the idea of how to use these people for Germany's advantage. Only during the period of September to November 1944 did the Germans make the first full-scale attempt to co-ordinate all their anti-Soviet resources, including representatives of the many nationalities of the Soviet Union.

The whole affair was in the hands of Himmler, *Reichsminister* for Internal Affairs, *Reichsführer* of the SS, Commander-in-Chief of the SS forces and the reserve army. The squabbling and bickering over these matters between Himmler, Rosenberg, to some extent Ribbentrop, the Minister of Foreign Affairs, and also Goebbels, went on right up to the end of the war. I must also emphasise that all these Ministers made two common mistakes. They all lacked information about the real situation in the Soviet Union and they misunderstood what they did know. This delighted the leaders of our State Security Service and they exploited the situation to our own advantage in many ways. The expansive major, my own direct superior, on several occasions when he received new information almost began to dance the Lyezginka.[1] I am sure that the leaders of anti-Soviet organisations on the other side of the front line felt like anything but dancing.

The most important of them was Lieutenant-General Vlasov, who in 1944 was made Chairman of the Committee for the Liberation of

[1] Lyezginka—a Caucasian dance.

the Peoples of Russia, and Commander-in-Chief, albeit only on paper, of the Russian Army of Liberation (ROA). He had formerly been Deputy Commander of the Volkhov Front and Commander of the Second Soviet Strike Army. His main helpers were Major-General Trukhin, former Chief of the Operational Branch of the Baltic Front, Brigade Commissar (Brigadier) Zhilenkov, previously First Secretary of a District Committee of the Moscow Party organisation. There were other leaders of anti-Soviet movements in Germany as well. The chief of the Main Administration of Cossack Troops, attached to the SS, was General of Cavalry Krasnov, whose title went back to the days of the Czar. He was a former *Ataman*[1] and a well-known Russian writer, but by then an old man. In Smersh I was soon to meet both him and some of his closest helpers, in circumstances which for them were very tragic. Bandera,[2] the leader of the Ukrainian nationalist liberation movement and Lieutenant-General Shandruk, the military leader of this movement, were also among them. Many of these people were far from being in agreement with one another and had not even worked out a general plan of action. In many ways they were prevented from doing this by the Germans, who did not wish to allow them to escape from the control of the various German ministries responsible.

There were, however, among the Germans one or two people whose attitude to the anti-Soviet movement made our own leaders rather anxious. These included the Chief of the Foreign Armies Branch of the German General Staff, Major-General Gehlen, Colonel Stauffenberg, Chief of Staff of the Reserve Army, and Captain Strik-Strikfeldt, a German liaison officer attached to General Vlasov. They helped this movement in every way they could by putting its point of view to the top German leadership. Soviet propaganda, for example, has tried in the past, and still tries, to present them as either convinced fascists and SS hangmen, or, as in the case of Stauffenberg, who made an unsuccessful attempt to explode a bomb under Hitler's map table, even as pro-communist. As an officer of Smersh, I was all too well aware that they were neither. They, and certain others like them, were simply Germans with a capital G. I have no time for any kind of sentimentality of phoney pathos, but someday, in a Russia set free from Soviet power, a monument should be erected to these men, to commemorate their assistance and understanding during a difficult period and the fact that they saved many Russian lives.

[1] *Ataman*—Cossack chieftain.
[2] Bandera—1909–59. Ukrainian nationalist leader.

During those years they saved a large number of people from both the Gestapo and the NKGB.

It would have been very strange if our State Security bodies had not exploited to the maximum the situation in Germany. There were in the German armed forces around one million Soviet citizens serving in combat and auxiliary units, spread throughout all the countries which were under German control. I can't, of course, state the exact number of agents we had among them, but there was no shortage of them. Apart from professional Chekists themselves, there were many former Soviet citizens living locally whom they recruited. This could be done in various ways. They might be promised complete forgiveness for all past sins and an honourable homecoming to their Motherland. They might also be threatened with reprisals and of course threats would be made against their families, if they happened to be in Soviet hands. At that time the intelligence-sabotage and particularly the secret political administrations of the NKGB carried out the vast, laborious task of seeking out the families, relations and even close friends, of all such people. Within the Soviet army this work was the concern of the First Administration of Smersh.

There were also other methods of recruiting. These people were held under the threat of being compromised with the German authorities and then handed over to the German security services. This threat was carried out in more than one case. Some agents were bought for money, others paid in service to us for their own ill-calculated drunkenness and moral depravity. We used special female personnel for this. Other out-of-the-way methods also existed for key individuals. We had our own representatives, often long-term permanent residents in all institutions and formations of the anti-Soviet movement in Germany, including the Committee for the Liberation of the Peoples of Russia, its main military headquarters, the top brass of the Cossack units, Ukrainian committees and military formations. The same went for the other national organisations. I must say that the anti-Soviet movement of those years, in particular the organisation of General Vlasov, which had the most clear political platform, found many supporters among our officers and men, in spite of the cruel, but effective control of Smersh. Many Soviet soldiers continued to go over to the Germans right up to the end of 1944 and the beginning of 1945. Those who fled presumably believed in the reality of the anti-Soviet struggle and had no idea of the true situation on the German side.

Then came a powerful blow from our First Ukrainian Front. We passed through the rest of western Poland within a few days. At the same time, the First Belorussian Front was attacking from further north. To our great envy, it was offered the honour of capturing Berlin. This was why Marshal Zhukov, the First Deputy of the Supreme Commander (i.e. Stalin), became its commander.

Still we moved forward very rapidly. It was very hard to find any time at all for personal matters, let alone for affairs of the heart. One of my favourite poets, Tvardovsky, was right when he wrote:

> On the road to Berlin in '45,
> The front rolled west in a splendid sweep,
> There was no time to eat or sleep.

Since then there have appeared in the western world many reports, about the rapes and atrocities committed by the '*Russian*' forces in Europe. All sorts of things happened, but I disagree with many of the hypotheses made about our troops. The people who were writing and speaking did not know, or chose to ignore, a number of very simple things. The behaviour of the Germans themselves in those areas of my own country which they occupied can hardly be compared to that of the members of old-fashioned, aristocratic London clubs. The only thing that it can be compared with is the way that their fellow Germans behaved in Poland and Yugoslavia. Both the Poles and the Yugoslavs, and for that matter other nations who had first-hand experience of German occupation, paid the Germans back whenever they had the opportunity, on the Mosaic principle an eye for an eye and a tooth for a tooth. This is how many of my fellow countrymen behaved. In our 'invading armies' there were a great many criminals, like the people with whom I'd been working in the camps at Tatishchevo. They had managed to get through the war successfully. Even bullets seemed to keep out of the way of many of them. I find particularly unjust, however, many of the writings of western specialists on the matter of cases of rape and atrocities committed by the 'Asiatics from Russia', i.e. the Kazakhs and Uzbeks, etc. I knew many representatives of these nationalities and I would like to assure all such specialists, that the behaviour of the average Uzbek or Kazakh is no worse, and perhaps even better, than the behaviour of the average inhabitant of western Europe or the USA. However, there was no justification for the behaviour of many of our officers and men at that time, nor can there be.

Our advance on Berlin and Dresden had gone on successfully so far, but soon, in the area of the rivers Oder and Neisse, it began to lose impetus and grind to a halt, ruining all the meticulous calculations of our High Command. It wasn't that we were short of manpower. On our First Ukrainian Front alone there were five armies of infantry, two tank armies and one air force army, amounting to about half a million men. There was no shortage of armaments. We alone had about fourteen thousand pieces of ordnance, over two thousand tanks and about two and a half thousand aeroplanes. On the contrary, too much equipment had been amassed in a relatively narrow space. To the north, with Marshal Zhukov, in the main strike area, the picture was the same. They had even been sent heavy siege guns from the Leningrad area.

There is no point in enumerating all the corps and armies of our forces who assembled in the spring of 1945 in the approaches to the German capital. This data is now known to very many people and there is nothing secret about it. The best thing I can do is to quote the poet Tvardovsky:

> Westward along the highway,
> With sound of groaning steel,
> Six abreast, we packed the way
> With serviced vehicles, night and day.

It had been decided that Berlin would be taken at the beginning of February. It was taken, however, only at the beginning of May. The political administration of the Front sent out freshly printed posters to all regiments and divisions: 'We are in Berlin!', but we weren't. What was the reason for this?

Soon after we had entered German territory our Smersh administration began to receive alarming reports from our representatives with the troops. Their content was very plain and monotonous: 'Such and such a unit (or detachment) had not achieved its strategic objective, the personnel had dispersed in (or near) such and such a town (or village). There had been cases of wholesale drunkenness, theft and looting. The measures taken by the commander of the unit (or detachment) to put an end to these occurrences had turned out to be insufficient and ineffective. The measures which had been taken to the same end by the unit's (or detachment's) political bodies had also been unsuccessful.' Then followed the signature of some operational representative of the particular OKR (Branch or Section of Counter-Intelligence) Smersh.

The measures which were usually taken by commanders and political officers were the imposition of disciplinary penalties of punishments. Just try to imagine putting ten or fifteen soldiers and sergeants in the guardhouse while an attack was going on! Another measure was the threat to use firearms. Just try and imagine using them against a large number of soldiers! They might also threaten to destroy all alcohol. It would indeed have been necessary to destroy all forms, because in addition to vodka and schnapps, the men drank eau-de-cologne and industrial methylated spirit. There could be no question of destroying supplies of the latter. Some individuals even extracted the alcohol from spirit-based paints and drank that. All this information was collected and summarised in the Third (Secret) Branch of the Smersh Administration of our Front and sent off in coded messages, by word of mouth or by V Ch (high frequency) lines of communication to Colonel-General Abakumov in Moscow. From him it was passed on to Stalin. Things were no better for our neighbour, Marshal Zhukov. At that time we were working in particularly close contact with the Smersh administration of the Front under his command. The top brass of our own Front was beside itself with rage. I'm sure that Stalin himself was hardly ecstatic after his informational chats with Abakumov.

In addition to everything else, at that time Stalin received a number of alarming coded messages. Apart from the ones coming via Abakumov's network, they also came via Kuznetsov at GRU of the General Staff and, I think, from Pitovranov in the NKGB's Main Administration of Foreign Intelligence. Once again these coded messages were brief and to the point. The western allies, in particular the British, had got terrifyingly close to Berlin. We had precise information from our agents that in allied headquarters the problem of whether or not to take Berlin before our forces arrived was being seriously discussed. This gave us all food for thought. What could we do? Any notion of mass repressions or punitive measures against our troops by the NKGB and NKVD was shelved at once. When we were standing on the doorstep of Berlin we could not do anything which would play into German hands, and possibly the hands of our western allies too. And, moreover, how would we ourselves have fared, as a result of any such actions? Possibly there were enough NKVD troops to do the job. They were always to be found, attached to the HQ of all Fronts, wearing ordinary army uniforms. Their number could easily have been increased by bringing in more from the main reserve. But the difficulties lay elsewhere, even if we disregarded the fact that an enormous number of troops were involved in the drinking, debauchery and looting. That it was large is an inescapable fact, otherwise the attack on Berlin would not have petered out. This was the most difficult aspect of the problem which Stalin and the High Command had to face.

They were perfectly well aware that what was happening was not in any sense an anti-Soviet protest. It was simply that soldiers and sometimes officers too, who were often veterans of Moscow, Stalingrad and other major battles, were so exhausted by the war and so overjoyed, finding themselves on German territory, by the proximity of victory, that they were unable to control their feelings any longer. Moreover, to many of our workers and peasants in 'grey overcoats', the ruins of conquered Germany seemed like the promised land. They had never seen such houses, such comforts, such furniture, such clothing, or even such an abundance of food. In the towns of Germany the food situation was very bad. In the countryside, however, there were cattle, pigs and poultry, to say nothing of strong drink. There could be no talk of rebuking and punishing the Soviet veterans who commanded each unit or detachment. They were the ones who were doing everything possible to maintain discipline and order. They were not magicians, and had been unable to foresee that the troops would run wild to such an extent. As a matter of fact, many of the officers meted out their own punishment and committed suicide in order to escape shame and disgrace, and the fear of being punished by the top brass. All this I knew through the nature of my work in Smersh.

There were many urgent, on-the-spot conferences of top brass during those days, one of which I remember particularly well. I was myself standing not far away from the participants of the conference and heard something of what they said. We were in the Breslau area, not far away from the aerodrome. All around were damaged buildings save one single large shelter, which had remained intact. There were a few jeeps and Dodges. Something wet and revolting was dropping out of the sky! God, what a climate! A large map had been opened out across the bonnet of one of the vehicles. Close by stood groups of NKVD forces carrying sub-machine guns and with knives in their belts. To one side stood a group of Smersh officers, myself among them. Round the vehicle where the map was stood a group of top brass. The thickset man with the large head and short legs was Marshal Zhukov. Beside him stood General of the Army Petrov, Chief of Staff of the First Ukrainian Front. For some reason Marshal

Konev was not in evidence. I think he was with the troops. Petrov was wearing pince-nez. His head kept twitching and from time to time a grimace contorted his face. This was the effect of shell shock. The first members of the Military Council of our Front and Zhukov's First Belorussian Front were also there: Lieutenant-Generals Krainyukov and Telegin. Close beside them stood two more Lieutenant-Generals: Korolyov, chief of Smersh for our Front, and Vadis, who was Zhukov's chief of Smersh and who had probably flown in with him. Next to them, on the side nearest to me, was a man of less than medium height, wearing the shoulder boards of a colonel-general. It was Serov, the second deputy People's Commissar of the Soviet Union for Internal Affairs.

Even before Serov's arrival Zhukov, as a high-ranking non-Chekist, had been completely surrounded by Chekist generals. These included Telegin and Antipenko. The higher a man's rank and the stronger his apparent power, the more he was kept under surveillance by the security services.

Zhukov was speaking and I could just catch the odd word now and then.

'. . . here we ought to . . . but there . . .'

He spoke energetically and waved his leather-sleeved arm above the map. Then I heard Petrov's light tenor speaking voice.

'. . . no, Comrade Marshal . . . we can't manage that . . .'

Zhukov went on waving his hand. The rest of them were silent for the most part. Vadis, whom I saw then for the first time, had a half-smirk on his impassive Latvian face. As far as I can remember Serov didn't say a word. At that time he used the completely fictitious camouflage title of Deputy Commander of the First Belorussian Front (i.e. Zhukov's deputy). The purpose of this ploy was to conceal his real job from the uninitiated. In Germany he had other tasks and duties, which were altogether different from those of Smersh, but more of that anon. The meeting at the aerodrome soon came to an end. A little later a Douglas, with an escort of nine fighters, droned noisily overhead, slowly gaining height and flying in a north-easterly direction.

I would like to quote extracts from certain secret orders and reports made by Marshal Zhukov during that period. Their originals are in the archives of the Ministry of Defence in the Soviet Union.

'If the left flank under K. K. Rokossovsky[1] stays in the same place

[1] Rokossovsky, Konstantin Konstantinovich. Marshal of the Soviet Union. Was active further north on the Second Belorussian Front.

for much longer, the enemy will undoubtedly go into action against the over-extended right flank of the First Belorussian Front. I request that K. K. Rokossovsky be ordered to attack in a westerly direction with the 70th Army, without delay . . .'

'2. I request that Comrade I. S. Konev[1] be made to advance towards the river Oder more rapidly.'

F.233 OP. 2307. D.194, L.48

Signatures—Zhukov, Telegin. Addressee—Stalin.

One further extract, giving only the important instructions:

'I request you all to realise your historical responsibility to fulfil the mission you have been given . . . and to demand from your troops exceptional steadfastness and courage. 1. Dig yourselves in deeply; . . . 3. Go over to night attacks, each time aiming at limited objectives; 4. Fend off enemy attacks during the day time.'

F.233 OP.2307, D.194, LL. 100–101

Signature—Zhukov. Addressee—Military Council of the Fifth Strike Army and Corps and Division Commanders of the Fifth Strike Army.

Even the most naive, with a smattering of knowledge about Zhukov, would realise that he did not write these documents because everything in the garden was lovely.

Phrases like 'I request that Rokossovsky be ordered', 'that Konev be made . . .' are somewhat out of character. Zhukov was, after all, Stalin's First Deputy in all military matters. What did all this mean coming from a man who himself knew perfectly well how to give out orders. Or 'dig yourselves in deep', 'fend off enemy attacks in the day time', 'attack limited objectives'. If all this had referred to the battles of Moscow or Stalingrad it would have been more understandable, but it referred to the approaches to Berlin. The date of the first document is 31st January 1945. The second is undated, but refers to a still later period in the spring of 1945. This was hardly the time when one would have expected Marshals to talk about 'digging in deeply' or 'attacking limited objectives'! We were then better off than the Germans in many respects, both in manpower and equipment.

I must quote just one more statement. It is not in any archive, and it is not altogether respectable. It has stuck in my mind, as we all found this unpleasant hold-up on the road to victory a very painful experience. It was made by the Caucasian major, the chief of my Smersh operational group at First Ukrainian Front HQ.

[2] Konev, Ivan Stepanovich. Commander of the First Ukrainian Front.

What a bloody caper!
The little dog got the big one
And then began to rape her.

It wasn't actually quite as bad as that, but the Germans, sensing
something odd in our hesitancy, more than once staged counter
offensives. The most important of these was in eastern Pomerania,
but it was quite clear that they had neither enough spirit or enough
strength to make any serious impact. All the excuses and explanations that Soviet historians and the Marshals themselves offer today
are not worth the paper they are written on. It is, of course, true that
at that time our forces did experience certain difficulties with the
supply of equipment and ammunition, but one can't compare these
difficulties with the difficulties experienced during, say, the battles of
Moscow, Stalingrad or Belgorod-Kursk. Any schoolboy knows, for
example, that there is a slight difference between German roads and
the average road in central Russia, and this difference is accentuated
at the time of the spring thaw. The Russian name for this time of
year literally means the time of 'roadlessness'.

Our Higher Command did, however, have one further reserve
plan. If Eisenhower and Montgomery had not turned out to be
reasonable people and had tried to take Berlin before Stalin could get
there, then we would have put this plan into action. Our mass tank
forces on three Fronts (the First Belorussian, Second Belorussian
and First Ukrainian) would have converged on Berlin from three sides
and, under the massive protection of our air forces, would have swept
everything off the roads. There were enough tanks to do this, in
fact about six thousand. They had been supplied with fuel too. Their
communications and their rear supply lines would have been guaran-
teed by NKVD motorised troops. Two whole armies had been brought
in as an emergency measure. Two Marshals of the tank forces,
Marshal Rotmistrov and Marshal Rybalko, were responsible for
controlling the tank side of this operation. Colonel-General Serov
was in charge of the NKVD involvement. Special detachments of
sabotage paratroops had been formed, not only on our two main
fronts, but also in the area of our southern neighbour, the Fourth
Ukrainian Front. In the event of any unexpected developments they
would have been thrown in to the attack. On Zhukov's Front, Vadis,
and on Konev's Front, Korolyov, were responsible for their preparedness. In the south, General of the Army Yeremenko's area, his
Smersh chief, Lieutenant-General Koval'chuk, was responsible. The

general terms of this plan which was never put into operation were known to me through my work in Smersh. But Eisenhower and Montgomery turned out to be reasonable chaps, as did all the top leadership of Great Britain and the United States of America. Luckily for Soviet power the allied armies waited patiently at the River Elbe until we arrived.

In 1945 everything ended relatively peacefully. The binges and mass debauchery gradually abated. Some of the out-and-out shirkers were put into penal companies. The extra reserves of NKVD troops were withdrawn from the second echelons of the Fronts on to Soviet territory.

These troops played, and today still continue to play, a very important part in all spheres of Soviet life. NKVD troops are as old as Soviet power itself, although sometimes they have been called by other names. ChON[1] for example (special purpose units), were formed by Dzerzhinsky at Lenin's behest. From 1946 onwards there have been two Main Administrations of these troops within the NKVD system. The NKGB is represented in their structure on the same basis of branches, sections and representatives of the Special Branches or Administrations in peacetime, and of Smersh in wartime, just as is the case in all the ordinary arms of the Soviet armed forces. One administration is the Main Administration of Internal troops. It includes operational troops, escort troops, signal troops and transport troops.

The operational troops are the most numerous. In every large town in the Soviet Union there are at least two battalions of these troops. At present in 1971 a division of these troops, the so-called Dzerzhinsky Division, is stationed permanently in Moscow. The main task of the operational troops is to ensure the success of all operations undertaken by the State Security bodies, or, more precisely, by the Main Operational Administration of the NKGB as it then was, or the KGB as it is today.

These operations range fairly widely from mass arrests, assembly of specific groups of citizens and their removal to certain places, to the suppression of anti-Soviet sentiments expressed in any form, from a demonstration to a revolution. There are no strikes in the Soviet Union, since the workers themselves are in power. Both the premise and the conclusion are, of course, purely theoretical.

The other duties of operational troops of the NKVD include mounting permanent guard on certain buildings or installations. Half

[1] ChON—*Chasti Osobogo Naznacheniya.*

a company of these troops, for example, is on guard duty round the clock in the building of the Central Committee of the Communist Party and the building of the Council of Ministers. The same situation obtains in a number of other buildings, though the quantity of troops is smaller. There is also, of course, a special list of country residences, belonging to Party and State leaders, which are guarded by these troops. Guarding prisons and labour camps is not one of their duties.

A typical operation carried out by these troops was the liquidation of the Polish officers at Katyn, near Smolensk, before the war. I say typical because the whole operation, which has led to such violent controversy in the west, was considered entirely routine and un-remarkable in Soviet Russia. I did not work in the State Security system at the time of that massacre, but during my time in the State Security Service body, GUKR Smersh, and in particular when I was working in its Third Administration, I met people who participated in and helped to organise this mass murder.

No outsider knows the exact date of the massacre of the Polish officers at Katyn. I am sure that this information is preserved in the KGB archives, under the heading Kh.V.[1] (All details of important operations are preserved in these archives. They are housed in underground premises, which can be immediately destroyed at any time, both by electric acid and high explosives. There is one entrance to the archive, in Furkasov Lane in Moscow, not far from Dzerz-hinsky Square.)

I do not believe the Soviet version of the Katyn story, namely there there was not time to evacuate the Poles from the camp where they were held in 1941 because of the German advance. The advance actually was a rapid one and in Smolensk a part of the Party and State archives fell into German hands. The NKVD, however, managed not only to remove its archives from Smolensk, but also to blow up a whole series of installations in the town. It also had time to remove from the area all Soviet-born, civilian political prisoners. Several thousand Polish officers, a substantial part of the flower of the officer corps of Poland, were of far greater concern. For such criminal negligence, the head of the Operational Administration[2] of the Main Administration of the State Security Service of the NKVD[3], Com-

---

[1] Kh.V.—*Khranit' vechno,* to be kept in perpetuity.
[2] Operational Administration—as it then was.
[3] NKVD—as it then was.

missar of State Security, Third Rank, Raichman[1], would have suffered. The same goes for the warden of the camp where the Poles were held, a major in the State Security Service called Vetoshnikov. The whole of his evidence to the Soviet commission was a fiction, designed to delude the uninitiated. Western conclusions that Vetoshnikov was, of course, liquidated as an inconvenient witness are untrue. There was no reason at all to liquidate Major Vetoshnikov. I don't say this out of any feeling of compassion towards him, as I never met the man. But he couldn't in any sense have been an inconvenient witness. He was a well-schooled Chekist, who knew how to keep his mouth shut and held a rank equivalent to that of a general. The last point underlines the importance of this Polish problem in the eyes of the Soviet authorities.

I myself have seen Raichman and met other persons involved in this incident, including Major-General Zarubin. During the Katyn affair, since he had to deal with the Polish officers, he used the rank of brigade commander. I very much doubt whether he ever was, in fact, a brigade commander, a rank equivalent to that of major-general, since within the NKVD this rank was only to be found in the internal and frontier troops. Even then there were only a few individuals left who continued to hold it until the beginning of 1943. Zarubin had nothing to do with these troops whatsoever. There were also brigade commanders in GRU of the General Staff, as in the rest of the Soviet army, but only until May 1940. Zarubin did not, however, serve in any of the aforementioned institutions. He became a 'brigade commander' for the sake of the Poles, so that they should not feel awkward in his presence, and so as not to arouse any unnecessary suspicions. He had no intention, as many in the west have written, to re-educate the Poles and convert them to the Soviet faith. How can one possibly re-educate a large number of grown-up intelligent people who are the enemies of Soviet power by conviction and who, into the bargain, are confined in a camp in bad conditions? Perhaps people in the west have other ideas, but Stalin and the top brass of the NKVD had no such illusions. The small group of Poles such as Berling, which the NKVD needed as decoys to put in their shop window, had already been picked out.

Zarubin was an important official of the Foreign Intelligence Administration of the GUGB[2], with orders to carry out, with his

---

[1] Commissar of State Security of the Third Rank—as he then was.
[2] GUGB (*Glavnoye Upravleniye Gosudarstvennoi Bezopasnosti*)—Main Administration of State Security, as it was then called.

operational group, a final 'sucking dry' operation, i.e. to collect from the Poles military and political intelligence data. This is what he did, without, of course, taking the Poles into his confidence. He and other members of his group gave the Poles the impression that they were interested in quite different matters. In my time Zarubin was still working in the same administration—the Main Administration Foreign Intelligence, no longer then of the GUGB, but of the NKGB.

Because of the importance of what I am describing I won't state his exact position, since I am not quite sure of it. I think that he was Deputy Chief of the Military Intelligence Agents' Administration of the Main Administration of Foreign Intelligence of the NKGB. In GUKR Smersh we maintained constant contact with GRU of the General Staff, though the Main Administration of Foreign Intelligence had even closer contacts with them. Zarubin was one of the Chekists whose job involved the practical realisation of this contact. He worked with Lieutenant-General Onyanov, the chief of GRU of the General Staff's Administration of Agents in Enemy Armies. The decision whether to kill the Poles was not Zarubin's. It was decided by Stalin and Beria, with the possible inclusion of Merkulov, who was at that time Beria's First Deputy and the chief of GUGB. I hardly think that they were tormented by doubts. Should they annihilate at a stroke most of the officer crops belonging to a regime of known hostility to the Soviet regime? There were no grounds for doubt here. One last thing about Zarubin. The official public confirmation of his rank, major-general in the State Security Service, saw the light of day in July 1945. This was a pure formality, however. Zarubin, like the other leaders of the NKGB, NKVD held this rank throughout the war from the spring of 1943 onwards.

I would like here to touch on certain other details connected with the Poles, which are not so important in themselves, but I mention them simply for the record. At the time when Anders and his few remaining surviving officers emerged from Soviet prisons, the chief of GULAG of the NKVD was not Nasedkin, but Nedosekin, who was then a Commissar of the State Security Service, Third Rank, and later on a colonel-general. He continues to be referred to as Nasedkin in all written sources in the west. He had no connection with the murder of the Polish officers and neither did his predecessor, who held the post at the time of the massacre. I am not altogether sure of my memory here, but I think this was Commissar of the State Security Service, Third Rank, Kravchenko.

Finally there are probably many Poles, and for that matter people in the west in general, who do not know that Panfilov, a Major-General who often dealt with Anders and Sikorski, was something more than just one of the Deputy Chiefs of the General Staff. He was also at the time the chief of the GRU of the General Staff.

I think there is no particular point in spending any more time on the internal forces of the NKVD in an attempt to establish precisely which detachments of their operational troops carried out the massacre of the Poles. It is possible that the escort troops of the NKVD took part in this affair. Mixed detachments, part escort, part operational, do in fact exist. There are no differences whatsoever in their uniforms or badges. I am quite certain that regular units of the Red Army did not take part. For understandable reasons the NKVD would allow the regular army no such an authority.

The main duty of the escort troops is to guard all types of prisoner, when they are being moved from place to place, on the territory of the Soviet Union, including movement of prisoners by air. It is also part of their duties to guard labour camps, but only from the outside. These troops enter the camps only in exceptional circumstances, in large groups, often accompanied by operational troops. They do not guard prisons.

The third type of internal troops are signal troops. They do not always wear the emblem of signals personnel, crossed flashes of lightning and a small star, on their shoulder boards. In peacetime these troops are responsible for government communications of all types. In addition to this they guard important communications installations throughout the country against saboteurs, wreckers and all unauthorised personnel. Such installations include high-voltage lines of communication, both above and below ground, certain plants and factories which produce communications equipment, and government field post centres. Personnel of these troops also staff the radio signal detection service of the State Security Service. The so-called corps of government messengers or *Feldjagers* belong to these troops. In wartime the activities of these troops remain the same, but embrace wider fields of state communications, which in peacetime are the purlieu of the People's Commissariat (Ministry) of Communications of the USSR. The duties of the transport troops of the NKVD internal troops are very much like the duties of the signal troops.

The Main Administration of Frontier Troops of the NKVD, now

the KGB,[1] has a special structure. Its administrations include a Maritime Administration, an Air Administration and an Administration for the Breeding and Training of Dogs and others. There is a central dog-training school in Alma Ata, and an intelligence administration (intelligence of all kinds) covering Soviet frontier zones and frontier zones of countries adjacent to the Soviet Union. There is also the Main HQ of the Frontier Troops with various branches, operational, signals, etc. Frontier troops normally are not made up of companies, battalions, regiments, etc., as are internal troops. They are divided into Frontier posts, a smallish unit, 'Komendatury' (Commandant's units), detachments and regions, which is the largest unit. In the areas of Soviet territory adjacent to the frontier, mixed regions of NKVD troops were stationed, including both internal troops and frontier troops. By the time the war began, stretching from north to south along the western frontier of the Soviet Union, there were eight such regions, amounting in all to more than a hundred thousand men. In the Far East there were three regions but since I had nothing to do with these, I do not know how many men they comprised, nor do I know all the details about the southern regions of NKVD troops.

NKVD troops are not subordinate to the High Command of the Soviet Armed Forces. It is true that Soviet newspapers regularly print orders of the Ministry of Defence concerning the demobilisation from and calling-up of troops into the armed forces. Frontier and internal troops are mentioned in these orders. This is however a pure formality for the uninitiated, so as not to draw unnecessary attention to these troops. After all, they are known to every Soviet schoolchild, and to certain people in the west. Consequently, without going into unnecessary details, they were included in general military orders. In practice, however, neither the Ministry of Defence, nor the Chief of the General Staff, can ever order a single soldier from these troops to be moved from the third storey of his barracks up to the fourth. They live a special isolated life of their own. Not only are they isolated from the Soviet army, but from the Soviet population in general. The war disturbed and upset their precisely arranged lives. In cases where they did not have time to retreat when the Germans struck, the personnel of Frontier posts actually fought to their last bullet and their last gasp. They understood perfectly

[1] At the present time, for reasons which are unknown to me, the Main Administration of Internal Troops belongs to the MVD system, and the Main Administration of Frontier Troops to the KGB.

clearly what would happen to them if they fell into German hands. Others dispersed, having changed into civilian clothes, and joined up with the Party section of the undercover partisan movement.

A few days after the beginning of the war, in June 1941, yet another Main Administration of the NKVD was formed in Moscow, the Main Administration for Guarding the Home Front. On the very same day administration of the rearguard, subordinate to this Main Administration, appeared at all the Fronts. In my time its chief was Colonel-General Apollonov, who became one of Beria's deputies in the NKVD network. Among the other duties of this administration was the organisation and maintainance of blocking detachments. All the officers and men belonging to this administration were re-equipped with ordinary army uniforms, just as we were in Smersh.

In my opinion our Anglo-American allies meted out an undeserved insult to Apollonov. He was responsible for the protection of Churchill, Roosevelt and, of course, Stalin himself, during the conferences at Tehran, Yalta and Potsdam. The British and Americans gave their high decorations to Colonel-General Kruglov, First Deputy People's Commissar of the USSR for Internal Affairs and Lieutenant-General Novikov the deputy chief of the Main Operational Administration of the NKGB, who were present at these conferences of the Big Three. I think that at some of these conferences Novikov stood in for the chief of his administration. Kruglov's presence at the conference was actually nothing more than decorative. He represented Beria, who was unable to leave Moscow due to pressure of work. Novikov, of course, took part in the control of operational guard duties at these conferences.

But the main burden of the security of Churchill, Roosevelt and Stalin lay entirely upon Apollonov. He was responsible not only for the safety of all premises used by participants of the conferences but also for the immediately adjacent streets and gardens, etc. And he was responsible for the whole territory, in all more than a score of square kilometres, around the sites of the conferences.

During the critical days of the defence of Moscow, when only ten or so kilometres stood between the Germans and the Kremlin, Stalin issued a special order. In accordance with this order, which was not secret, all authority for maintaining order and security within the city limits was placed in the hands of the Moscow City Military Commandant. His men were given the right to shoot on the spot all panic-mongers, pillagers, saboteurs and the like. The whole of the internal forces of the NKVD stationed in Moscow were placed under his control. The Military Commandant at that time was Lieutenant-General Sinilov. Western specialists claimed that in Moscow Stalin had put all power into the hands of the military. This has also been recorded in many western printed sources. Nevertheless, in some respects western judgements have misrepresented the situation. Sinilov was a professional Chekist, a brigade commander, and subsequently major-general in the internal troops of the NKVD. Before taking up his appointment in Moscow he had been the chief of the Murmansk region of NKVD troops, both internal and frontier. Sinilov remained Military Commandant of Moscow right up to Stalin's death.

On 8 May 1945, on the day when the Germans signed the act of unconditional capitulation in the dining-room of the former German School of Military Engineering in Karlshorst, the guard duty for this ceremony was carried out by NKVD troops. They also guarded the aerodrome at which the supreme military leaders of the western alliance and the German delegation from Flensburg arrived. Colonel-General Serov was entirely responsible for the NKVD side of everything connected with the capitulation, including the transportation of the German prisoner-delegates. He was representing Beria. Stalin was represented by Zhukov and Vyshinsky.[1] However, before all this happened there were certain other things that had to be done. Things were moving slowly with Zhukov on the First Belorussian Front, where the Germans were putting up stubborn resistance. On 18 April a coded message arrived at Front HQ of the First Ukrainian Front: 'Direct the mobile part of the Front northwards in the direction of Berlin. Stalin.' That very day, in order to implement this coded order, Konev threw the Third Tank Army of Guards in the direction of Berlin. On the evening of 21 April, units of this army burst into the southern suburbs of the German capital. At almost the same time detachments from Zhukov's Front also arrived. Now final victory could not be far off.

---

[1] Vyshinsky, A. Ya. At that time First Deputy People's Commissar for Foreign Affairs.

6

Then the barrel of every gun
Roared out a salute as one,
Proclaiming that the war was won.

From a poem by Alexander Tvardovsky

I FIXED THE THIRD small star on my shoulder boards. Now I was
a first lieutenant. It was pleasant, but nothing special. It would still
be some time before I became a Marshal of the Soviet Union!
Within the State Security Service only one man held that rank and
that was Beria. He had only received it in July 1945. In any case, I
had already realised that in Chekist circles the influence of some
senior officers and generals often had nothing to do with their actual
rank.

Many of my colleagues in Smersh had received promotions and
decorations. My immediate superior, the Caucasian major, became a
lieutenant-colonel. His closest colleagues, of whom I was one,
celebrated his second star with a friendly evening's drinking. Despite
the large quantity of old Armenian brandy which was disposed of
during that evening, none of those present lost his head, or said
anything that he shouldn't. It's true that one of the lady officers of
our group got very drunk. We took her into the next room, undid
her dress and her suspender belt, and applied a wet towel to her
forehead.

On the following day, however, I had such a terrible headache that
I vowed there and then never again to drink cognac, whatever the
brand. I have kept to this.

On the same day my chief, the lieutenant-colonel, told me that
he had been given a new assignment. He had been appointed deputy
chief of the Third Branch in the Smersh Administration of the First
Ukrainian Front.

'I would like,' he said, 'to take a few of my own people with me.

Why don't you come? You'll come to no harm with me. I'll make a great man of you.'

He finished with these words from a famous Caucasian anecdote. Despite my dreadful headache, I was very moved and flattered by the lieutenant-colonel's suggestion. In the first place, it meant that he regarded me as one of his own sort. This was not to be sneezed at. I knew of his authority and influence among the Chekists of our administration and even among the leadership of the Smersh Administration of the Front. Also working in the Third Branch carried the most responsibility. It was Smersh's Holy of Holies. It was the confluence of streams of information from all the other branches of Smersh. To the Third Branch came, via the Third Administration of the Main Administration, all the orders, instructions, briefings and data from Abakumov's Main Administration in Moscow. I owe it only to my Abkhazian lieutenant-colonel, Beria's fellow countryman, that I, a fairly humble Smersh officer, got to know incomparably more about what was going on than a senior Soviet army general.

Then came the long-awaited day of victory. The war was over. Like everyone around me, I was in an elated, joyous mood. But I cooled slightly at a victory party in our Smersh Administration. All the Chekists free from duty in the Administration gathered that evening in our main hall. The chief of the Administration, Lieutenant-General Korolyov, was away in Moscow. One of his deputies, Colonel Yevdokimenko, made a short congratulatory speech. He began with a 'Gloria' and ended with a 'Requiem'—a requiem for our western allies, the British and Americans. He said, more or less, that for some people, perhaps, the war was over, but for us Chekists this was not so in any sense. The real war, to bring about the final destruction of the capitalist world, was only just beginning. We had annihilated what was simply its ugliest manifestation—Hitler and his empire. The fight to annihilate the rest lay ahead.

The colonel's speech disheartened me. Was it really necessary, I thought, for us to tackle the British and Americans at once? We had, after all, just achieved victory and peace. There was so much joy and happiness in the air. Surely we could relax and enjoy ourselves? In any case, the British and Americans had fought on our side and helped to bring about Hitler's downfall. They too had made many sacrifices. Like us, many of them had lost their relatives and their loved ones. But I soon came to, and put these depressing thoughts out of my mind. All about me was a hive of activity. Our officers and men were firing salutes to victory with weapons of every shape and size. Even our anti-aircraft guns were firing. As I learnt later, they all but shot down one of our own planes with a number of important officials of the People's Commissariat for Foreign Affairs, assistants of Vyshinsky, on board. In those days I was aflame with love for all men, even diplomats. I say 'even' because my love for them soon evaporated.

My liking for my boss, the lieutenant-colonel, increased further when in June 1945 he took me with him to Moscow for a three-day visit to attend the Victory Parade. Of course, neither he nor I travelled there for that reason officially. We travelled to Moscow to hand over to the Main Administration of Smersh a number of important documents and to take the German colours and standards which we had collected to the capital for the parade. (Long live the lieutenant-colonel!) The Smersh Administrations of all Fronts had actually helped to collect these colours. The order that they should be sought out had come from Stalin himself. Once in Moscow, the rest was fairly simple.

It was a rainy morning and I stood in Red Square with a group of other officers. It turned out that I was by no means the only one with an intelligent and quick-thinking boss. The light blue card of GUKR Smersh, to which I still belonged, worked unfailingly whenever I took it out of my pocket. In fact on my way to Red Square it was more frequently in my hand than in my pocket. Heaven knows how many times I showed it at the innumerable patrols and police cordons. To get to the centre of Moscow one had to pass through several cordoned-off zones. The first one was manned by NCOs of NKVD Internal Troops, the next by Chekist officers. The nearer one got to the Kremlin and the Lenin Mausoleum, the higher were the ranks of the officers manning the cordon. In front of the guests' stands, shoulder to shoulder in an unbroken line, stood officers of the Main Operational Administration of the NKGB. A second line of officers of the same administration, none below the rank of major, stretched the whole length of the façade of the Mausoleum. Behind and beside the Mausoleum stood officers of the Special Operational Group which formed Stalin's personal bodyguard. Walking slowly up and down by the steps leading up to the balcony of the Mausoleum was a shortish stocky general. It was the chief of this group, Lieutenant-General Vlasik. Close by him, frozen to attention with bayonets fixed, stood two soldiers from the NKVD. Everybody was in full-dress uniform. Amongst the guests on the stands, however, there were many Chekist operational officers in plain clothes. They were also on duty.

Of course, I had not counted on, or even dreamt of, a place on the guests' stand. After all, Moscow was a far cry from my home town. The people standing here held far bigger jobs and higher ranks than I did. Among the many foreigners there were British, French and American officers representing our wartime allies. I thought back to that day in Tatishchevo when I'd taken a group of bedizzened criminals for our western allies.

Those in the Red Square were genuine representatives of the allies and looked quite different. I and the rest of the group I was with were found a place quite some distance from the Mausoleum and the guests' stands, not far from the Spassky gates of the Kremlin. The square, packed with troops, one regiment from each Front, was tense with expectation. The clock in the Spassky Tower began to strike. At its last stroke Zhukov and his adjutant—who was, I think, Major-General Minyuk—rode out from the tower gates at a field gallop. The Marshal's white Arab horse was in a mood for showing-off and kept on trying to rear up on its hind legs. Zhukov was, however, a cavalry man of long experience. They dashed past some twenty or thirty yards from me, heading for the centre of the square.

Not very long after this Zhukov was banished to a provincial military region and accused of many sins; among them, as I later learned in Chekist circles, was the accusation that he had tried, by galloping about on his white steed, to set himself up as some kind of second St. George, the slayer of dragons. Zhukov was in fact a George, Georgy Konstantinovich.

Certain things that I saw and heard that day in Red Square I shall never forget. Glinka's triumphant melody, 'Hail, hail',[1] which seemed to clutch at one's very soul, was one. But the rain never stopped. Water streamed down everybody's caps and faces. I think that many faces on that day were wet not only from the rain. There were none of us, not a single family, that had not suffered irreplaceable losses, near ones, relatives, old friends. This was certainly one of the things I was thinking about then. I didn't listen to the short speech from the Mausoleum. The Soviet National Anthem thundered forth, drowned at times by the salute of the Kremlin battery. I almost felt like laughing. El'-Registan, who was widely known as a connoisseur of pretty girls and spicy jokes, had collaborated with the poet Mikhalkov in writing the words. This national anthem was first

[1] From Glinka's opera *A Life for the Czar*.

played in public in 1944. It took the place of the *Internationale*, so as not to cause unnecessary embarrassment to Churchill, Roosevelt and other distinguished guests from among the western allies. The *Internationale*, after all, calls openly for the destruction of people like them and the regimes they represent, although, as distinct from *Horst Wessel*, it does this in perfectly respectable terms. The effect of playing it after 'God Save the King', was nevertheless somewhat ambiguous.

The *Internationale* was, and in fact still is, the official party anthem of the CPSU. In El'-Registan's new anthem, however, there were the words 'Stalin reared us . . .', but they have now been removed and the anthem has been turned into a *Lied ohne Worte*. I learned from a trusted friend, that when in 1942 a project for new guards' colours was submitted to Stalin for his approval, after a little thought he decisively crossed his own profile off the colours, leaving only that of Lenin and said: 'At this point in time, that will be quite sufficient.' Now, in June 1945, it was clear from the words about Stalin which were included in the anthem that things had changed.

The ceremonial march began. To the accompaniment of the thousand-strong band, regiments of all the Fronts marched past the Mausoleum, not in an order that in any way reflected their role in the war but arranged geographically from north to south. The regiments were led by the marshal in command of the Front they served on. Each saluted before the Mausoleum with a sweep of his drawn sabre. The band played the tune

> Volga, Volga, mother Volga,
> Volga, river of the Russians,

which had been specially adapted as a march. Along came my own Front, with Marshal Konev at its head. He strode out with precision, holding his sabre at his chin. I heard from my boss the lieutenant-colonel, who had good connections and knew a great deal, that Stalin's order that Rokossovsky and not Konev should command the parade had deeply offended the latter. Konev's First Ukrainian Front was indeed more important than Rokossovky's Second Belorussian Front. There was only one candidate for taking the salute, however, and that was Zhukov, Stalin's first deputy, and he in fact did so. Strictly speaking, the Supreme Commander himself, Marshal Stalin, should have taken the salute at the Victory Parade, but he was no longer young, and probably incapable of sitting astride a restive horse for a long time. I am not alone in thinking that, although Stalin came from the Caucasus, he had never sat on a horse in his life.

The regiments all passed and the band was silent. Peace reigned once again in the square. It was broken by the dull and insistent beating of many drums. A long column of soldiers was approaching the Mausoleum, carrying colours and flags of all kinds. They did not, however, bear these colours proudly, but half dragged them over the wet cobbles of the square, before throwing them down at the foot of the Mausoleum. The drums continued their insidious rattle. The first standard to fall on the ground was a fairly small square one on a wooden staff. It had on it a large swastika within a circle and the name 'Adolf Hitler' in Gothic letters.

Standing on the balcony of the Mausoleum was a short man with a moustache, wearing the uniform of a marshal. He was surrounded by other marshals. It was Stalin. I wasn't looking up there at him, however. I was deep in my own thoughts, about Yoska, about my grandfather. I recalled that beautiful summer day in June 1941 and my grandfather's prayer before the icon of St. Nicholas the Miracle Worker. The words of the prayer had been, 'Oh Lord, Save and preserve Russia . . .' I recollected Grandfather's answers to my questions on that far-off day. 'No one will ever conquer Russia, grandson . . .' I shook myself free from my thoughts and memories. Both Grandfather and Yoska were gone for ever. All that was left was a rainy day, a deserted Red Square, a heap of German standards thrown down by the Mausoleum and a first lieutenant of GUKR Smersh whose face was moist, perhaps not only from the rain.

Many changes had taken place in our First Ukrainian Front. Properly speaking, the Front, as such, no longer existed. It had served as a basis which, with the addition of units from other Fronts, had become the Central Group of Forces (the TsGV).[1] Demobilisation of older privates and NCOs began. We left the Dresden area and Germany. Marshal Zhukov's Front remained in Germany under the new name of GSVG.[2] Our new 'parish' was Austria and Hungary. The Smersh Administration of TSGV occupied a number of large houses standing in a secluded garden in the spa of Baden bei Wien. The basements of some of the houses were re-equipped as cells for prisoners

---

[1] TsGV—*Tsentral'naya groopa voisk*—Central Group of Forces.
[2] GSVG—*Groopa Sovetskikh Voisk v Germanii*—Group of Soviet Forces in Germany.

under investigation. In another part of Baden, on permanent attachment to us, was an operational battalion of NKVD troops.

I began to get used to the new place. Baden was a delightful little resort, full of trees and not far from Vienna, away from the main road to Wienerneustadt. The Austrians were lively, cheerful people, and, unlike the Germans, not at all frightened. I was soon able to substantiate this feeling through my own personal experience with a young Austrian girl. She was a student in Vienna, but at that troubled time she was living with her parents in Baden. I first met her in the public library and sensed that somehow she reminded me of the doctor captain from the Moscow hospital. It was her eyes, and her 'socialist property', in general. This time I suppose it must have been 'private property', since Austria was undoubtedly a capitalist country. My bosses in Smersh had often reminded me of that.

I asked her to show me the sights of the town, and wandered meekly after her through the squares and streets. The war had been kind to Baden and there was plenty to show and plenty to look at, including the central Kursal and many old houses. Each new thing I saw delighted me more and more.

At our first evening meeting in a garden near the officers' club we strolled decorously up and down the paths. She corrected my pronunciation of German words. I shall never forget the wretched word *naturlich*, which I seemed quite unable to get my tongue round. I saw her home, but all I managed was one modest kiss. We continued in this vein for a couple of weeks. She and I drank the occasional bottle of wine together in an Austrian restaurant and she visited my flat once or twice to give me German lessons. I had a room in the house of a retired Austrian railwayman. I chose this flat specially because it was some distance from our Smersh Administration. I informed my boss, the lieutenant-colonel, about my German lessons, but took care not to go into unnecessary details.

Certain officers of our administration, though not, of course, of the Third Branch in which I worked, were already working amongst the Austrian population. Forsaking their uniforms for mufti, they attended Austrian Communist Party meetings and those of the local municipal authorities too. They were also interested in many other things, such as the activities of other political parties.

My operation with the young girl student was rudely interrupted by another Smersh operation. The Caucasian lieutenant-colonel was busy collecting information about the leaders of certain anti-Soviet organisations active on German territory, and I too was put to work on this. At the very end of the war the leadership of the organisation which interested us most, that of General Vlasov, was situated in Czechoslovakia, near Prague, which was now under the jurisdiction of our Front. After the storming of Berlin the Czechs had staged an uprising in Prague. They seized the city radio station and put out many calls for help, both to us and to the Americans. The most advanced American units were nearer to Prague than we were. A single movement and the Americans could have been there. The American High Command, however, on this occasion too, did not feel inclined to irritate Stalin, and decided not to move its troops. Stalin sent a coded message to Konev, the commander of my Front, who dispatched to the south, towards Prague, the Third and Fourth Tank Armies of Guards, with cover from the Second Air Army.

Nevertheless, they did not liberate Prague. The Czech capital was liberated from the Germans by Vlasov's First Division, which was close by at that time. Vlasov's men took Prague by storm, took many German prisoners, SS troops in particular, and raised two flags on the town hall roof; the Czech national flag and the blue and white flag of St. Andrew, the flag of Free Russia. Vlasov was well aware that he and his men could not remain in Prague. Our tanks were already within a day's journey of the city. Behind the tanks came the Smersh operational groups of the First, Second and Fourth Ukrainian Fronts. They all had the same mission, to capture Vlasov and his men. With tears in their eyes, the Czechs thanked Vlasov's men for liberating their proud capital and saving it from the fate which Warsaw suffered at German hands. They put the finishing touches to their thanks in a somewhat unusual way.

Throughout the whole war there hadn't been a single serious partisan detachment in Czechoslovakia, with the exception of the Chekist partisans, who had been sent there from Moscow. Now however, after the capture of Berlin, a huge number of Czech partisans appeared, all wanting to wreak vengeance on the Germans. Vlasov's men, who wished to reach the American lines and surrender there, became easy prey for them. Not far from Pibran, the Czechs seized General Vlasov's assistant, his chief of staff General Trukhin, and handed him over to a Smersh operational group. The Czechs hanged Trukhin's deputy, Colonel Boyarsky on the spot. A local administration, with a communist majority, was hastily set up in Prague. One of the leaders of this organisation was Smrkovsky, who was later, in 1968, to be one of Alexander Dubcek's chief comrades-in-arms. Incidentally Dubcek, like Smrkovsky, was extremely short-sighted in 1968. Having grown up in the Soviet Union he should have known the workings of Soviet power very well. In 1968, however, it became clear that he knew and understood nothing.

The losses of 1968 were far smaller than those of 1945 and 1946, when the British and Americans handed over to Smersh former Soviet citizens and Russians from the old emigration. These people, many of whom had their families with them, found themselves at the end of the war in Germany and Austria. Only a very small percentage of them had actually been involved in crimes against the laws of God and man; namely participation in the punitive police activities of the Third Reich. Of course, old men, women and children hadn't been involved in anything at all. However, more than a few such perished. In the Austrian province of East Tyrol there is a town called Lienz, near to which stands a small Russian cemetery and chapel. Here in 1945 the British handed these people over to the Soviet authorities. They were beaten with sticks and rifle-butts. Some committed suicide. Mothers hurled themselves and their small children into the river Drava, others beneath the treads of British miniature tanks. I have spoken personally with people who survived this action and with English officers who were there.

Not long ago I spoke to a young Englishman who spent several years in a Soviet concentration camp. I once asked him whether he had ever been insulted in Soviet prisons and camps simply because he was an Englishman.

'Yes,' he answered, 'once, because the British forcibly handed over to Stalin many Russians who were his own enemies.'

Of course, amongst Soviet troops and the population, the NKGB and the Soviet propaganda machine exploited to the full the fact that these extraditions had taken place.

To this day neither the British nor the American authorities have done anything to make up for what happened. There has been no effort to remove the stains of shame from the colours of their victorious armies, who were compelled in 1945 and 1946 to take such unsoldierly actions. Nobody can, of course, bring back from the dead those who lost their lives in Germany and Austria, or, for that matter, in Czechoslovakia in 1968. The Czechs, however, should not even have raised their hands against Vlasov's men in 1945, not to speak of hanging then.

It is not surprising that I don't feel towards the Czechs the same sympathy as I feel towards the Poles, the Yugoslavs and the Hungarians. But not so, for the Czechs suffered too during the war.

There was one particular Czech village called Lidice, near Kladno. The Germans destroyed it completely, shooting in the process all the male population, about two hundred men in all. All the women from this village were sent to a German concentration camp. The operation was a punishment for the murder in Prague of one of the top leaders of the German Security Service, Heydrich. At that time, in 1942, he was Deputy Reichsprotektor of Bohemia and Moravia. All this is true, but it's worth bearing in mind two facts. Heydrich was killed not because of atrocities that he himself had committed against the Czech population but because he had organised Czech strategic industries efficiently and made them contribute successfully to the war effort of Nazi Germany. Heydrich had been able to establish quite good relations with a wide variety of circles in Czechoslovakia. The second fact is that he was killed by two Czechs, dropped by a British aeroplane. The whole flight was arranged by the British Secret Service. Finally, during the war years, a large part of the territory of Poland and Yugoslavia was Lidice on a grand scale, not to mention what happened on the Soviet territory which the Germans captured.

General Vlasov was seized in the American military zone of Czechoslovakia, near the town of Pilsen, by a Smersh operational group from my Front. American military were present and made no attempt to interfere. Vlasov was quickly transferred to Smersh Front Headquarters near Dresden. From there he was taken by plane to Moscow and the scaffold. I did not see him. On the basis of the large number of his papers, appeals, proclamations, etc., which I have read, both through my work and also out of personal interest, I am absolutely sure that he hated Hitler and his regime bitterly, and saved many former Soviet citizens from the hands of the Gestapo. I am convinced, too, that he was a Russian, though not a Soviet, patriot, and a great friend and admirer of the principles and social structure of the western democracies, in particular of Great Britain and the USA. One thing I remember which moved me particularly was the fact that in all Vlasov said and wrote there wasn't a single word against the Jews. To achieve this and remain important under Hitler's regime one had to be far more than simply not an anti-Semite. All the leaders, and I mean all, of the other national movements of those years were embroiled to some extent or another in anti-Semitism. This was not true, however, of Lieutenant-General Andrei Andreievich Vlasov. There were other close collaborators of Vlasov whom we received from Anglo-American hands during 1945–6. The same fate as his awaited them in Moscow.

On one occasion, in the late spring of 1945, when we were already in Baden, my boss the lieutenant-colonel invited me to accompany him, so that I should, as he put it, 'glimpse a piece of history'. I was in no mood for history. It was early morning, and I had still not learned to like getting up early. We got into the car.

'Bystrov's outfit!' the lieutenant-colonel rapped at the chauffeur.

Bystrov was a lieutenant-colonel of Guards, commander of an air force regiment belonging to the Sixth Bomber Corps of Guards, which was part of our group. 'Outfit' was the official camouflage title of all our units and formations then. The whole group, for example, was known as 'Konev's outfit' up to 1946. The Sixth Bomber Corps was known as 'Nikishin's outfit', after its commanding officer Nikishin, who was a major-general in the Soviet Air Force. Our Smersh Administration was known as 'Korolyov's outfit', and so on. It was a simple system, but confusing for outsiders. Bystrov's outfit was not far away at all, at Bad Voslau, a few kilometres from Baden. Most of Bystrov's aeroplanes were based at other aerodromes. This particular one was used for somewhat different purposes, including those of Smersh. In many respects this aerodrome was ideal from our point of view. It was handy, secluded and surrounded by a wide belt of forbidden territory. It also had good hangars. The NKVD Internal Troops who guarded it permanently took great care that no one, not even a member of our military personnel, should enter the forbidden area. Local Austrian peasants were not even allowed to pasture their cattle in that area.

An aeroplane was standing on the airfield, ready for take-off, when we arrived. Beside it stood a truck with a tarpaulin cover, and a group of Smersh officers, whom we joined. My lieutenant-colonel was the senior officer amongst those present.

'Well, then,' said a major from the Operational Branch, addressing the lieutenant-colonel, 'shall we start?'

The latter nodded. An old man climbed slowly down from the cab of the lorry, where he had been sitting next to the driver. He was wearing German uniform, but his shoulder boards were the broad shoulder boards of a Russian general. He also wore Czarist decoration in the form of a white cross.

'It's Krasnov,' said the lieutenant-colonel, nudging me.

I had already read Krasnov's book, *From the Two-headed Eagle to the Red Banner*, while I was still in Germany. It had somehow fallen into Smersh's hands, probably from the library of some Russian émigré. I had very much liked the description given in the book of the life of officers in the Imperial Russian Horse Guards. They didn't live at all badly and much more elegantly than us Smersh officers. They also knew a thing or two about women. There were certain other things in this book of which I'd approved. The only thing which I didn't like at all was the crude anti-Semitism. The old general who was now walking past me was not only a writer, however. Krasnov was a famous Czarist cavalry general and a Cossack. He had been one of the leaders of the White Army in the Civil War. In 1945 he was supreme leader of all Cossacks on Nazi territory.

'That one is Shkuro,' the lieutenant-colonel said.

He was a small man of good bearing, also wearing general's uniform. In the Civil War he had been one of the main opponents that Budyonny's cavalry had to deal with and into the bargain they had clashed right in my home town. I looked at them both with an interest that I, like the rest of our Chekist officers, was unable to conceal.

'They're a grand lot, the English,' laughed the lieutenant-colonel. 'They give Shkuro their decoration, called after some saints, Michael and George, I think it was. Now, if you please, they're quite happy to deliver him to our door.' All our chaps who were standing near began to laugh.

A further group of officers in the same uniforms emerged from the back of the lorry. They disappeared into the aeroplane, followed by a soldier of NKVD troops, armed with a sub-machine gun, and a major of ours from Smersh Operational Branch. The aeroplane picked up speed and soared up into the sky, heading for Moscow and the scaffold. The British handed over Krasnov and Shkuro to us in the Austrian province of Stiria. The British lured them, about two thousand men in all, into a trap by inviting them supposedly to take part in a conference with Field Marshal Alexander. I found out these details later from our NKGB agents, who had been with Krasnov for a long time. They had played the parts of anti-Soviet Cossack officers who had gone over to the Germans and were handed over to us along with the others. There were the same kind of agents in the Vlasov movement. One evening when I was looking through the lists of Cossack officers, before they were dispatched to Moscow (we received these lists from our investigation branch), I went over the whole affair in my own mind. How could the British have done this? Perhaps it was the work of their socialists, who, after all, were also in the government. But Churchill, the Prime Minister! You could hardly call him a socialist! I recalled my grandfather's words about Churchill, 'May the Lord help and preserve him ...' Yes indeed, there was a lot I couldn't understand. I needed something to take my mind off it all and cheer me up a bit.

I resumed my interrupted German lessons. An officer friend taught me an Austrian expression, completely Austrian, something like 'ABO KE, KE, TRADE'. He said that it worked infallibly with Austrian girls, particularly with girls from Vienna. I couldn't make up my mind, however, to try this expression out on my Viennese student girl friend. Who knows, perhaps my friend wasn't all that great a linguist. We'll call this girl Gilda, in honour of Rita Hayworth's performance in the film of the same name. I saw that film soon afterwards, and liked both it and Rita Hayworth very much.

Gilda seemed glad that I had reappeared on her horizon, but perhaps she was gladder about the food I used to bring in payment for my German lessons. The food situation in Austria then was quite wretched. Everything was rationed and the rations were extremely beggarly. Of course, our Occupation authorities kept up the spirits of the active Austrian Party members by supplying them with food from special stores. The senior Austrian civil authorities were also fairly well looked after. But Gilda's family did not belong to either of these categories. For me food was no problem. In the Smersh canteen we were fed as if we were being fattened for slaughter. Hardly any of the officers was able to eat all the food he was given. The canteen was open at nights too, and one could get supper there until midnight. One could also get tea or coffee, sandwiches and biscuits until three o'clock in the morning. This was a service which was of particular use to our investigators! Unfortunately, there were days, or rather nights, when my lieutenant-colonel kept me and others at work until four or five o'clock in the morning. This was usually caused by top-priority assembly of documents and data for the Third Administration in Moscow.

My resources for getting hold of food by no means ended in the Smersh canteen. We also had food warehouses, and there were certain other useful places in the Baden garrison, of which the best two were the food stores and officers' restaurant of the TsGV. There were special shops, too, where one could buy literally anything very cheaply indeed, even such splendid things as caviar, balyk, smoked salmon and chocolate. I could hardly have been described as a penniless suitor. A song appeared, which is now forgotten:

Junges hubsches Madchen
Und Russische Soldat,
Heute, ficken-ficken,
Und Morgen Shokolade!

In actual fact our army officers and men weren't all that well off for chocolate. Every one of our soldiers gave food to his girl friends in proportion to his means. It was all on a good Marxist basis.

Gilda and I had one slightly alarming surprise, of which my boss, the lieutenant-colonel, was the cause. As I felt quite sure that nothing could upset my particular apple-cart, I was peacefully strolling one day with Gilda, in one of the streets of Baden. My confidence was, after all, not entirely unfounded. It was hardly likely that any of the Commandant's officer patrols would come up and start asking questions. I was a Smersh officer on duty. If they noticed that I was with an Austrian woman they would assume that this was part of the job. My fellow officers in Smersh would hardly take an unhealthy interest either if they saw us. We were, after all, given all kinds of missions. As for Smersh top brass, the lieutenant-general and the colonels who were his deputies, they had enough worries of their own. I didn't ever meet any of them out of doors. On this occasion, however, Gilda and I had the misfortune to meet my lieutenant-colonel in the street. He nodded to me politely in answer to my salute, and gave Gilda a quick once-over. That evening the conversation went something like this.

'Is she the one who's teaching you German then?'

'Yes.'

'And what else are you teaching one another?'

'Nothing, yet.'

I already knew it wasn't a good idea to lie and dissemble when talking to the lieutenant-colonel.

'Yes,' he said, 'pigs have been known to fly. But just you watch out.'

In everyday speech this meant more or less 'Well, go ahead if you want to, but just see you don't land up in trouble'. I was very grateful to him for this. Before he left, however, the lieutenant-colonel could not stop himself telling me a quick joke. This time a Russian one.

A Czarist officer gave his batman three roubles and said, 'Go and find yourself a woman. I can see that you're in great need. But make sure she's a healthy one.' The next day he asked the batman whether he'd found a woman. 'Oh yes, sir.' 'And was she a healthy one?' 'Oh yes, sir. So healthy that I was hard put to it to get my three roubles back off her.'

I was well aware that my boss had no fears about the political consequences of my connection with Gilda. He was far from being a fool. He knew me inside out. He would hardly have believed that when Gilda and I were on our own she would teach me the theories of Hitler from *Mein Kampf*, or explain the constitution of Great Britain to me, if any such thing exists. I doubt whether he had any illusions that I for my part would teach Gilda Marxist-Leninist theory. Of course, not all our officers and men were fortunate enough to have a boss like him.

One afternoon Gilda and I were sitting on a sofa studying German and exchanging kisses. I used to work until four o'clock in the morning and was then free until the following evening. It was quite clear that Gilda had got used to me and was not in the least afraid of me. I had told her that I worked in the literary section of an army newspaper. There actually was such a newspaper in Baden, I knew a number of people who worked on it, and even went there myself from time to time. On one or two occasions Gilda had accompanied me to the door of the editorial offices. Of course, I told her nothing else about the nature of my duties. When Gilda was very close to me I finally had to give up my resolve to behave like Dumas' D'Artagnan.

It was only when I lay naked beside her that I heard my German teacher's embarrassed confession.

'I thought two things,' said Gilda. 'Either you didn't like me at all, or that you'd got something wrong "down there", perhaps the result of a wound.'

Bursting with laughter I managed to find the right words to assure her that till then no young woman had complained about my passivity. As for Gilda, she was the most beautiful and desirable girl not only in Baden, not only in the province of Vienna, but in the neighbouring province of Lower Austria too, and probably in the whole of the European continent. I think she was happy with this answer. I was in my seventh heaven. My German textbooks, dictionaries and notes were all put in the bottom of my wardrobe.

'Oh well,' I thought, recalling the words of Colonel Yevdokimenko, the deputy chief of the Smersh Administration of the TsGV, 'we shall study in capitalist Europe all that is new and interesting and useful for our Party.'

I spent several days doing a job for the lieutenant-colonel in a Smersh operational group, which was permanently based in Vienna. Among other things this group was responsible for collecting information from agents about the garrisons of our Anglo-American allies in Vienna. The allies had in the Austrian capital units of troops, officials of the Allied Control Commission, Commandant's groups, detachments of military police and certain institutions, like, for example, the American administration on Roosevelt Square, concerned with military administration. All the installations I have listed were under constant surveillance, internal and external. In its internal operations Smersh took advantage of the services of Austrian civilians working for our allies in various auxiliary capacities: cleaners, translators, secretaries, typists, and so on. These agents were recruited by a series of methods or 'keys' as we called them. A particularly popular 'key' was to promise an individual that any of his relatives who were prisoners in the USSR would be found and released as quickly as possible. Many Austrian families had relatives, who in many cases had disappeared without trace in the USSR during the war. Another way was to obtain work with the western allies for persons who were known to have pro-communist views.

Sometimes if we were lucky we even recruited allied personnel themselves. Smersh took into account the strong pro-Soviet feelings which were then current among citizens of the western democracies.

For external surveillance, or spying, Smersh used people of two basic types. The first was members of the Austrian Communist Party. Communists and their families who had been recruited would receive from our organisation all kinds of support in the form of money, food and, of course, administrative assistance. We would issue them with documents, which would guarantee that they were left alone by both the Soviet occupation authorities and the Austrian police. We would also provide them with documents which allowed them freedom of movement throughout all the zones of Austria. The second type of people from among the local population whom Smersh exploited for the same purpose were former Nazis, insignificant functionaries of Hitler's NSDAP.[1] Many of them were people, who, according to Soviet law, ought to have been in prisons and concentration camps. Smersh, however, preferred to close its eyes to their past peccadilloes, if they agreed to work for us. It's true that in

[1] NSDAP—*National Sozialistische Deutsche Arbeits Partei.*

this kind of case we really needed to have hostages who could be used as levers for blackmail. An individual's wife, children or elderly parents, if they lived in the Soviet Occupation Zone, could be used for this purpose. The local Smersh bodies in the place where these relatives lived kept them under permanent secret supervision, to prevent them escaping to the west.

These external observers usually carried out various activities near to where allied forces and institutions were situated in Vienna. Some might sell newspapers and magazines in a kiosk, others did business with allied personnel, buying and selling anything, from gold and carpets to pictures, or even pornographic photographs. These photos were often of some artistic merit. After my first trip to Vienna I got hold of a handsome leather photograph album. I perused it in my flat with great interest. It was my first encounter with a lovingly executed work of art of this kind. One day Gilda found me thus occupied and told me, indignant and offended, that I wasn't yet an old degenerate, that surely she, Gilda, should be enough for me and that in any case to spend money on something so disgusting was completely crazy. I calmed Gilda down and dispatched the album to the drawer of my wardrobe, where it joined a German grammar, a short history of the CPSU and selected works of Lenin in one volume.

Apart from the Smersh operational group I have described, the first branch of Smersh was also represented in Vienna by a staff of operational representatives. They had the usual jobs to do, with all the Soviet military units of the garrison, in the hospitals and in all the Soviet administrative and political institutions, like Colonel-General Zheltov's Allied Control Commission Administration, Lieutenant-General Lebedenko's City Commandant's Office and so forth. Representatives of the first branch of Smersh did not work directly against our allies, but, as previously, they were responsible for the political reliability of our own Soviet citizens, civilian and military, living in Vienna. Over and above all this, operational groups of Smersh and individual officer agents, carrying out missions for our Baden administration, were often active in Vienna. It might perhaps be a question of recruiting certain interesting individuals, either Allied or Austrian, getting hold of top-priority information on instructions from GUKR Smersh in Moscow, and so forth. The permanent group of Smersh in Vienna had its own reserve, which was based with the second echelon of the staff of TsGV in the town of Modling, not far from Vienna. The first echelon, the staff of the

Commander-in-Chief, who after 1946 was Colonel-General Kurasov, the political administration, the operational and intelligence branches of military intelligence and a series of other administrations and branches, these were all in Baden.

Among the Austrian agents whom Smersh recruited, the procurers of girls for allied military personnel worked with particular success. This 'roof' was a very convenient one. We had in Vienna a number of 'meeting houses' or brothels, which Smersh financed for the same purpose. Their clientele included soldiers, NCOs and junior officers of all our allies, the French, the British and a very large number of Americans, Negroes in particular. I personally took a great fancy to the Negroes. I was most fascinated to observe how they dashed about in their jeeps with their white teeth flashing and often with one leg tucked underneath them on the seat.

I knew from the briefings which came through the Smersh network from Moscow a certain amount about the counter-intelligence services of our allies in Austria and Germany. The Americans had the CIC, which had an administration in Austria, headed by a USA army brigadier. The personnel of this administration included a large number of officers, many of whom were young graduates of the east European faculties in American universities. GUKR Smersh in Moscow had a very low opinion of this system of training personnel, which was used by American counter-intelligence. It goes without saying that our administration in Austria did complain about it. On the contrary, our bosses were both pleased and grateful. It's true that officers of the CIC underwent a crash course in intelligence work abroad before taking up a European posting, but the opinions of them, or rather the teachers who taught on them, expressed in our Moscow briefings, were also not very high.

The British had two types of Security Service in Austria and Germany. The military counter-intelligence service, called the FSS (Field Security Service) and the system of PSOs (Public Security Officers), for work among the local population in the British zones. The PSOs had their own system of ranks. PSO1—colonel, PSO2—lieutenant-colonel, and PSO3—major. However, the people who bore these ranks were neither the first thing, nor the second, nor the third. They were selected from the British police force, often the London police force, in which they had usually been sergeants and inspectors. They were simply fitted out with special dark blue, army-type uniform and given the appropriate badges of rank. Among the FSS there were a lot of young people who had completed the same kind of special courses as their American counterparts.

The French Security Service and Counter-intelligence Service had in their ranks a large number of people holding pro-communist views. I learnt all this from studying data sent from our Main Administration. This seemed completely natural to me at that time. France had suffered more in the war than the other allies, since she had been occupied by the Germans. Moreover, France's Deputy Prime Minister, Maurice Thorres, was also the leader of her Communist Party. This being the case, it didn't seem at all unusual to have members of the Party in the Security Services.

In the allied zones of occupation there were what were known as 'Auxiliary Guarding Detachments and Battalions'. The people who served in them were Poles, Yugoslavs and even Russians from the old emigration, who did not want to return to their own countries. Later, Soviet citizens, who had escaped being handed over to the Soviet authorities, found their way into these units. Of course, both they and the old *émigrés* used assumed names and nationalities, often passing themselves off as Poles. These detachments, however, although they were made up of people with anti-Soviet views, were not used by our western allies in the work of their Security Services. On the whole, battalions like these simply did guard duty at warehouses, goods depots and the like. So as not to irritate their Soviet ally, the British and Americans and, in particular, the French, kept them well away from the frontiers of their zones. The French were most circumspect and dispensed altogether with all kinds of military ranks in these battalions. Their numbers were simply designated as 'worker, categories 1 and 2', 'technician', 'engineer' and so on. The French didn't even call these bodies of men battalions, but referred to them as 'working groups'. Smersh was perfectly well aware that such detachments existed, and I would think that it maintained permanent contact with certain of their members.

Because of my business trips to Vienna in particular, I had to acquire civilian clothing. My first suit was made from dark blue serge by an Austrian tailor, under my directions and was very much to my taste. When I put this suit on at home I gazed admiringly at both myself and it for a long time, and thought with regret of Yoska. Indeed, he and I had worn suits like that when we conquered the hearts of our girl friends at school: wide, padded shoulders and extremely wide trouser bottoms. We had also had them on when we had abused the good name of the pilot Nikolai Petrovich Kamanin,

Hero of the Soviet Union, to help us pull off a disgraceful financial operation. By the way, in 1945 Kamanin wasn't far from me at all. He commanded the Fifth Corps of Storm Fighters, which was based in Roumania, and had by then become a lieutenant-general. Yoska, sadly, was no longer around.

My recollections were disturbed by Gilda's arrival. She gave me a cursory glance and said something like: '*Um Gottes Willen!*' observing further that I might do well to bear in mind that I was not a sailor in Kaiser Franz-Josef's navy.

'The trousers are too wide,' she said, 'and what's the point of all that padding on the shoulders of your jacket? You've got a perfectly good pair of shoulders of your own, that God gave you.'

Her remark about my own shoulders pleased me, but I decided not to pay any attention to the rest of what she said.

'The cheeky minx,' I thought to myself. 'She knows as much about men's fashions as a pig does about oranges.'

I quickly took off my new suit and suggested to Gilda that she also get undressed. The next morning I put it on to go to work. My Caucasian lieutenant-colonel rose from behind his desk, stared hard at my pale face with dark circles under my eyes, walked round me and said.

'Yes, if I were a young woman, I wouldn't be able to resist a suit like that either.' He then informed me that the sight of me tore his poor heart with memories of his native Sukhumi. 'In that suit,' he said, 'you look just like a Merited Shepherd[1] of the Georgian republic, who's just been given a large cash prize. And still more you remind me of a Caucasian *kinto*[2] who used to entertain on the promenade at Sukhumi.' He ended his remarks by stating officially that he categorically forbade me to show my face in any public place in that suit, not to mention Vienna. 'It would be difficult,' he said, 'to think of a better way of attracting the attention not only of all the western intelligence services but also of every friendly dog in Austria, than by showing your face in that suit. It would be possible, but difficult.'

Those were his very words. Invoking a curse both on him and all the multitude of his Caucasian kin, I set off home.

---

[1] Merited Shepherd—a civil decoration for exemplary professional work.
[2] *Kinto*—comedian.

7

The war hadn't finished, it was just lying low.

From a poem by Leonid Pervomaisky

THE DEMOBILISATION OF THE older privates and NCOs was over in TsGV. The Smersh administration of our group now began a new job: checking the personal files of all officers, NCOs and privates who had been left for further service in eastern Europe, in our case in Austria and Hungary. During the war the State Security bodies had had to come to terms with a huge influx into the Soviet army of not altogether desirable elements. This was particularly so in the officer corps. Some officers had close relatives such as brothers and sisters who had been convicted as 'enemies of the people' during the pre-war purges. Others had themselves been arrested for some period on charges of anti-Soviet activity. Of course, their cases had subsequently been closed and they had been set free, but none the less for the rest of their lives they remained marked men. A third category came from families which were unacceptable to the State Security Service. Either their own parents or the parents of their wives had been 'unpersons' or class enemies.

During the war, when every man with two hands, two feet and two eyes was required for service in an army of many millions of soldiers, the NKGB had allowed such people in, making the appropriate note in their personal file as it did so. Many of them had been decorated for bravery and commissioned. It was with this huge mass of personal files that our Smersh administration now had to work. Our First Branch in Baden received a vast number of them, which were sent to us by our operational representatives in all the regimental sections of Smersh via the branches in the larger military units. From the Main Administration of Smersh in Moscow we were sent precise, detailed instructions as to which categories of army officer had to be demobilised at once into the reserve, who could be transferred to less senior posts, etc. The whole of this briefing passed through the Third Branch of Smersh in which I worked. Of course, I can't remember all the details, but only certain isolated points. All officers, for example, who had been imprisoned in connection with the case of Marshal Tukhachevsky[1] had to be demobilised into the reserve at once. We also had to demobilise all officers who had had relatives in any anti-Soviet movement or formation during the war. One such taboo formation was the movement of General Vlasov. I remember a number of queer cases cropping up in connection with this point of the instructions. The surname Vlasov is fairly wide-spread in the Soviet Union. Operational representatives of our administration in each military unit studied with particular care the personal files of all officers, NCOs and men who had this surname. It was necessary to discover whether they might be even the most distant relative of Vlasov, the traitor. For many this was no laughing matter at all, as they were summoned to Smersh premises for protracted interrogations both by day and night. They had to recount with the most minute details, the genealogical tables of their families, going back for years and years. In our group of forces in Austria and Hungary we were unable to discover a single relative of General Vlasov. I heard, however, from a colleague of mine in Smersh, a regular NKGB officer, that before the war there had been many cases when relatives such as brothers of prominent Czarist officials, had been imprisoned on a political charge simply on the strength of such a relationship. On the documents of some such cases there were notes saying, 'To be held in prison until he repents completely.' I am certain that he was serious.

Smersh itself did not demobilise a single officer from the army into the reserve. There existed for this purpose a specifically created commission, attached to the staff of the group of forces. The members of this commission included the chief of the group's political branch, in our case a lieutenant-general, the chief of the group's personnel branch, in our case a major-general, two or three more members who held the rank of general or a colonel. Smersh itself was represented at the commission only by a single major from the First Branch. This was all that was necessary, as our major's task was a very straightforward one. He sat modestly at one end of the table, and observed that the decisions of the commission coincided completely with Smersh's resolutions. The resolution was

[1] Tukhachevsky—First Deputy People's Commissar of the USSR for Defence. He was shot after being tried for espionage in 1937. Rehabilitated at the 20th Party Congress, 1956.

written in each case on the cover of the personal file of each officer who had been sent for. I can remember that these resolutions came in three varieties: 'Demobilise from the army', 'Transfer to less important work' and 'To be left on active service'.

All these resolutions were reviewed and confirmed long before the commission began its work, by the chief of our Smersh administration or his first deputy. It's true that Moscow made an exception in the case of a number of senior army ranks. I can roughly remember the texts of two coded messages from GUKR Smersh.

'Refrain from demobilising into the reserve, personnel holding the rank of general or colonels serving as acting generals, unless you received special instructions from us. Abakumov.'

It was clear that a special top-level Smersh group was at work in Moscow deciding the fates of generals and marshals. We soon received a supplementary briefing:

'The following persons are to be demobilised either into the reserve or on to the retired list, according to the appended instructions. Chernyshov.'

Chernyshov was the First Deputy Chief of GUKR Smersh until 1946. Everything with Marshal Konev, the First Commander-in-Chief of our group of forces, TsGV, up to the spring of 1946, turned out to be in order. Only a very small number of generals in the group were put on the retired list. The remainder were demobilised into the reserve. One of the Deputy Chiefs of Staff was among them, one or two administration chiefs, and the rest were all commanders of divisions. About the same number of colonels was involved.

I knew that in our group, as well as in the other groups of occupation forces, there were many generals and senior officers who had been involved in 1937 and 1938 in the Tukhachevsky case. The most famous of them was the outstanding hero of the war, the conqueror of the Germans at Stalingrad, the liberator of Belorussia, Marshal Rokossovsky. In certain circles, and not only among Chekists, it was well known that Rokossovsky had been in prison and under interrogation for quite a long time. He had been cruelly tortured, and it had been demanded that he confess to treason and espionage. To this end he had sacrificed most of his teeth, had a chair leg driven up his rectum and undergone a number of other similar brutalities. All this didn't appear to have left any perceptible traces, for I saw Rokossovsky personally at the Victory Parade gallop dashingly on horseback to Marshal Zhukov to present his report. They met in the centre of Red Square, immediately in front of where Stalin was standing on the Lenin Mausoleum. It was Stalin who had ordered Rokossovsky's 'case' to be closed, and Rokossovsky himself to be released immediately before the war. Marshal Zhukov interceded personally with Stalin on Rokossovsky's behalf. They knew each other well and had served together for a long time.

Later, however, when I mixed in a circle of people who were close to Marshal Voroshilov, I established definitely that he had played a decisive part in setting Rokossovsky and a number of other military personnel free. In the first post-war purge of the Soviet army Stalin ignored both Rokossovsky and the majority of the other generals who had formerly been in prisons and concentration camps.

But Rokossovsky himself went on from strength to strength. After being Commander-in-Chief of the Soviet group of forces in Poland he soon became Polish Minister of Defence and Marshal of Poland, at the same time retaining his title of Marshal of the Soviet Union.

Some officers, who at that time were either demobilised into the reserve or put on the retired list, were fortunate. They managed to land reasonable posts in civilian life. I remember hearing from an air force officer, whom I met on one of my trips, the true story of a close friend of his who had been demobilised into the reserve. This officer applied for a job as security chief at one of the large works in his home town. The director of the works, a prominent Party figure, said that the officer seemed to be just the man he was looking for. When he read, however, in the man's personal file the words 'Imprisoned at such and such a time, for such and such', the director became noticeably more serious and appeared to lose interest.

'What were you imprisoned for?' he asked gloomily.

The officer replied that he had been imprisoned for being one of a group of spies which had illegally crossed the Polish and German frontiers with certain secret information. When he heard this, the work's director, who was an old communist, beamed and sighed with relief.

'Oh, that was what it was!' he exlaimed happily. 'Excellent, I'll have you, you can start tomorrow. I thought you were some Trotskyite or Menshevik.'

Of course, by no means all those who were demobilised from the army managed to find such realistic directors. The majority had to content themselves with poorly paid labouring jobs.

The fates of privates and NCOs demobilised from the army because of notes about their unreliability in their personal files were decided on the same principles by Smersh officers and officials of army personnel branches on a lower level. Demobilised personnel were sent to groups to the nearest reserve regiments and transit stations. They were placed under the armed surveillance of the so-called Commandant's groups. These groups did not belong to the NKGB, NKVD system. They were made up of officers, NCOs and men from the Commandants' administration of the occupation forces. Smersh was represented in the branches of this administration and in all municipal, district and village Commandant's Offices, in the usual way, by operational representatives. They played no part, however, in the transporting of these groups owing to shortage of personnel.

One such reserve regiment was stationed not far from Vienna, just across the frontier on Slovakian territory. The usual troop train was being sent up there, to dispatch the demobilised troops back to the Soviet Union. Unexpectedly, a group of those being dispatched discovered that they would not be sent to their families in the areas they had come from but to some top-priority building site, so far as I can remember, in Central Asia. A group of soldiers and NCOs of between 150 and 200 men began an angry protest. Others, who were destined to be passengers on the same train, and also some who were to remain behind in the reserve regiment, came out and supported them. All the efforts of those in charge, the regimental commander, the political officers, and other officers, to explain the situation and persuade the men to obey orders, were useless. The soldiers started getting off the train, forming in crowds, creating scenes and holding meetings. There was a whiff of rebellion in the air.

The regimental command had to retire hurriedly into the HQ building. The Smersh permanent regiment representative telephoned to the Smersh branch of the division to which the regiment belonged, and informed people there. Then, he and his assistant, a junior representative, leapt into their car, and left the camp. They returned very quickly accompanied by two or three battalions of NKVD internal troops, who were stationed in the Vienna district. The Chekist soldiers cordoned off the regimental camp and the troop-train departure point. All this area was rapidly sealed off both from the local population and from other units of the Soviet army. The Chekist officer, who was in charge of the operation, shouted a proposal to the soldiers who were in revolt that they should either disperse to their huts or board the train. His appeal was ignored completely.

On the contrary, the insurgents produced a handful of rifles and some sub-machine guns. The vast majority of the men and NCOs were unarmed, however, as it was part of standing orders to surrender weapons before being transferred to regiments of the reserve. Then, on the order of their officer, in accordance with the statutes, the NKVD troops fired a first salvo into the air above the heads of the insurgents. This salvo was fired from sub-machine guns and by some soldiers lying prone round the area armed with light machine guns. The second salvo was not fired into the air. This time the NKVD troops' heavy machine guns began to chatter from the lorries on which they were mounted. Some of the insurgents were killed and wounded. There was a third salvo, and then, still firing, the Chekist soldiers cut through the insurgents, breaking them down into isolated groups. Everything was over very quickly.

Some of the insurgents, the wounded among them, were herded into the carriages of the train, which was already standing by with a locomotive coupled to it. The waggons were shut and padlocks hung on their doors. NKVD soldiers armed with sub-machine guns and machine guns, carrying hand-grenades on their belts, leapt up on to the brake platforms. A waggon of NKVD soldiers was hastily attached to the back of the train. The train left the station and travelled direct to the Soviet Union. The soldiers who were left in the regiment were dispersed to their huts, which were cordoned off by soldiers armed with machine and sub-machine guns. A group of officers from our Fourth Investigation Branch, and representatives of the Fifth Branch, the tribunals, came post-haste to the regiment. The soldiers who had been killed were buried in a mass grave. The regimental commander and a number of other officers, including political officers, were reduced to the ranks and sentenced to various terms of imprisonment. The regimental Smersh representative was demoted both in rank and status and sent to work in the State Security Service system in the Soviet Union. As I learned later, a number of the soldiers and the NCOs of this reserve regiment took advantage of the general mêlée and sensibly disappeared.

This is the only incident of its kind, in either Austria or Hungary, which I remember during my service in Smersh. All sorts of things happened, including minor disorders and isolated incidents involving shooting, clashes between the authorities and small groups of our soldiers, but there were no more cases, as far as I know, of a full-scale revolt in a whole military unit. Smersh did not allow things to get as far as that. As my boss the lieutenant-colonel told me soon afterwards, that particular revolt cost the lieutenant-general who was the Smersh chief in our group of forces a decoration. He also got a full-scale wigging from Abakumov, the chief of GUKR Smersh. According to what the lieutenant-colonel said, Abakumov said to our general, 'You're like a bull in a china shop.' Meanwhile, Smersh agents set about spreading rumours among the local population of the nearby Slovakian villages, that in the area where this regiment had been stationed temporarily, manœuvres involving firing had been taking place. This revolt triggered off not altogether cheerful thoughts in my own mind. If we were annihilating, shooting, hacking down, blowing up Germans, and our own traitors who had sold themselves to the Germans as police minions, that was one thing. But when our soldiers began shooting at their own comrades-in-arms, veterans of the war which was only just over, then that was something quite different. Of course, I kept these reflections to myself. When Gilda, my Austrian girl friend, noted my sullen face and asked me what was the matter, I simply answered that it was a bad twinge from old wounds in my leg. I nevertheless declined her offer of a poultice.

Throughout the territories which had been liberated from the Germans there were scattered millions of Soviet citizens. Some of them, the so-called *ostarbeiters*, had been deported by the Germans for forced labour, men and women, youths and girls, who were often young enough to be of school age. Others had left the Soviet Union voluntarily, either in the period of German occupation or during the retreat, often in whole families. Many men who had served either in the German army, or in the anti-Soviet military formations such as General Vlasov's units or General Krasnov's Cossacks, were handed over to us. Our western allies handed such people over forcibly. Certain Soviet citizens who had had a very bad time in the 'New Europe' of the Nazi Empire returned voluntarily. Others were drawn by an acute feeling of nostalgia for their native country and the families and friends they had left behind there. There were also such reasons for returning as apathy and indifference.

On the other hand, a lot of people had heard all about the reprisals we had taken against returnees. They had also learned from their bitter experience of the treachery and far from democratic treatment meted out to them by the western democracies, and consequently scattered to remote towns and villages throughout the western zones, as far away as possible from the Soviet occupation zones. They began to claim that they were Russian *émigrés* from the post-

Revolutionary emigration. Many said that they were Poles, Czechs, Yugoslavs and sometimes Germans, Spaniards and even other nationalities. In this way they hoped to save themselves, and in many cases their families too, from being sent back to the Soviet Union. Of course, Stalin was perfectly well aware of all this from the information and briefings of GUKR Smersh. Smersh had clear instructions from Stalin. We were to bring back the maximum possible number of Soviet citizens into the Soviet Union, if possible all of them, regardless of whether they wanted to come or not. It was not a good idea to have such a large number of our citizens outside Soviet frontiers. Including women and children there were between five and six million. In the first place they were undesirable witnesses against communism and the Soviet system. Secondly, the Soviet Union had suffered colossal human losses in the war and was short of manpower.

The Main Administration for the Repatriation of Soviet Citizens, attached to the Council of People's Commissars of the USSR, was formed in Moscow. Colonel-General Golikov was appointed chief of this administration. He was not a Chekist. It would have been impossible to appoint a Chekist to such a post for a number of reasons which were connected mainly with 'image' and propaganda considerations. Golikov, however, was well known to Stalin and was more than an ordinary army general. Before the war, and at its very beginning, Golikov had been chief of the Main Intelligence Adminis-tration (GRU) of the General Staff. He then became head of the Special Soviet Mission in London, and subsequently commander of an army, deputy commander of the Stalingrad Front and Com-mander of the Voronezh Front. He gave no intimation, however, of being an outstanding strategist or second Clausewitz.

Even when he was removed from command Golikov retained Stalin's favour and trust, a detail which in those days impeded no one's progress. In his new job of dealing with repatriation Golikov was happily not overburdened with work. Everybody who knew what was what realised that Golikov was no more than a 'front', a man who signed official documents, reports and appeals. The repatriation administration was also a 'front' to delude outsiders, our foreign allies in particular. All the real work in this sphere was done by GUKR Smersh and the Main Secret Political Administra-tion of the NKGB.[1] We worked outside the country and they worked inside it. Being on its home ground, GSPU NKGB had much less

[1] *Glavnoye Secretno—Politicheskoye Upravleniye* NKGB (GSPU NKGB).

reason to feel constrained or stand on ceremony with repatriated Soviet citizens. Smersh had a far harder job of it. In the first place the vast majority of Soviet citizens living abroad hadn't the slightest desire to return home, and went to any lengths to avoid meeting Soviet representatives. Again these expatriates lived on the territory of our allies, in the British, French and American zones of occupation. Even Smersh was obliged at that time to observe certain polite formalities with the official representatives of these countries.

Our western allies treated with complete sympathy and co-operation the request of the Soviet government, which came to them via Golikov, that a large number of Soviet military missions should be permitted to exist in their zones. These missions were, after all, devoted to a noble, humanitarian aim, that of helping the Soviet authorities seek out and repatriate their fellow countrymen and women, who had become displaced persons as a result of the war. Our allies were apparently unaware that the members of these missions were regular Chekist officers from Smersh. These officers travelled freely about the western zones, at one time without even being accompanied by allied representatives, and collected a mass of useful information about the location and strength of allied troops, etc., in addition to doing their basic job of rooting out former Soviet citizens. Any trips our allies made in our zones contrasted sharply with the facilities we enjoyed in their zones. They were given specific routes, solely to enable them to support their lines of communication. During such trips they were kept under constant overt and covert supervision, both by our Commandant's office and by Smersh. It only needed the slightest deviation from the prescribed routes for the offender, regardless of his rank, to be hauled in to the nearest Commandant's office. I happened to see one such offender, a British major, brought in his own jeep to our Municipal Commandant's Office in Baden. There ensued a polite but stern interrogation, with a warning that the officer's mistake should not be repeated. A sharp protest was also made to the Allied Control Council in Vienna.

Things were rather different for us in the western zones—by God's grace a calm sea and prosperous voyage! Our western allies did in fact gradually begin to realise that the very existence of an enormous number of Soviet citizens who stubbornly avoided the official representatives of their country's authority was far from normal. Some, albeit a depressingly small number, even began to think that something must be seriously wrong with Soviet power itself if hordes of its citizens preferred to live in poverty and obscurity in some foreign countries instead of returning to live under its protection. Unfortunately, such thoughts and conclusions surfaced in the consciousnesses of our allies only at a much later date, when the greater part of these Soviet citizens had already been returned to the Soviet zones.

Our allies assisted us very generously in this work. They laid on transport and food, organised assembly points and transit camps and were helpful in many other ways. The whole thing was in accordance with the law as set down in the treaty signed at the meeting of the British and American delegations. At that conference were adults who had stopped playing with toys years before. There were also undoubtedly among them the most able specialist advisers on 'Russian' affairs that these countries possessed.

What is most important is that from what other things we know of them all the members of the western delegations were people who believed in the traditions of democracy and humanitarianism. Two of the cornerstones of these same traditions are the right of every man to choose for himself where he wishes to live and that right to be granted asylum against religious, political or ethnic persecution.

In view of the huge influx of Soviet citizens into our zone from the west the Soviet administration had to open a large number of camps where they could be housed and where it could work with them. Former *ostarbeiters*' camps, the buildings of such factories, works, warehouses and schools as were still standing, sometimes large Austrian farms, stables and cowsheds, even tents, were used as premises. All these places were quickly surrounded with barbed wire. Some NKVD troops were posted to guard the perimeter and others patrolled the immediate area in groups. No one was allowed into them. By the term 'our own people', I mean the members of the hastily constituted Smersh Vetting and Screening Commissions (PFK). There were not enough people in our Baden administration for such an enormous operation. All the reserves from the town of Modling were drawn in, but even then we were shorthanded. GUKR Smersh urgently sent special groups of PFK staff to Austria, Germany and Hungary from their own reserves on Soviet territory, but even then there were nowhere near enough of them.

At GUKR Smersh, Abakumov had to borrow people from other main administrations of the NKGB, such as the Secret Political Administration, the Industrial or Economic Administration, the Investigation, Administration and even from the Operational

Administration. I know from the documents which went through the Smersh Third Branch in which I worked that at the request of Merkulov, People's Commissar for State Security, Beria also helped out with personnel, and loaned us officers from the NKVD Police Administration, Investigation Administration and to some extent from the Third Administration of GULAG. Of course, when all these officers reached us they were already kitted out with army uniform.

They all had the same job to do: namely to screen all Soviet citizens who had for a time been outside Soviet supervision, sorting them out at the same time into a number of categories: enemies of Soviet power of all kinds, relatively clean people in the political sense, and more or less reliable people. The ones who belonged to the last category were people who had engaged in active anti-Nazi activity which they could substantiate with irrefutable evidence, and untested youth, but not all of the latter. After the people from the west had been divided into these three categories they were sent to their several destinations. The 'enemies of Soviet power' were dispatched in prison trains to labour camps and in specially serious cases to top-security political prisons. The 'relatively clean', depending on the degree of individual cleanliness, either went home where the local security bodies would be asked to keep an eye on them or were sent for two or three years' forced labour on some top-priority reconstruction site in any part of the Soviet Union. The most fortunate people were the more or less reliable ones who belonged to the last category. The young men were given jobs by the occupation forces in the building, servicing and administrative and maintenance units. The young women and girls were also accepted for work in military units and institutions. Some went to work in service kitchens and canteens. Others worked in warehouses, on livestock farms and market gardens belonging to the units of the armed forces which were stationed abroad. Finally, some went as servants to the families of senior officers and generals. Of course, unofficially many of them had a second role as mistresses for our officers. The officers had a very wide choice.

The work of the PFKs took up a great deal of time. Camps for Soviet citizens from the west existed for several years, getting gradually smaller and closing one by one. The Chekist officers who worked in them were a sorry sight to look upon. They looked harassed, short of sleep, and pale, and their mood was permanently bad. There was too much work and it was obvious that they couldn't keep pace with it. Into the bargain, the whole responsibility for any persons set free after vetting lay on these officers. Their names figured in all the personal documents of the people who had passed through their hands. Those being vetted, however, were an even sorrier sight. They lived in cramped quarters, under guard. Their food supplies left much to be desired. Officially they were fed in accordance with Number 3 Army Ration, which was meant for the home front and auxiliary units, but there were often hold-ups and interruptions in food supplies and the ration itself was somewhat different from a general's.

I personally then came into contact with only two of our citizens who returned from the west. The bandmaster of TsGV HQ band was a close friend of my lieutenant-colonel. I think their sense of humour was the main bond between them, for they were both extremely witty and great lovers of jokes and anecdotes. The band-master's love of alcohol of many years standing kept him at the rank of captain. His passion was writ large on his nose. He was a tall, slim man with the true bearing of a Guards officer. I firmly believe that in an army only one encounters this kind of bearing either among elderly military bandmasters or army horse doctors.

The captain's band played everything splendidly, from 'Hymn to Stalin' to the cheerful, rollicking tunes of the Odessa carters' songs. On one occasion the captain burst into the lieutenant-colonel's room in a state of great excitement. I happened to be there, and heard the captain announce to the lieutenant-colonel, in a dramatic voice, that he had discovered among the returnees a genius of a musician, and that if he were unable to obtain this man for his band, then he would throw a fit on the spot. The lieutenant-colonel advised the captain to go and have a talk with the chief of PFK in the camp where the musician was, and earmark him for his band—if, of course, the musician was reliable and had survived the screening process.

'It's too late!' said the captain, assuming an Othello-like pose.

The musician had in fact been screened, but the authorities had baulked at some detail and were sending him back to the USSR, not to prison, but to work on some building project. My boss sighed deeply and picked up the telephone receiver.

'Comrade Lieutenant-General, this is Lieutenant-Colonel ... reporting.'

In a few brief words he had told the chief of our Smersh Adminis-tration all about the musician who was being sent to the Soviet Union. After listening to the general's answer, the lieutenant-colonel said, 'Yes, sir, very good, sir, that's quite clear, sir . . .' and replaced the receiver.

He then explained to the captain that he could go and collect his musician and mobilise him for military service in the band.

I then saw this musician. He was a real virtuoso on several instruments. He was completely remote from any kind of politics and lived only for his music. The Germans had deported him to Germany. The only blot on his copy-book was the fact that he had played in Germany for the last two years in a cabaret which was visited by Wehrmacht officers.

A second incident concerning a returnee from the west did not have such a happy ending. One of the 'identifiers' at our operational branch was a certain young woman, who was a repatriated Soviet citizen. The work of Smersh 'identifiers' hinged on the fact that their earlier life and work enabled them to pinpoint persons of interest to Smersh. As a rule our identifiers had had fairly close connections with the intelligence service of other countries. I recall that this particular woman, who was then between twenty-eight and thirty, was a Russian and a former student of languages. She had worked as in interpreter in one of the branches of German foreign political intelligence. It was said in Smersh that at the same time she had been the mistress of an important officer in that intelligence service, some *Oberführer* SS. Smersh was in no hurry to imprison her. I met her several times, always in the company of our plain-clothes officers. She was tall, with a boyish figure and her skin was the colour of white marble. Her eyes were always well made up. A captain friend of mine told me that in bed she was capable of tricks that simply took one's breath away. He also said that she smoked either hashish or opium, I can't remember which. She often travelled with our officers to Vienna and to other towns, some in the western zones. The last time I saw her she was getting into an Opel Admiral with Austrian number plates, which belonged to our operational branch. She was wearing a magnificent fur cape and had diamond rings on her fingers. Her escort, who was a Chekist officer, was dressed in a typical 'western bourgeois suit' of an entirely different cut to my creation in blue serge. It must have been about a month later that she shot herself with a pistol she had snatched from a driver-sergeant whose attention had wandered for a moment. The sergeant was subsequently tried by a Smersh tribunal.

The lieutenant-colonel sent me and one of our other officers, a captain, on an assignment which involved calling in at GUKR Smersh in Moscow. We also visited Odessa and Sevastopol. We went to collect and verify information about new troop formations. At that time Smersh administrations were busy implementing one of Stalin's secret orders. The gist of this was that tables should immediately be compiled listing military personnel in two particular categories. Firstly were persons who had served in the navy in any capacity whatever; and secondly persons suitable for service in NKVD internal or frontier troops. As a result of our administration's work, long lists of figures and other data emerged. All this had to be tied up with the data provided by the Smersh administrations in our fleets. My particular concern was the Black Sea Fleet. As I soon discovered, the situation in the Soviet Fleet gave real cause for alarm, and the skilled manpower situation was even worse.

It is well known that our fleet as such played no part in the decisive battles of the Second World War. During the first years of the war a large number of our sailors, including ratings, petty officers and officers, were formed into maritime brigades. These brigades were deployed like normal infantry brigades on the most important and critical sectors of the fronts. The sailors turned out to be poor infantrymen, but courageous human beings and soldiers. Because of their courage and the colour of their uniforms, the Germans referred to them as the 'Black Death', a name they really earned. An order came from Moscow that top priority should be given to issuing these maritime brigades with ordinary field-green soldiers' uniforms. This helped very little, however. The vast majority of the sailors in these brigades were either killed or maimed in battle. Now, after the war was over, Stalin had resolved to create a powerful navy, and the higher command beat their heads in despair when they totted up the number of sailors who had either been maimed or had lost their lives during the war.

The situation of the NKVD interior and frontier troops was not catastrophic, although certain of their units had also participated in war. Stalin had been obliged, probably against his better judgement, to use them at highly crucial stages in the first period of the war. In the main, NKVD frontier troops had been used in this way, partly because many of them were out of work due to Soviet territorial losses. More than twenty thousand soldiers and NCOs, for example, served as top-class snipers. Units of NKVD frontier troops also took part in the battles of Moscow, Stalingrad, Leningrad and the North Caucasus.

Of course, they suffered certain losses in personnel. There were also fatal casualties in the top brass of the frontier troops. The commander of the Ukrainian region, Major-General Khomenko, was one such casualty. NKVD internal troops played no active part in the fighting. They had more than enough to do with their usual work on the home front.

At the end of the war it became clear that existing numbers of interior and frontier troops were insufficient for the extra duties which were allotted to them. In all the countries captured by the Soviet Union these troops were used as rear guard for all army units, for supporting lines of communication to the Soviet Union and for guarding all important Soviet institutions and personnel in foreign countries. They were also employed fighting anti-Soviet partisans in Poland, the Baltic and the western Ukraine. Finally, NKVD troops were responsible for keeping the peace, that is for averting and/or suppressing any uprisings against Soviet power in eastern Europe. For this reason there was an urgent need for increases in these forces. Some of the new recruits came in the usual way from the Soviet Union, having been selected specially from civilian youth by local State Security bodies. Others were drawn from army units, after being carefully chosen and screened for political reliability. The screening was done solely by Smersh and my assignment in the Soviet Union was connected with it.

At the same time, a series of changes had taken place in our NKGB/NKVD system. From the beginning of the autumn of 1945 all orders and documentation passed through the NKVD chain were signed not by Beria but by action People's Commissar for Internal Affairs, Kruglov. I think that the official edict relieving Beria of his responsibilities as People's Commissar for Internal Affairs was published early in 1946. Colonel-General Kruglov took his place as chief of the People's Commissariat. He had worked as Beria's first deputy right from the moment when the NKVD was divided into NKGB and NKVD in 1943. I had known from my work that for a long time Kruglov had been handling all routine matters in the running of the NKVD. Beria had quite enough on his hands. During the war, as Stalin's deputy in the State Committee for Defence, he had been responsible for the work of a number of People's Commissariats for strategic branches of industry (arms and ammunition, etc.). It had been his job to make operational as quickly as possible aviation, tank and artillery factories which had been evacuated from the west of the country. He was also responsible for the uninterrupted supply of labour for the economy, not only with the aid of GULAG NKVD, and both for the movement of troop trains and equipment up to the front and for the whole system of

State Security under the NKGB and NKVD. For these services he became after the war a full member of the highest Party body, the Politbureau, a Marshal of the Soviet Union and 'A Hero of Socialist Labour'. This supreme honour was granted to Beria in the autumn of 1943. Even in his capacity of deputy chairman of the Council of People's Commissars (from 1946 Ministers) Beria, as before, remained in supreme charge of the NKVD NKGB systems (from March 1946 MVD MGB). To all these duties was added a new, secret duty. Beria was put in charge of a new Soviet industry whose job was to make an atom bomb, and to handle all affairs associated with this task, such as the selection of scientific personnel, and obtaining information from all over the world.

After Stalin's death and Beria's execution there appeared both in the Soviet Union and in the west a plethora of all kinds of writings, works of research, learned treatises, lectures and even works of fiction about the personality of Beria, his depravity, his cunning, his acts of sabotage and so on. I have no desire to dispute all this, or to enter into moral arguments about his political actions. I would simply like to set down what I myself know about Beria's personality. All the remarks made below became known to me largely through my work in the Third Secret Administration of GUKR Smersh, and from 1946 onwards, in the same administration of what was then called GUKR MGB. I also learned a lot from mixing with people who had known Beria for a long time before he was transferred to Moscow in 1938. I cannot claim that I had close personal contact with Beria as I did, for example, with Abakumov, the chief of GUKR Smersh.

But I saw and heard Beria speak on more than one occasion, the first of which was when I was still a cadet at the State Security Service school. Although he was really a Caucasian, more precisely an Abkhazian, like the lieutenant-colonel, Beria actually looked like a Jewish intellectual. It's true that after the war he noticeably put on weight and ran to fat. He spoke Russian well, with far less of a Caucasian accent than, for example, Stalin had. Some young Chekist officers, friends of mine, used to say that if one had a small dimple on one's chin it was a sign of heightened sexuality. Of course, they weren't thinking of Beria, our top man, when they said this, although he did in fact have a small dimple there.

I was aware that Beria had actually had mistresses. My lieutenant-colonel pointed one of them out to me in the theatre, rolling his eyes ecstatically and clicking his tongue as he did so. I can't remember much of what this woman looked like. She was a Russian, married, and well beyond school age, contrary to what one might expect from the writings of people, both in the west and in the Soviet Union. I know for a fact that Beria behaved very well, not only to his women but also in certain cases to their relatives. I have heard of instances where he helped to get them not only a Moscow residence permit but a nice flat in the capital too. . . . Both of these were and still remain the dreams of every Soviet citizen. I find it hard to believe that Beria not only enjoyed the company of schoolgirls, although this is possible, but also drugged them by putting something in their wine before he made love to them. Such stories become particularly implausible when it is suggested that these same schoolgirls were the daughters of the Chekists who formed the bodyguard of Beria's colleagues in the Politbureau, which is what Khrushchev is alleged to have said in his revelations on the subject.

In the west, pages have been written on this particular topic, in which it is stated that Beria went hunting on the streets of Moscow for pretty schoolgirls, drugged them, raped them and was then filled with a horror of having caught venereal disease. It is even alleged that he called in doctors other than his regular ones to make the necessary examination of his person. Even in the Soviet Union people have written extraordinary stories about him. The Soviet poet and 'angry young man' Evgeni Evtushenko has described in lurid detail how a limousine drove slowly through the streets of Moscow. In it sat a monster on the look-out for fresh schoolgirl victims.

Beria was known widely in Chekist circles as a man of exceptional self-control. Two things he could not bear were wordiness and vagueness of expression on the part of his subordinates. This, by the way, went for the whole top leadership of the State Security Service, although not all of them possessed these qualities in equal measure. I often heard that the implementation of this style of working came from Stalin himself. In the NKGB school we were also frequently told that the founder of our service, Dzerzhinsky, considered brevity and clarity of speech the necessary qualities of a Chekist.

I find myself altogether unable to agree with Svetlana Alliluyeva, Stalin's daughter, in her description of Beria. Svetlana herself I regard with feelings of sympathy and pity. To be Stalin's daughter is by no means an easy thing. In our circles we often talked about Svetlana, in general, in a sympathetic way.

I well remember the anecdote, once told by a Jewish Chekist

major, whose name was, I think, Krishtal. A Moscow Jew, who had no son of his own, persuaded his Jewish woman neighbour to agree to her son marrying Svetlana Stalin.

'No,' she said at first, 'my Moisha is used to kosher food. Who'll give it to him in the Kremlin?'

'Nonsense,' said the Jewish neighbour, 'they'll set up a special kosher kitchen in the Kremlin, run by Chekist cooks.'

'No,' she said, 'my Moisha will feel very out of place with the members of the Politbureau.'

'Nonsense,' said the Jew, 'there is no class snobbery in the Soviet Union! We're all comrades and brothers, building communism together.'

'No,' said the woman, 'my Moisha hasn't got the right education. He doesn't know how to do anything.'

'Nonsense,' said her neighbour, 'he won't have to do anything. There'll be Chekist officers even to open the doors of his limousine.'

Persuaded by these arguments, the Jewish lady agreed. Her neighbour was ecstatic and exclaimed, rubbing his hands with glee, 'Marvellous. That leaves only Stalin to convince!'

While I was working in an operational group of KRU MGB, collecting information for Marshal Voroshilov, I got to know some of our leading fliers very well, including Krasovsky, who was in charge of the Air Force at TsGV, and his wife Sylva Rudolfovna. He is now a Marshal of the Air Force, but was then a colonel-general. I learned a great deal there about Svetlana's brother Vassili. At that time he was serving in Germany in a nearby fighting force. Many other people were also sympathetic towards him. He behaved badly only when he was drunk. Vassili was quite a good pilot and not in any sense a coward who hid behind his father's back. Alcohol was his downfall.

Let me return, though, to the points about Beria in Svetlana's books with which I disagree. When one reads what she has to say about the interminable dinners and drinking bouts at Stalin's house there are certain facts that one ought not to forget. For Stalin, Beria and the others, these dinners were almost the only rest and relaxation from their work, and some of these were working dinners. Beria and the others worked between fourteen and sixteen hours a day during the war.

An impression has grown up in the west that the Soviet leaders are no more than stupid, ill-mannered and narrow-minded. This impression is very alluring and lulls the west into a false sense of security. If this were in fact so, then today the west would be in a far better position than it is, and all that would be left of Soviet power would be a memory.

Svetlana, of course, knew Beria far better than I did. She had known him since she was a little girl. There is even a photograph which I have seen in the west of Beria dandling a very young Svetlana on his knee. I, of course, never got on to Beria's knee at any age. I simply came across him through my work. Nevertheless, despite my natural disadvantages, I don't agree either with her conclusions about Beria's behaviour immediately after her father's death. As soon as he was convinced that Stalin was dead, Beria at once sent for a car and went off to work. There were no further ways in which he personally could be useful to Stalin. Stalin's death had, however, caused a large number of acute problems. Beria realised this. The others, like Bulganin and Khrushchev, remained by Stalin's body and wept and so forth. The chief of the whole MGB MVD system could not permit himself such a luxury.

Neither can I agree with Svetlana's statement that Beria often urged Stalin to hound innocent people by playing on his unhealthy suspicions. I am sure that Beria simply acted as a person in his position had to do. He informed Stalin about highly placed or famous people, who, as a result of something they had said or done, had aroused the suspicions of his MGB MVD system. Beria did not inform Stalin about simple, insignificant folk, but merely dealt with them himself. I agree entirely that the system itself was inhuman. These, however, are the facts.

As for the whole official Soviet indictment of Beria, I accept only one point, namely that he was a British spy. I have one slight reservation. In 1921–2 Beria and other Chekists worked with the Secret Services of Mussovat[1] and of the Menshevik government of Georgia. I can easily believe that the British Secret Service controlled and assisted these services, although both their control and their assistance were insufficient. The Soviet indictment of Beria sensibly omitted one small detail, that Beria and the other Chekists penetrated these hostile services on the orders of their own Soviet Chekist top brass.

During my trip to Moscow, while I was in a Smersh building in Kuznetsky Most, a Chekist major in early middle age approached me. It was evening, and he asked me whether I was going to GUKR Smersh that day. I said that I was, whereupon the major asked me

[1] The nationalist Azerbaijan government.

to do him a favour. A close friend of his, a captain who had been a representative of one of the Special Branches, from which Smersh had been formed somewhere on the southern front, had apparenlty been killed during the first year of the war. He had left a son, who then, in 1946, was I think between fifteen and seventeen years old. The boy's mother had remarried and the lad himself managed to scratch along on·a small pension, which he got through his father, in some provincial town which I don't remember. His only other relative was an aunt in Moscow. The boy was very quiet, well behaved and able at school, particularly in chemistry and maths. I remember the major saying, 'The young pup will be a second Mendelyeev[1] or a Lobachevsky.[2] He'll go straight on to the "Baumanokva".'[3] Unfortunately, the way to the Baumanovka was blocked, and all because the boy lacked a residence permit allowing him to live in Moscow. Even the fact that his father had been a Chekist, albeit a fairly humble one, was of no help. There were too many people who wanted to live in the capital. This had always been the case. At that time, after the war, a permanent government commission was in session to decide Moscow residence permits. A huge queue of many thousands, often armed with various pieces of paper from important people in high places, was waiting to appear before this commission. Nevertheless, most of the petitioners were doomed to be refused. Without them Moscow was bursting at the seams and there was a tremendous shortage of living space.

The young man in our story was living illegally in the communal flat where his aunt was a tenant. A police check, of which there were many, had already discovered him there. He had been told to clear out of Moscow in twenty-four hours. The major himself was only spending a day or so in Moscow, in transit to his place of service in a local MGB administration beyond the Urals. He had talked to the boy on the telephone, consoling him as best he could, and offering advice. He couldn't do much more. He could hardly telephone the Moscow Police Administration, which controlled residence permits and expulsions from the capital, and make demands on the boy's behalf. In the eyes of that administration a provincial Chekist was nothing out of the ordinary. When he saw that I was listening with interest and a certain amount of fellow-feeling the major brightened, and thrust his hand into his pocket.

[1] Mendelyeev, D.I.—an eminent nineteenth-century Russian chemist.
[2] Lobachevsky, N. I.—a famous nineteenth-century methematician.
[3] Baumanovka—the Bauman School of Advanced Engineering in Moscow.

'Here,' he said, 'I've written a report to Abakumov. After all, he's in charge of the administration where the lad's father used to work.'

I read his short report. I liked its brevity and most of all its business-like approach. There was nothing obsequious in his style. This is more or less what the major had written:

'An official of Special Branch GUGB NKVD was killed on the southern front in such and such a year. A son survives him.' Then followed the bare facts about the son wishing to live and study in Moscow, and about his exceptional capabilities and diligence. The report ended with the words, 'I consider it my duty to inform you of this matter, Major so and so.'

The report was addressed to the chief of GUKR Smersh, Abakumov. Abakumov became Minister of State Security a little later, in October 1946.

'The problem is,' the major said, 'how to get this straight to Abakumov, and to let the boy know what happens. He might be thrown out of Moscow at any moment.'

Such doubts as I had were fast vanishing. The major had to leave for the aerodrome immediately, whereas I was free until the following morning. Abakumov's staff could hardly eat me alive, and when all was said and done I wasn't asking for either a decoration or promotion for myself. What really made me take this errand on was a feeling of anger that the lad had been badly treated. I was only too well aware that rats and parasites from the home front, who had never even got the smell of war, dolled-up whores, fixed themselves up in Moscow for life, on the basis of protection, enormous bribes, or having slept with sufficiently highly placed individuals. I took the report and wrote down the boy's telephone number.

'Don't chicken out!' was the major's parting remark. 'I've heard that Abakumov is approachable. See if you can manage to talk to him face to face.'

I had more than once been in the complex of buildings in Dzerzhinsky Square. Among ordinary folk this place is still known more often than not by its pre-Revolutionary name, the Lubianka. As I walked over to the telephone, I tried to raise my spirits by thinking of a joke about this building. Before the Revolution it had housed insurance companies called 'Russia' and 'Anchor'. The single Soviet insurance company, which had taken over the functions of these two, and other Czarist companies, was called *Gosstrakh*. This was an acronym from the words *Gosudarstvennoye* and *Strakhovaniye*. The first word means State and the second insurance.

In Russian the word *Strakh*, the second part of the acronym, means terror, and people used to say jokingly, 'It used to be *Gosstrakh*, now it's *Gosuzhas*', which we must translate as, 'It used to be state terror, now it's state horror.'

I dialled the number of the first deputy minister's reception room. The duty adjutant, a captain, whose name I have forgotten, answered it.

'An urgent personal matter,' said the adjutant, repeating the words of my brief report. 'All right, First Lieutenant. In about fifteen minutes "Himself" will have a few free minutes. You'd better get a move on.'

I made my way to a remote part of the building. This is where the offices and next to them, the reception rooms, of Merkulov, my own minister, Kruglov, the Minister of the Interior, Serov, Kruglov's First Deputy, Chernyshov, Abakumov's First Deputy, were situated. There was also a conference-room for meetings of the collegiums, and a closed-circuit government communications link. There was no one in the large reception room, apart from the duty adjutant. He was a little older than I.

'Sit down and wait, and when you get in there,' he nodded towards an upholstered leather door, 'don't bugger about. He doesn't like it. Say what you've got to say quickly. Got that?'

I nodded gratefully. A bell on the adjutant's table rang softly and a red light came on. He leapt to his feet and disappeared through the door. He soon reappeared and beckoned to me to enter. I looked myself over, straightened my jacket and looked at my boots. Hell, they were slightly splashed with mud! I went forward.

The first thing I noticed in the well-lit, fairly small office was a desk. On it stood a table lamp with a green shade, just like the one my father had had on his desk at home. Beside the table was a tall man in a completely plain, dark green jacket. He was wearing ordinary trousers, not riding breeches, with pale blue, general's stripes running down the outside seams. It wasn't the first time I'd seen Abakumov, but I had never before been alone with him. I looked at him with great interest. This man was, after all, one of the very few who had free access to Stalin at any time of the day or night. All he had to do was to pick up the phone and say that something urgent had cropped up and Stalin would be sure to receive him. Standing stiffly to attention, I made my report: 'Comrade Colonel-General . . .' As he was in uniform I could address him only by his rank and not by his office. It was a fairly modest rank, as we had plenty of colonel-generals. As they sing in Odessa, 'There are all kinds—healthy and infectious.'

When he had heard my report, and taken the major's written report, Abakumov sat down, nodding to me to take the armchair beside his desk. There was no doubt that the chief of GUKR Smersh was a very handsome man. He had an athletic build, just a shade overweight. He had in fact been an active sportsman and was still a fervent patron of Dynamo, the sports club of the MGB MVD staff and troops. He had a round, open face, with regular features and one eyebrow just a shade higher than the other. His thick, dark hair was brushed back. On that particular night it was slightly damp. He'd apparently only just got washed and shaved before his night's work. The top buttons of his tunic were unfastened. I could see his snow-white linen undercollar, a narrow strip of material sewn on to the inside of the collar. I myself always wore a celluloid one, which I found far more practical. All one had to do was rub it over with one's handkerchief and it was clean again. Hearing the calm, unhurried tones of the colonel-general, I forsook my thoughts.

'You know what our father[1] used to say in situations like this?'

'No, Comrade Colonel-General,' I answered.

'He used to say that a Chekist who needs help should always get it from another Chekist. You ought to have known that. You did the right thing in trying to help the son of this captain who was killed. You were right too in coming straight to me.'

Abakumov took his fountain pen and wrote something deliberately on the major's report. I took a quick look round the office. There was a beautiful thick carpet, leather armchairs, a sofa and an open door leading, probably, to his rest room and his bathroom. There was also a bust of Dzerzhinsky, a portrait of Stalin in military uniform, and one of Beria in his marshal's uniform.

'You,' said Abakumov, dropping into the familiar form of address 'are a Cossack, as I am. Yes, we Abakumovs come from quite near where your people come from. Just a little bit higher up the Don.'

'Here you are,' he said, holding the major's report out to me.

I formally asked his permission to leave, 'Am I free to go?'

He made a slight motion of his head. I about turned smartly and left his office, wondering as I did so about the man whose other decisions—taken possibly that same day—might send thousands to their deaths without compunction.

The duty adjutant smiled amicably and said, 'I didn't quite know what to do. Whether to send for an escort armed with sub-machine guns for you, or to wait a bit.'

[1] This was how many senior Chekists referred to Dzerzhinsky.

I thanked him gratefully, for it was, after all, he who had made it possible for me to see Abakumov. He could easily have put a spoke in the wheels if he'd felt so inclined. When I reached the corridor I looked at the report. On the left-hand side the resolution was written across it. 'Comrade Romanchenko![1] Issue a residence permit without delay. Abakumov.'

I rang the number that the major had given me. It was already very late. For a long time nobody answered, until eventually an irritable man's voice said, 'Who do you want?'

I mentioned the boy's name. I've forgotten now what it was, but I can remember his first name, which was Grisha, short for Grigori.

I received the brusque answer, 'Everybody's asleep here. I'm not his servant.'

In a furious voice I shouted into the receiver, 'I am not anybody's servant either. I'm an officer of the MGB and I need this comrade (i.e. Grisha) urgently, on a matter of business. What is your name?'

From the receiver came a strangled sound, a cross between a croak and a wail, 'Oh, just a minute, please, I'll get him.'

I waited and finally heard a frightened piping boy's voice.

'Is it Grisha?' I shouted. 'Everything's all right. This is a colleague of your late father's speaking. You're to stay in Moscow. Only I'm in rather a hurry. Get your clothes on. I've got to see you immediately.'

He lived rather a long way away, somewhere near the Paveletsky station, so we arranged to meet there, at the booking office for military personnel. I stopped a lorry and requested a lift. When I got to the station I saw a lanky, skinny youth in a tatty old overcoat and large spectacles. So this was the future Mendelyeev! I thrust the report into his hand, explaining that he was to take it next morning to the nearest police station, straight to the officer in charge. Grisha seemed somewhat uncertain. He was clearly afraid of even going to the police, let alone approaching the officer in charge. After all, he had been given twenty-four hours to leave Moscow. I explained in language he could understand that the man who had signed his paper had only to wave his finger to make any Moscow police officer turn turtle for ever. Finally I told him that he'd be as safe with this piece of paper as he would be in the arms of Jesus.

All this obviously had a beneficial effect on Grisha, because his face began to shine, and he started to thank me. I wasn't in the mood

[1] Romanchenko. Police Commissar, Third Rank. Moscow Chief of Police at that period.

for that. I was rather tired and somewhat over-excited by my meeting with Abakumov. In any case, I was short of time. I forced open Grisha's clenched fist and pushed a wad of notes in it. I had more than enough. At that time I was on triple salary. I was paid one salary in roubles, and a double salary in Austrian schillings. In all it amounted to about eight times as much as the earnings of the average Soviet doctor or engineer. Grisha somehow hadn't got the look of either a Rockefellar or a Rothschild, and life in Moscow was by no means easy. He had a pension, it's true, but that didn't amount to much.

After he was shot, which is supposed to have happened in 1954, Abakumov too became a target for writers and historians, both in the west and in the Soviet Union. Some fairly famous people have written that Abakumov and Smersh were responsible for Trotsky's murder. When Trotsky was killed in 1940 Smersh did not in fact exist, and Abakumov was busy in the State Security system with quite different matters. There are many equally absurd descriptions of his appearance, where he is described as 'huge', 'bloated', 'like a gorilla', and of his abilities—'semi-literate' . . . and so on. In reply I will simply say that even in the Soviet Union only a very small number of people knew what Abakumov looked like. I am almost certain that his photograph appeared in the Soviet newspapers no more than a couple of times, I think when he was standing as a candidate for election to the Supreme Soviet. And one could hardly call those photographs! The other candidates were photographed in normal close-ups. Abakumov and Merkulov were photographed from the waist upwards, from a distance and with their faces in shadow. Their own mothers would not have recognised them. This was done on purpose. People in jobs like those of Abakumov and Merkulov were not supposed to be film stars and were not in need of publicity. Beria, who was a leading political figure as well as being a Chekist, was quite a different matter. Here again I am not indulging in political or moral judgements, but merely describing how the presentation of a man's physical image may be used to distort the truth.

I want to quarrel with only one literary portrait of Abakumov. Solzhenitsyn, winner of the Nobel Prize, gave a detailed description of Abakumov in his remarkable book *The First Circle*. I admire Solzhenitsyn immensely, both as a man, for his very real and moving courage, and as a writer. I don't, however, accept his version of Abakumov. In *The First Circle* Solzhenitsyn says that Abakumov made a huge personal fortune by bringing in from abroad, probably from Germany and Austria, a mass of looted trophies. This couldn't have been the case. Although in his heart of hearts Abakumov might have been a scoundrel, which I myself doubt, being chief of Smersh, and subsequently a minister, he wouldn't have taken either a single rouble or a single towel that wasn't his own. I am all too well aware that for the uninitiated, particularly in the west, this is difficult both to understand and to believe, but it happens to be a fact. For Abakumov, as Solzhenitsyn admits in his book, neither things nor money had any meaning whatsoever. He was short of nothing. If then, as Solzhenitsyn writes, Abakumov had been unable to restrain his feeble urge to thieve and had begun to rob from a simple desire to perfect his technique, then he would never have become either chief of Smersh or Minister of State Security. Let me make just one more small point for precision's sake. Solzhenitsyn describes how, when Abakumov was stealing, he avoided the supervision of the Ministry of Finance, which he feared. This couldn't possibly have been true, for the simple reason that all the employees of the Ministry of Finance, from the minister downwards, shook in their shoes whenever Abakumov's name was mentioned.

I cannot accept the scene in *The First Circle* between Stalin and Abakumov. If the latter had behaved in his dealings with Stalin in the way that Solzhenitsyn describes, then he wouldn't have held the post of Minister of State Security for ten minutes. Stalin would not have put up with either his long, diffuse monologues or the scenes of cringing fear and dissimulation from a man to whom he entrusted the country's most important instrument, the State Security Service. It is well known that Stalin sometimes liked to play the fool and relax with people from the world of entertainment, writers and certain of his colleagues, but never with people in jobs like Abakumov's. Of course, any writer is free to write as he thinks fit, particularly a writer as famous and talented as Solzhenitsyn. This is precisely the reason why I have dared to make this criticism. Many people in the west have, after all, read Solzhenitsyn. When they read his description of Abakumov in *The First Circle* they also come to the wrong conclusion that the Soviet system of espionage and oppression is headed by stupid, crude thugs. It is possible to reproach the Soviet Security system, but let us have grounds more relative than these.

To return to the personality of Abakumov. There is one particular circumstance which I regret. If I had known then that I would ever write a book, I would have collected more information about him.

In Chekist circles people used to say that Abakumov had worked with Dzerzhinsky, the creator of the State Security Service. I should think that this is possible. Let us suppose that like the majority of senior Chekists he was born about 1900, give or take five years. Dzerzhinsky died in 1926. Of course, Abakumov could hardly have been his closest assistant, but he could have been one of his junior colleagues. Marshal Tukhachevsky, for example, successfully commanded a whole army at the age of twenty-five. There were several people of his age in positions of only slightly less importance. This people in the west find difficult to understand.

I disagree with many views prevalent both in the west and in the Soviet Union that the State Security Service system initially contained a predominance of Jews and later, in Stalin's time, of Caucasians. I can myself vouch for the fact that within our system there were plenty of both, but at no time was there a predominance of any particular nation in the MGB MVD. During my time the leadership of the MGB was made up of the representatives of the various nations of the Soviet Union. For example:

Russians

Chernyshov, Colonel-General, Chief of GUKR Smersh, Chief of GUKR MGB, Deputy Minister of MGB.

Abakumov, Colonel-General, Chief of GUKR Smersh, Minister of MGB.

Ivashutin, Lieutenant-General, Chief of UKR Smersh of the Third Ukrainian Front.

Ukrainians

Strokach, Lieutenant-General, Chief of the Undercover Partisan movement in Ukraine, the Minister of State Security of the Ukraine.

Bel'chenko, Colonel-General, Deputy Chief of the Partisan Main Staff of the USSR.

Koval'chuk, Lieutenant-General, Chief of UKR Smersh of the Fourth Ukrainian Front.

Caucasians

Beria, Marshal of the Soviet Union, Head of the whole MGB MVD system.

Kobulov, Colonel-General, Deputy Minister of the MGB of the USSR.

Jews

Raichman, Lieutenant-General, Chief of the Main Operational Administration of the MGB

Belkin, Lieutenant-General, Chief of the UKR MGB in Austria and Hungary, Deputy Minister of MGB of the USSR.

Latvians

Vadis, Lieutenant-General, Chief of UKR Smersh of the First Belorussian Front.

Belorussians

Korolyov, Lieutenant-General, Chief of UKR Smersh of the First Ukrainian Front.

The same picture held good for the sphere of internal affairs—the MVD. The majority of the top leadership, the minister, his deputies, heads of the main administrations, were Russians (who, after all, make up the greater part of the population), Ukrainians, occasional Jews, Caucasians (from the various Caucasian ethnic groups), Belorussians. The situation was much the same lower down the scale.

I am afraid that I shall have to disillusion many people about their external appearance as well. They were nothing whatsoever like characters in popular films and television plays about espionage. Merkulov or Abakumov could easily have been taken for successful, middle-aged company directors if they had happened to walk into the bar of some first-class hotel. The same could be said for Kruglov, whose appearance is well known to the heads of western intelligence services, from seeing him at the conferences of the Big Three. Serov, who has been seen by many Londoners and inhabitants of the other capitals which Khrushchev visited, could easily escape notice in the crowd at a football match or the greyhound stadium. Probably the only one who could have attracted particular attention, because of his head, which like Yul Brynner's was completely shaved and as shiny as a billiard ball, was Chernyshov.

Of course, their appearances changed with passing years. The life and work of the leaders of the Soviet State Security Service were hardly likely to improve their chances of a peaceful, untroubled old age. The question arises whether any of them lived to be old at all. Of the five examples I've just quoted, two were shot, one, Serov, fell into disgrace, another, Chernyshov, died a natural death, but long before he was old, and only one, Kruglov, managed to reach old age.

Yet many of my former bosses are not only still alive today but still occupying key posts in the State Security and similar bodies. Lieutenant-General Ivashutin, Chief of Smersh for the Third Ukrainian Front in those days, is now in charge of the GRU of the General Staff. Not very long ago he was made a general of the army. Up to the latter 1960's (1965–7) he was First Deputy Chief of the KGB of the USSR. The Chief of the Main Administration of Foreign Intelligence of the MGB (as it then was) Pitovranov is now First Deputy Chairman of the All-Union Chamber of Commerce. This institution maintains trade contacts with many countries in the western world. My direct superior in Smersh and KRU MGB in those years, Yevdokimenko, is now Chairman of the Kazakhstan KGB. The Minister of the Interior in Kazakhstan up to the 1960's was a man called Moskov, whom I have known since my early youth. The head of the whole partisan sabotage movement, Bel'chenko, was a Deputy Chief of the KGB of the USSR in Moscow until the first half of the 1960's. Kruglov, Beria's First Deputy in the NKVD hierarchy in my time, managed to survive his patron and remained minister at the MVD until 1956. Beria's Second Deputy, Serov, was for several years head of the KGB of the USSR and then prior to Ivashutin, from 1965 to 1967, head of the GRU of the General Staff. The former chief of the Maritime region of NKVD troops, Zyryanov, whom I knew personally, is now the Chief of the Main Administration of the Frontier Troops of the KGB. Only in 1971 I saw the obituary of a certain Yatsenko, who in my time was the Deputy Chief of the Main Administration of MVD troops.

There are working in the KGB today many people whom I knew, and who in my time occupied relatively minor posts in the State Security Service. Western specialists often go into great detail to claim that the KGB system is quite different from what it used to be, that all Beria's and Abakumov's former comrades-in-arms have been liquidated, and that the present-day leadership of the KGB is under strict Party supervision. In general they suggest that an altogether different type of person now works there. This may well be. I, after all, am not a specialist and have not had access to secret material for many years. Who can tell? Perhaps the people I have just mentioned have attended special crash retraining courses at Soviet finishing schools. But I think it likely that the basic organisation and personnel of the KGB has not greatly changed since I was myself a member of the Soviet Security Service.

8

Bulgaria is before us
And the Danube at our backs

From a song by Isakovsky

SMERSH AS SUCH WAS no more. It had played its part as a concentrated mobile organisation. The war, or at least the visible war, was over. The running of the Security Service in our considerably reduced armed forces was put into the hands of the Main Administration of Counter-Intelligence of the MGB. At the head of the MGB was a new minister, the former chief of Smersh, Abakumov. Our Main Administration, GUKR, was headed by Chernyshov. This work was not new to him. He had been in charge of security work in the armed forces before Abakumov. We, of course, also knew Chernyshov extremely well. During the last few years he had been Abakumov's First Deputy in Smersh. I personally, however, did not know very much about Belkin, Chernyshov's new deputy. I had seen and heard him several times with groups of other Chekist officers. Now I got to know him better.

During one of my trips to Budapest my boss, the lieutenant-colonel, and I were sitting in the room of the Third Section of our OKR (Counter-Intelligence Branch) in the MGB building on Andrasi-Ut Street. A middle-aged lieutenant-general entered the room. We sprang to attention. It was Belkin making an inspection trip of eastern Europe. I can no longer recall what particular difficulty we were wrestling with on that day. I can remember that there were some sets of figures which should have coincided and didn't. We were collecting information initially for the Baden administration and ultimately for Moscow. Belkin listened to the report of the senior officer present, which was my lieutenant-colonel, frowned, and lapsed into thought. Then he snapped his fingers gleefully and exclaimed to the lieutenant-colonel with a smile, 'Christ is risen.'[1] I

[1] *Khristos voskresye*—An Easter greeting among Orthodox Christians after the church service. The answer is '*Voistinu voskresye*' (Christ is risen indeed).

was perplexed. I knew that Easter was a long way away and that neither in Smersh nor in the MGB, even at Easter, did anyone use this greeting. Into the bargain Belkin was a Jew. My lieutenant-colonel, however, looked gratefully at Belkin and said guiltily, 'Of course, why didn't I think of it myself? It'll be done right away. I'll go and check.' He then left the room. In the general's mouth '*Khristos voskresye*' was not an Easter greeting. The letters Kh.V. on certain documents, cases, etc., stood in our service for '*Khranit*' *vechno*'.[1]

But I had heard the words '*Khristos voskresye*' from my grandfather when I was a child more than once.

The disappearance of Smersh had no effect whatsoever on either my service or my personal life. The rights and obligations of GUKR MGB were the same as those of Smersh. We did in fact lose our Fourth and Fifth Administrations (Investigation Administration and Tribunals). The work of investigators in military units was now done by our regular operators. Only a few senior Chekist investigators were left in our Baden administration for specially important cases. On the other hand, in Moscow the Main Investigation Administration in the MGB was considerably increased in size. The tribunals were now under the jurisdiction of the Main Military Collegium of the Procuracy of the Soviet Union. The Main Military Collegium was, of course, a military institution and so contained our permanent operational representatives, who were responsible for the surveillance of officials of the collegium. Territorially speaking, the nearest tribunal to us was in the second echelon of TsGV in the town of Modling, not far from Vienna. This was all that was necessary, as we were not at war and our units were in permanent quarters. There was no need for haste in the pronouncement of sentences or for tribunals to be urgently dispatched everywhere.

In Budapest I had to work with our officers who were registering personnel and collecting information in an assembly camp for war criminals. The camp was in the centre of the city, in the building of one of the former charity hospitals. When I think of my stay there I shudder even today, and all because of the smell, which was a mixture of human ordure, pus, dirty clothes, long-unwashed bodies and boiled cabbage. It permeated even the offices of our group, which were by the entrance from the street, a long way away from the other buildings. The MVD soldiers who were guarding the station sprayed themselves liberally with eau-de-cologne, sometimes

[1] See footnote page 136.

with ladies' perfume too, and smoked scented tobacco. I simply spent as little time in the station as possible. One day, when my Caucasian lieutenant-colonel dropped in, he wrinkled up his nose and exclaimed, 'Yes, this place really does smell of charity, and no mistake.'

The most important members of the Hungarian pro-fascist Party, the 'Crossed Arrows', were at the station, waiting for their fates to be decided, along with officers of the German and Hungarian gendamerie, officers from the SS troops. Our clientele also included minor officials from the Gestapo and the Hungarian counter-intelligence service, 'Kemelharito'. Among them were quite a number who were suffering from slight wounds, or simply the after-effects of beatings-up they had received when they were caught. I think that a lot of them were held there for many months. There was no reason to hurry with them and they didn't possess any highly important information. Moreover, we were short of personnel.

Medical treatment in the station was the responsibility of the Budapest City Commandant, Major-General Zamertsev. He had very few doctors or nurses. However, there were several Soviet military hospitals and medical evacuation stations in Budapest. The MGB leadership had ordered an improvement in our people's conditions of work so as to avoid any kind of epidemic and so Zamertsev began periodically to send teams of orderlies to disinfect the place. They walked about the station with tanks across their shoulders and splashed everything with strong smelling liquid, carbolic I think. This brought no noticeable improvement in the smell. It's true that permanent residents of the station, that is to say prisoners, were put through a field disinfection chamber to kill their lice. Many also had the bandages changed on their wounds.

The station gradually began to empty. There weren't many ways out of it. One led to an anonymous hole called the cemetery, where some went, having died either from wounds or from illness, or after a trip to the gallows, like the leader of the 'Crossed Arrows' Party, Ferenc Szalasi, and his closest comrades-in-arms. Another road led to the prison in the town of Sopron for an extremely long stay. For the small number who were of interest to the MGB a third road led to the military aerodrome, Aksyonov's outfit, near Budapest, followed by a flight to the Soviet Union and then either prison or a labour camp. I can't remember any statistical data which I or any other officers of the Third Branch got from the MVD personnel in charge at that station. I should think that when I arrived there were over fifteen hundred men imprisoned there.

In the Budapest city district of Kispest beside the Ferencvaros goods station there was a transit station for NCOs and privates from our forces. Anybody who had been separated from his unit was sent there. Some were discharged there from hospital, or perhaps their units had been re-formed, or moved to another place. Some of them were left over from already packed troop trains, others had been picked up by patrols. All this information was given to me by my lieutenant-colonel. He also informed me at the same time, that I had been appointed deputy chief of an operational group which had been formed to carry out a top-priority mission at this station. The lieutenant-colonel stated quite openly that since I had had some experience of this kind of thing at Tatishchevo at the start of my career, he had approved my appointment. He emphasised, however, that I had, as before, to carry out my basic work, which was the collection of information for the Third Branch of KRU to which I belonged. I was given two weeks to complete my assignment.

The chief of our group was a major, unknown to me, who had recently arrived from Moscow. The transit station was bursting at the seams. Most of its inmates were privates and NCOs, who had been detained by patrols from our Commandants' offices, not only in Hungary, but in Czechoslovakia and Roumania as well. The detainees had wilfully 'separated themselves' from their units, and enjoyed a free, nomadic life. I could understand them all too well. At the end of the war our units had been put on a permanent garrison regime in eastern European towns and villages. Strict discipline had been established. The right to leave the confines of the unit was very restricted, and it was not at all easy to obtain for privates and NCOs. Selection of men for service in special-purpose detachments had already begun. These detachments were not part of the MVD troops. They were officially regarded as the reserve of the commanders of groups of occupation forces. Their job was to carry out special missions. They might be dropped behind the enemy lines, to destroy selected key installations and carry out other acts of sabotage and subversion.

The supposed enemy was our Anglo-American allies. Propaganda against them had been conducted consistently in one form or another throughout the war. As soon as the war was over, the Main Political Administration of the Soviet armed forces stepped it up fiercely. The usual channels—press, radio, political study groups and talks to the troops—were used. The basic idea was that the allies had the atom bomb and were ready to use it against us. So far we hadn't got this bomb, but soon would have. We must therefore be particularly vigilant. The best alternative open to us was to capture the whole of western Europe, including the British Isles, at a single swoop. If we did this sufficiently quickly and successfully, then the Americans would be left holding their bomb looking rather silly. They would hardly be likely to drop it on Britain, France and the other European countries. The greater part of our troops would by then be mixed with the local population in these very countries.

MGB bodies in the forces also took part in this propaganda, but in unorthodox ways. Our representatives in the units sent for individual soldiers, NCOs and sometimes officers too, and instructed them to spread certain rumours among their fellow soldiers. Often the most amusing things would happen. The soldiers took the people who were spreading these rumours for anti-Soviet provocateurs, and informed on them to those same KRU MGB representatives. It then had to be explained via a private chat with the informers, that what he had heard from X was unfortunately the truth. Churchill and Truman, for example, were said to be not one whit better than Hitler, and just dreaming of the chance to attack us unexpectedly. We therefore had to be ready at any moment, not just to defend ourselves, but to attack, so as to forestall our former allies. It was added that for this very reason, our Party and government were forced to keep such a large army under arms and build the atom bomb with all speed. It was all very sad, but what else could we do?

At the Budapest transit station in Kispest we were met by the permanent counter-intelligence representative. He was a young-looking captain, who was childishly overjoyed at our arrival. Twelve of us arrived together. In his own words, the station was a complete shambles. The permanent staff of officers and NCOs, who were simply army men and not from the MVD, was completely unable to cope with its duties. In the first place there were nowhere near enough officers and NCOs. In the second place the vast majority of troops in transit were far too energetic, far too resourceful, much too fond of adventures and in fact of everything else in the world apart from routine army service. The major in charge of my group listened to all this, took a walk round the station, had a good curse, jumped in his car and drove off to KRU MGB to demand more men for his group. He left in charge of the station his deputy, who happened to be me. When I had instructed the members of our group to make a preliminary selection from the documents of the men in the transit station I closeted myself with the captain who was the station's permanent representative. He was the only man who was aware of our group's actual purpose. He also had received an order through his own chain of command, that of the First Branch of Counter-Intelligence, to leave all other matters and give us all the help he could in every respect. As far as everybody else was concerned, including the station CO, we were ordinary army officers recruiting NCOs and men for military units. This gave rise to no suspicion, as recruiting officers of this type were visiting the station all the time.

I soon grew weary of the captain's flood of complaints, although none of them was unfounded. How could one hope to conduct the normal business of counter-intelligence when there were only two officers (the captain and his assistant, a lieutenant) to deal with a vast number of constantly changing and undisciplined privates and NCOs?

I can no longer remember the overall total of the inhabitants of this station. I think there were about five or six multi-storey buildings which were packed tight with people. To add to all our other troubles, the CO of the station at that time was an ageing captain—why this should have been so I could not for the life of me understand—who had just received the Order of Lenin for many years of unimpeachable service in the army. In those days, it was accepted practice to give the Order of Lenin for twenty-five years, the Order of the Red Banner for twenty, etc. In the words of my new colleague, once the station CO had received this high decoration he rejected completely any further thought of carrying out his duties. For about three or four weeks he had been drinking celebratory toasts to his decoration and putting in an appearance at the station only intermittently, by and large, late in the evening.

'Alas,' said the Chekist captain, 'these appearances are in no way connected with his work.'

At the station there was a sick bay, staffed by girl medical orderlies, NCOs in the medical corps. The station CO used to retire with some young lady, and entertain himself as best he could.

I only saw this station CO once or twice. His face was the same colour as the brightest red ribbon of his Order of Lenin. He made a brave effort to salute us, and reeled off in the direction of the sick bay.

All practical matters, on which our work depended, were handled by his deputy for matters of registration, and by various clerks and secretaries. The chief of my operational group, the major, managed to get six more Chekist officers as reinforcements.

It very soon became perfectly clear to us that the population of the transit station was not interested in any kind of political activity, either anti-Soviet or pro-western and capitalist. These people were simply enjoying a relatively free life, illegal trips into town, drinking bouts, games of cards, hunting for Hungarian women and girls. There was nowhere near enough of our own women medical personnel to go round. They were all snapped up by the permanent establishment of officers and NCOs, just as the CO chose his favourites to help him with his little pursuits. The activities of station residents had consequently to range far beyond the confines of the barracks and far beyond Kispest itself. For a booze-up, a game of cards and most other things, one usually needed money. Our transit station therefore acquired a certain unfortunate reputation, both in Commandant's-office circles and among the local Hungarian population.

It was physically impossible to keep an eye on everyone. The large number of sentry posts were merely furniture. Anybody who wanted a night out slipped out through small holes in the fences. Most of them usually came back by morning, give or take a few hours, and peacefully slept off the after-effects in the barracks, until the following evening. Only a tiny minority of really wild characters fled from the station without any thought of coming back. This kind of escape amounted to a formal act of desertion from the army, which was covered by Article 193 of the Criminal Code. Soldiers were sentenced under this article by military tribunals to impressive terms of imprisonment, as every private and NCO in the station was well aware.

The station's fame, in terms of complaints from Hungarian citizens about robbery and rape, and demands by the Budapest City Commandant that 'this den of thieves should be removed from the garrison', reached the chairman of the Allied Control Commission in Hungary, Marshal Voroshilov. The allied ingredient of this commission did not amount to very much, apart from the official representatives of Great Britain and the USA. For all practical purposes, power in Hungary was concentrated in Soviet hands. All that our western allies could do was to try to put a brave face on things, which they managed quite well. Voroshilov sent his senior adjutant, Major-General Shcherbakov, to the station, to acquaint himself with the situation there. This visit had two results: a slight increase in the permanent staff of officers and NCOs, and a slightly better supply of troop trains to the left-hand side of the station, i.e. to Ferencvaros goods station. These troop trains, each one amounting to approximately battalion strength, transported groups of men from the transit station to reserve regiments in Hungary, Slovakia and

Austria. They were replaced at the station by new men and NCOs who had been brought in by Commandant's patrols.

During those first post-war years there were plenty of chaps in our forces who wanted to have a good time and get about a bit. A captain colleague of mine was right when he said of the station, 'The holy place is never empty.' The work of our operational group in choosing candidates for detachments of special-purpose troops went ahead very quickly. Sixteen of our officers were directly involved in the work of selection. The major who was in charge of the group resolved cases which were uncertain, organised the lorries in which the candidates were transported to Austria, and jollied along the special medical commission which had been set up at the station.

The qualifications we were looking for in candidates were excellent health, political reliability and active service during the last war. It was also considered desirable that the candidates should have served in reconnaisance units or in the paratroopers or sabotage units with experience in laying minefields. We had to come to terms with the fact that most of the candidates we selected had been severely disciplined during their previous service for such offences as hooliganism, looting and being AWOL. On the other hand, no one could have accused any of them of cowardice in battle, lack of physical agility or gumption. The lie was clearly given to any such suggestion by the medals, decorations and stripes for wounds which adorned their chests.

As I was the deputy chief of the group, I was not much involved in direct selection or questioning. I assisted or involved myself only when our officers encountered some problem and were uncertain whether or not to select. I soon became convinced that it was much more pleasant to supervise the work of others than carry out dull, monotonous work oneself. I was also flattered by the fact that I, a mere kid of a first lieutenant, had a number of captains who were older than me working under me. Of course, I was well aware that this was a consequence of my working in the Third Secret Administration of KRU MGB and of my having graduated from one of the State Security Service's best schools, but probably most of all by the fact that I had worked closely with the deputy chief of the Third Branch of KRU in TsGV. All the same, it was very pleasant. The major and I shared the duties equally between us, as one of us had to be at the station all the time. I spent my spare time in excursions exploring Budapest night life. The city had suffered very badly during the war, but there was plenty of night life left if one knew

where to find it. Thank heavens that on my first visit to a night club
in some basement I was accompanied by a Chekist captain, who was
an old hand in Budapest.

On that occasion a Hungarian girl, with luxuriant chestnut hair,
and 'good property on all floors', very much caught my eye. The
cabaret orchestra was playing a dashing Kukaracha. Tokay wine and
Hungarian vodka called Palinka flowed freely. In addition to all
this, my new lady friend spoke quite reasonable Russian. In those
days my Hungarian was confined to the knowledge of words like
'How do you do', 'Wine', 'Beer', 'Girl', 'I love you very much' and
a few more similar expressions. And suddenly here was a pretty
girl who spoke Russian into the bargain. To have asked for more
would have been a sin. I rapidly began making plans. A few more
dances, followed by a stroll with her along the nocturnal boulevards
which would end in my room in the officers' hotel. The captain,
completely disregarding my seniority of position, dragged me
roughly into a corner and said, 'She's a good-looking chick, and she
likes Russians, but you listen to me, and you'll live to say thank you.
Every officer in Budapest garrison HQ has marched his way through
her. You can count on a dose of clap.'

Clap was the last thing I wanted. I thought of my Gilda in Baden.
A dose of clap would be a real present to bring her from Budapest,
and no mistake. What a way to celebrate our reunion! I remember
one occasion when we sent about four hundred men to Austria from
the station. The top brass in Baden sent at once for the major who
was in charge of the group. I stayed and took his place. The first
thing I did was to appoint a deputy, and I chose, of course, the
captain who had saved me.

I began to have more and more free time. The work of the group
ran on oiled wheels. I knew that the people we selected were sent
to an area near the Austrian railway station of Zvettl, or, to be more
exact, to the Allenstein Training Area near the Czechoslovak
frontier. We had inherited this vast training area from the Wehrmacht.
There the Germans had set up one of their most massive troop-
training centres. There was everything there, including settlements
(without, of course, anyone living in them), fortifications of all kinds,
unbridged rivers, artillery ranges, systems of earthworks, aerodromes
and tank exercise areas. Selected candidates, not only ours but from
elsewhere, were trained there for service in subversive sabotage work.
The training was supervised by experienced instructors who had spent
the war on the territory of Germany or her allies, as subversive agents.

I was obliged to remain in Budapest until the work of our operational group there was completely finished. I didn't regret this at all, but on the contrary soon began to seek pretexts to pay visits to Budapest from Baden. Directly opposite the station in Kispest was a large park with shady paths. It was in this park that I met Maryjka, which is a very popular Christian name in Hungary. She was a little older than I. A student whose studies had been interrupted by the war, she was now working in some firm or other and preparing for her final university examination. All this was not the main point, however. The main point was that she was small and very *chic*, with light brown hair, a slim waist and wonderful legs. I complained bitterly to her, after joining her on the bench on which she was sitting, that I, the literary correspondent of a Soviet Army newspaper, based in Vienna, was having a difficult time in Hungary, where I'd been sent to collect material for some articles. I knew no Hungarian and had to use German to communicate, I didn't know the town, and so on.

Maryjka turned out to be a kind, open-hearted person. She began to twitter animatedly in German, which was far, far better than mine, about Hungary, about her beloved Budapest, which had suffered so in the war, about human cruelty, and about the war itself. We ended the evening in a restaurant. Good God! How difficult it was for me to persuade her to go there! She wouldn't even hear of coming to my room. She stamped her foot angrily, her eyes flashed and she told me that her fiancé had been reported missing in the war and she was no prostitute. I soothed her as best I could, saying that although I had never had a fiancé, I wasn't a prostitute either. We shook hands and agreed to meet again.

Thus it came about that thanks to Maryjka I developed a burning interest in Hungary and the Hungarians. Later, when Maryjka was no longer with me, this interest grew into real love and affection for the country. By historical tradition, Hungarians should hate all Russians. All the Hungarians I met at that time were not in any sense my enemies, nor was this because I wore the uniform of a Soviet officer. None of them made the least attempt to curry favour with me, and we often discussed very delicate matters together. The road from such conversations had anybody overhead us, led only in one direction, to a labour camp in Siberia, and perhaps for me worse still. I tried simply to follow the advice of my grandfather, who had been perhaps closer to me than any other person: 'Always, wherever you are, be a human being and everything else will fall into place.'

In those days, because of my youth and stupidity, I did some very risky things, which were often clear breaches of service discipline. Since I had been a child, when we used to pasture the horses at night near the construction site which my father looked after, I had loved riding. After all, on my father's side I am of Cossack descent. Both in Austria and Hungary I was able to go riding. Our forces confiscated a large number of riding horses which had formerly belonged to German and Hungarian Nazis, and major landowners. The horses were kept in stables, some of which were in Baden, and were looked after by our staff. It wasn't anything like so interesting to go for a gallop in the outskirts of Baden, because that area was fairly thickly populated. Hungary was quite a different matter. I would take a car and drive an hour out of Kispest to the military stables, from where I could gallop to my heart's content. Travelling on horseback from there onwards the country was like what Sandor Petofi describes in 'Oh plain, Oh wild steppe Feldverneki'.

At first I used to go riding with a cavalry orderly, a Kazakh corporal, as was the rule of the stables, but then I began to go riding alone. I didn't care for trotting, I never knew how to and always got jolted. I liked to go at a real Cossack gallop. The Lord only knows how many places I used to drop in at. Sometimes I would stop in remote Hungarian villages, or at forester's cottages, to let the horses have a rest and a drink of water and have a drop of wine myself. I know there had been cases of our officers and men being murdered when they were on their own. All I had with me was a pistol. Probably mostly out of stupidity or lack of experience I used to sit down with Hungarians whose house it happened to be and talk a dreadful mixture of German and Hungarian. An awful lot of Hungarians understood German. Soon, over a glass of wine, they would be showing me their family albums with photographs of people in uniform in them, the uniform in fact of my enemies. People used to ask me what would become of Hungary. That I didn't know. I could hardly answer with the words of my Chekist bosses and teachers: 'We shall do whatever needs to be done for the sake of our Party, and destroy the existing order, whether it wants to be destroyed or not.'

But by this time I had certain doubts, there were certain things I wasn't clear about. Possibly isolated words and expressions which I had heard earlier from my grandfather and my father were beginning to assume a more definite form in my mind as a result of all I'd seen and experienced during my service. Of course, there was no one with whom I could share my thoughts and feelings, neither among my professional colleagues, nor the Hungarians.

Only a few years later I would have had time to become disillusioned about many aspects of life in the west, its lack of principles, its dull-wittedness and smugness. Never, however, did I feel more pain and shame because I was a citizen of the western world than one November day in 1956. I was sitting by my radio set. Words of excitement and hope were pouring from it. 'Many tanks are moving in on us . . . where is the help that the west has promised us . . . this must be the end . . . we have no more ammunition left . . . long live freedom . . . long live Hungary . . .' Then came the sound of the Hungarian National Anthem, followed by complete silence. Even now when I hear that anthem, tears come into my eyes. Perhaps this is because I can remember so well an action in the Polish forests at the end of the war, when our partisan detachment was breaking out of encirclement. Taking advantage of the cover provided by the trees, the Germans had been able to attack us unexpectedly. We had one way of escape, which was across the mountains. With us were wounded men and valuable military material. Somebody had to hold the Germans up, to give the rest of us a chance to escape. The detachment commander left about a platoon of soldiers armed with machine guns. Certain death awaited them. The rest of us began to move off quickly. Behind us we could hear bursts of machine-gun fire and exploding grenades. One of us, a young lad like I was, looked back with a wry grin.

'Now they're really giving them the works.'

Our commander, who was usually a reserved person, lashed out at him furiously.

'Shut up, you. Can't you understand that those men are heroes?'

The same could be said of Budapest in 1956. I later learned that the Hungarian uprising had been suppressed under the leadership of Lieutenant-General Grebennik, whom I had known, and who was deputy chief of MVD troops. These same troops undoubtedly did the actual suppression.

I had plenty of official reasons for making trips to Budapest. A group of buildings in Andrasi Ut kept on growing and taking in more and more of the ones which surrounded it. This was where the headquarters of the Security Service of Socialist Hungary was housed also our MGB administration and its many branches. As previously, the top leadership of our service was based in Austria, in Baden bei Wien. The chief of the KRU Administration of the

MGB, Lieutenant-General Korolyov, was based in Baden, and made
only flying visits to Budapest. One of his deputies, a colonel, was
based permanently in Andrasi Ut. The whole responsibility for the
state security of the new Hungary lay on these two persons. A little
later, for camouflage purposes, the letters MGB disappeared altogether from Hungarian official jargon. The organisation was known
simply as The Inspectorate, having a chief, and a staff of inspector-
advisers. These advisers were well represented in all spheres of
Hungarian life, in the government, in the life of the Party, in the
educational system, in industry and in the Church.

At the same time the meticulous training of Hungarian personnel
for the Security Service was under way. The higher ranks of this
service were not novices, or people whom the Soviet system did not
know. Many of them had spent the war in the Soviet Union and were
scions of the Seventh Administration (of counter-propaganda) of
the Main Political Administration of the Soviet army. They included
Matthias Rakosi, for example, Ferenc Munnich and other future
leaders of the new Hungary. There were also representatives of other
'People's Democracies', like Walther Ulbricht from East Germany,
and others still. The middle and lower links of Hungarian State
Security were trained on the job in branches and administrations of
the MGB in Hungary and Austria. The town of Modling, near
Vienna, was one of the places used for this purpose. The task of us
Chekists and the Hungarian service was one and the same. We had
to set up in Hungary a regime which was submissive to the will of
our Party, to put it even more simply, in the words of a witty friend
of mine, we had to 'feed and fan the flames of world revolution'. He
was thinking of the old joke which I had known since I was a child.
It concerned two Jews, who met in Moscow after not having seen
one another for a long time.

'Ah, Srul'. How are you getting on. What have you been doing?'

'I am fine, Nathan. I've got a responsible job—I'm a skin
examiner in a fur company.'

'Phoney. That's what he calls a responsible job! Just you listen
to what I do. I've got a really responsible job! I sit up in the Spassky
tower of the Kremlin and watch out for the flame of the fire of the
world revolution.'

Once again I came to Budapest on official business. On instructions
from my lieutenant-colonel, I was collecting information in the First
Branches of KRU MGB of army corps and divisions which had
recently arrived in Hungary. Naturally as soon as I had finished my

business, which was I think in the town of Papa, I dashed off to Budapest. I got in touch with the lieutenant-colonel in Baden via the communications link in Andrasi Ut, and hurried to Kispest to see Maryjka. She was working temporarily in the accounts office of some private firm. At that time they still had such things left in Hungary, which were unheard of for us Soviet citizens. The owner of the firm greeted me with great respect and a certain amount of awe, when he saw my new pilot's officer's uniform. Maryjka too was surprised by this change. I managed to explain to her that my army newspaper had sent me to write some pieces about pilots, hence the uniform. I could hardly tell her the truth, that I had been given a mission by the Third Branch and attached to an operational group, which was working in the district of the Air Army's HQ. In a pair of very full riding breeches and a field shirt of fine green cloth, but most of all in the cap with its sky blue band and its golden badge, known as a 'cabbage', I thought myself quite irresistible. In keeping with the latest fashion among young officers in those days, the holster with my pistol was not on my right side, as the statutes said it should have been, but almost at the back.

Maryjka had one shortcoming. She peppered me with streams of questions on politics, economics and other very tricky subjects, often when she was in the most unsuitable positions for discussing serious matters. On this particular day she looked critically at my air force uniform, which I had dropped hastily on the carpet, and said thoughtfully, 'How drab and grey all your things are in comparison with what our officers used to wear in Horthy's day. Nobody would have let you in to one of Horthy's receptions in clothes like that.' Having learned a lesson from my bitter experience in Austria with the serge suit, I endured her criticisms in silence and merely remarked that we felt that what was inside the uniform was more important than the uniform itself. She went on with further questions. Why were most of our officers so crude and uncultured? Why were there so many cases of rape and theft among our soldiers? Maryjka worked every bit as hard as an experienced MGB investigator. I simply parried her questions with jokes, and tried to get her into a situation where even the prettiest and most elegant girls are usually silent.

On another occasion I came to Budapest with my boss the lieutenant-colonel in his BMW. He stayed there for five or six days. I was ordered to return on the following day to our group's base near the Viennese suburb of Mauer. That time I managed, not altogether officially, to spend the greater part of the night with Maryjka. I could

not spend the whole night with her, because I would not have got to
Mauer on time, which would have been a breach of service regula-
tions. I fear that it was on that night that the delving, curious Maryjka
began to guess that I was a rather unusual army journalist. The fault
for this lay with the reaction of a night patrol of MVD troops, a
sergeant and a soldier, who stopped us to check our papers. As a
resident of Budapest, Maryjka had seen enough of the unceremonious
way that these patrols treated our officers. This was even true of Commandant's patrols, and not just MVD troops. The alert young woman
also knew to which service these disdainful, lordly soldiers, in their caps
with the light blue crowns and bright red bands, belonged. After the
war MVD troops had begun to wear their own uniforms openly.

This then was the scene. A first lieutenant, a very young army
journalist in pilot's uniform, was pulled up late at night with a typical
Hungarian girl, whom he was taking home from his hotel. The
journalist shoved a small identity card in the face of the senior member of the patrol. The sergeant looked at it and sprang to attention,
saluted and murmured some respectful remark to the journalist. Even
today I curse the memory of the two men in that patrol, although
they, of course, were only doing their duty.

That night a sharp change took place with my relations with
Maryjka, or, more accurately, in her attitude to me. For the rest of
the way to her home she kept on looking at me strangely, and although
it was very warm, her shoulders kept shaking as if she were cold, and
she no longer peppered me with her customary questions. Maryjka
was a dear, brave, wonderful girl. I can remember how frightened
she was on my behalf when that damned patrol appeared. If need be
she was prepared to protect me from them and take the blame herself
for my being on the street so late at night. She wanted to say that she
had asked me to see her home as it was so dark. She whispered all this
into my ear when she saw the sky blue caps. I tried to explain to her
lightheartedly that all Soviet journalists enjoy this kind of respectful
treatment from the NKVD. Like most Hungarians, Maryjka knew
this organisation by its old name. My joke, however, fell flat. Then
I told her that I was the fifth or perhaps it was the sixth illegitimate
son of Count Andrasi, for which I hope the count will forgive me,
which was why I was treated with such respect. This idiotic joke was
a failure too. Saying goodbye to her at her flat was difficult. I realised
that I had lost Maryjka for ever. During the whole of our relationship
she had regarded me as a cheeky, talkative boy, with whom she could
talk about everything.

During my years of service in the State Security network I had firmly grasped the fact that a Chekist's identity document opens every door for him. Practical experience now taught me that this same document possessed a different kind of strength too. It could cause the doors of people's hearts and minds to slam in one's face. I travelled to Hungary several more times on official business, but no longer with the old feeling of elation. I knew that in Kispest, the southern suburb of Budapest, no one awaited me.

Once, when I was travelling by night in a train, somewhere near the town of Djor, I was awakened by noises and shouts in the next compartment. Most of the passengers were our officers and men, but there were also some Hungarian men and women scattered up and down the train. I got up and went off in the direction from which the shouts had come. It was a woman's voice and the screams turned suddenly into stifled groans, just as if she had had something stuffed into her mouth. By the pale electric light of the carriage I distinguished three of our soldiers. Two of them were holding a woman down on the seat. Her skirt was pulled up above her waist. The third was in the process of raping her. I'd heard a fair amount about this kind of activity on the part of our soldiers in all the countries I'd passed through. In Poland I had even been present at a public execution when one of our officers was shot for just this. For a few seconds and no longer these thoughts ran through my head, then a flood of the foulest language poured from my mouth in the direction of the rapists. One thing I had long since learned how to do was curse. When he saw my gold officer's shoulder boards, and my pilot's badge, one of the men who was holding the woman, I think he was a sergeant, gazed at me dumbfounded, without however letting go of his victim. I slid my right hand into my trouser pocket, where my bone-handled Browning lay. The first shot went into the wall of the compartment above the heads of the rapists, the second went into the ceiling. They leapt to their feet and the woman, a young Hungarian peasant woman, dropped her brightly coloured skirts and collapsed into the corner of the seat, covering her face, and shaking with sobs and terror. Another passenger, a major, leapt out of the next compartment with one or two other people, also in uniform. Seeing the pistol in my hand, the major started to rebuke me indignantly. My answer was a further flood of filthy back street curses. I thrust my left hand, holding my identity card, in front of his nose.

'I suppose you know,' I asked him, without stopping swearing, 'what *we* used to do in this kind of situation?'

He just about had time to read the large letters on my identity card—GUKR MGB. Nodding silently, the major turned pale and stony-faced to the soldiers who had caused the shooting. They also had turned pale and were standing in the middle of the compartment in an untidy group. A sergeant and a soldier armed with sub-machine guns and with red bands on their sleeves came running up to the scene of the firing. It was the train's Commandant's men who had been sent for. I told the sergeant who I was, praised him for the exemplary order he maintained on his train and told him to take the rapists to the service compartment and to hand them over to the Commandant's office at the next station, making sure when he did to get a receipt. I took down in my notebook his name and the number of his unit, promising that I would ring and check that he had carried out these orders. Someone, I think it was the major, nipped off and brought a mess-tin of water, which he handed to the woman, who was still sitting in the corner. I went back to my own compartment without even looking at her properly.

Right up to the end of the journey the major never left me in peace, and tried in every possible way to draw me into conversation. He excused himself by saying that he had been sound asleep and heard nothing before my bullet went crashing through the compartment wall above his head. Of course, he was lying, because he'd been very close to the scene, and the woman had been screaming very loudly. The major was simply afraid that I might keep my promise. I think I had shouted at him that I would deal later with him as an accessory to the rape. I thought my own thoughts and listened to his wheedling voice with only one ear. Normally the sight of naked women delighted me, especially if they were pretty and I was on my own with them. Here, however, I kept on putting Maryjka, Gilda and all the girls I had known in the place of the girl in the railway compartment. This led to some very uncomfortable thoughts.

That major, who was serving in Hungary, was years older than I was, and probably had a family of his own. He could hardly have approved of the actions of our soldiers when they raped that girl. In an effort to amuse me, however, he said that for soldiers hungering for a woman's body every girl or woman seemed to be something to satisfy their desires. When a girl said '*Hogyvan*' (in Hungarian 'How are you'), a soldier thought he heard '*Hod*' Ivan' (in Russian, 'Let's go, Ivan'). All this was perfectly true, but how could one understand and forgive such treatment of a young girl?

9

'We shall build our new world.'

From *The Internationale*

To Klim Voroshilov
A letter I wrote,
Comrade Voroshilov,
People's Commissar.

THIS IS FROM A poem by Lev Kvitko, which I learned as a child. Kvitko was a Jewish poet, who along with many others was shot by the MGB, during the purge of the Cosmopolitans, i.e. Jews, after I had already come to the west. I was included in an operational group of Chekist officers who were collecting information for this man who stood so close to Stalin. He was one of Stalin's deputies in the government and First Marshal of the Soviet Union, a member of the Politbureau, and a member of the Military Council, etc. Voroshilov's official reason for periodic trips either to Budapest or to the outskirts of Vienna was one further job of his, that of Chairman of the Allied Control Commission in Hungary. However, in view of his special place in the Soviet system and his closeness to Stalin, Voroshilov concerned himself with many other matters which had nothing to do with Hungary.

Because I had a light flesh wound I didn't come into contact with Voroshilov immediately. I had taken part in some shooting between some MVD troops and some of our own soldiers near Uipest, a northern suburb of Budapest on the Danube. The soldiers forcibly abducted as pilots two Hungarians, and attempted to cast off and sail away in two barges loaded with stolen goods. So far as I remember the cargo was sides of fat bacon, flour and rum. The means of transportation had been chosen very intelligently, as on the roads the system of control was very strict.

The wound was only superficial, but my face remained swollen and

I wore a bandage for about ten days. I spent this period doing paper work at group base and wandering through the parks in the vicinity of Mauer, which is a beautiful place, full of magnificent villas set in their own gardens. The Zoological Gardens stand nearby, and if you face away from them, on the left is the road to Vienna, to the British sector, on the right more gardens and parks, and down below, at the bottom of the hill, the road to Modling via Liezing.

It was at Liezing, near the famous brewery, that the headquarters of our Air Army was situated. Closer to us on the hillside was the villa belonging to the Commander of this army. Just below it were the houses of air force generals. Next door to our HQ was a regiment of MVD frontier troops. They were responsible for guarding every inch of these parks and the secluded villas standing in them. There were certainly people worth guarding.

Here was the permanent residence of Zheltov, the Soviet representative on the Austrian Control Council. And chief of the Administration of Soviet Property in Austria the Deputy Minister of Trade, Borisov. This administration worked on the principle, 'I take what I want, while I can.' The main thing was, however, that this was where important guests like Beria, Molotov, Mikoyan and Abakumov used to stay. They lived modestly, without their presence being advertised and without any parades. Neither our troops nor Soviet citizens in general knew of their arrival, not even the officers in charge of our checkpoints on the roads. Only one—the State Security Service was fully informed of what was going on in the area of the Zoological Gardens and on the roads which led there. There was a daring joke which one could crack only among one's closest friends. 'Where's Mikoyan? In the Zoo, where do you expect?'

Usually on the day when any important guest arrived a Chekist operational officer visited all the checkpoints on the road from the aerodrome in Baden-Voslau to Mauer. He gave instructions that a high state of preparedness was to be maintained at these posts, without however mentioning the names of the important travellers. Soon afterwards three powerful limousines with the usual TsGV registration number, beginning with E, roared past along the road at high speed. All the passengers were in civilian clothes. The important guest sat in the back seat of the middle car. In the two other cars were Chekist officers. When the first limousine approached the checkpoint it made a squawking sound with its klaxon horn, which was commonly known as its 'duck'. The sergeants at the checkpoints waved down all other vehicles with red flags and held out green flags for the limousines. They roared by without ever having to use their brakes, on up the hill, where they were eventually hidden by the high walls and trees of one of the villas.

Voroshilov also arrived in this way on some occasions. At other times his aeroplane would take off from an aerodrome near Budapest and land near Liezing, close to the headquarters of the Air Army.

Not knowing what to do with myself in all the free time I suddenly had through the enforced isolation on account of my wound, I spent a lot of time wandering about near our building. I could easily tell by the number of patrols, soldiers and NCOs of MVD frontier troops, whether there was anybody important staying next door. They had their own uniform caps; a very dark blue cap band and an emerald-green crown. Their methods of working were special too. They patrolled in pairs. When they approached a soldier of any rank, even generals, whom they did not know, the senior member of the pair stated briefly, 'MVD duty detail. Your papers.' The senior member then took the proffered identity card, studied it carefully, comparing the description given with the owner of the card himself, at night with the aid of a flashlight. He approached from the side, leaving the subject of the check in the field of vision, and if need be, the field of fire of the second soldier. The latter stood a few paces away, with his sub-machine gun at the ready. To enter into an argument or dispute with these patrols was not advisable.

At that period I spent a great deal of time with Sashka, the orderly and bodyguard of the major in charge of my group. Sashka was a former athlete. For amusement's sake I used to practise with him Chekist arm exercises for developing speed and dexterity. You place your left hand on the table, with the fingers spread wide apart. You can use your right hand, but unless you're left-handed this isn't a good idea. In your other hand you take a sharp flick knife. Then, constantly increasing your speed, you have to embed the knife in the table between each pair of fingers in turn.

Many years later, in London, I played this game with the grandson of a former British Prime Minister. He didn't do at all badly and just cut one finger slightly. What a shame his grandfather is a Tory!

Sergeant Sashka knew another game, which was called 'Miaow'. He only played it a couple of times in a deserted summer-house in the garden, with some of his pals from the frontier troops. The more people there were playing this game, the more fun it was. These were the rules of the game, which had to be played in complete darkness. The people playing the game spread out all over the room and one of

them would miaow like a cat. The person who had miaowed was then
supposed, depending always on his inclinations, to change his position. The person who was running the game then fired his loaded
pistol in the direction of the sound. I myself never played at this
particular game and our major forbade Sashka to do so.

The swelling on my face soon went down and all that was left was a
small sticking plaster.

'How did you manage to get hit just there, my boy? I hope it
wasn't a duel over some beautiful lady?'

These were the exact words, which, of course, I have remembered.
The man who said them was a smallish old gentleman with friendly,
amused eyes. His appearance was known to millions of people all
over the world.

'No, Comrade Marshal of the Soviet Union, not in a duel,' I
replied, and briefly and quickly explained the real reason for the
injury to my face.

Voroshilov said something which was very similar to my father's
words at the beginning of the war: 'Don't worry, everything'll get
sorted out. We just need a bit of time,' though, of course, he didn't
call me 'son'. Afterwards in later visits, apparently automatically,
without even knowing how it happened myself, I used to call him
Kliment Yefremovich when I answered his questions. It seemed to
flow from the atmosphere which surrounded him. This is how all his
officers and my own colleagues in the group addressed him.

We were preparing for Voroshilov regular reports on various
subjects. They were something like the permanent secret bulletins
prepared exclusively for certain[1] members of the Politbureau. Tax
my imagination as I may, I can't ever visualise being able to say something like 'Yes, what a wonderful morning, just right for shooting a
few ducks, Viktor Semyonovich' to Abakumov, chief of Smersh. Nor
could I say the same thing, plus 'Vsevolod Nikolaievich' to Merkulov,
Minister of the MGB, or even to the other marshals like Konev and
Zhukov, not to speak of Beria himself. One might as well imagine Ian
Paisley marrying Bernadette Devlin today. With Voroshilov, though,
it was all completely natural. He was simply a different kind of person.
A real professional revolutionary, who had known Lenin and been a
friend of Stalin right at the beginning of the century. A delegate of
the early Party Congresses in London and Scandinavia, one of the
creators of the Cheka. A semi-literate worker who learned to understand all the subtleties of classical music and literature. A difficult,

[1] Some members of the Politbureau did not have access to these bulletins.

complicated mixture, he was an unusual man of great natural gifts. I have heard and read about Voroshilov, mostly in the west, a large number of unjust remarks. Krushchev too had a hand, and a mouth, in all this. I don't want to wean anyone from their convictions. What is the point? What I am doing here is setting down personal impressions photographically, and that is all. I met no one from among the Soviet leaders who was more humane, more kind, more straightforward, more ready to help others than Voroshilov.

A few years ago a fairly elderly woman died here in the west. She was the widow of one of the leaders of the Red Army who was shot in 1937. She was also the mistress of Voroshilov's first deputy, Marshal Tukhachevsky, who was subsequently executed. Right up to her death (I went to the funeral) this woman was one of my closest friends. She was more than twenty years older than I. When she lived in the Soviet Union and at various other times, the circle of her friends and close acquaintances included such differing people as Stalin, his second wife, Nadezhda Alliluyeva, Gorky, Ehrenburg, General Vlasov, Field-Marshal Paulus (before the Battle of Stalingrad) and . . . the American ambassador in London. I almost got down on my knees and begged her to write her memoirs. Being a very modest woman, she refused. I would have thought that a person of my stubbornness could have broken her resistance. Her second husband, now also deceased, said that she had already bought the paper, but cancer and death intervened.

I naturally spent hours asking her about Voroshilov, and comparing my own personal impressions of him with hers. She had known him for many years and of course her knowledge was on a different footing from mine. Voroshilov saved her life by getting her out of prison. He did this same thing for many commanders and generals of the Soviet Army, before and at the beginning of the war. In truth all the ludicrous accusations hurled at Voroshilov by Khrushchev, including his documentary proof, are falsifications from beginning to end. I have had plenty of experience in concocting this kind of proof. None of the Soviet leaders either inside or outside the army enjoyed the same widespread popularity as Voroshilov.

Even the leaders of the State Security Service listened attentively to what he had to say and did not risk getting into an argument with him. I heard several conversations between him and Chekist generals. No one used the same tone as he did when talking to them, neither the other Marshals, nor of course Khrushchev. Voroshilov's role in the Revolution and in the building of the Soviet state was recognised

by the Kremlin leaders of today. I shan't attempt to judge whether
from the point of view of world history Voroshilov was a good and
useful person. This I cannot do. It's simply that here in the west
people make facile judgements without having the experience of those
they are judging, or even understanding the context for their judgement. Of course, Voroshilov was an enemy of the western capitalist
world. The principles we lived by were at the root of my training in
the State Security Service school.

An aeroplane had just landed on the aerodrome at Bad-Voslau. A
small group of military personnel went up to the aircraft steps. There
was Zheltov from the Control Council, tall and bovine, Kurasov,
Commander-in-Chief of TsGV, who looked like an ascetic intellectual, Korolyov from our own MGB and one or two others. One by
one they went up to the visitor and reported to him. It was Beria,
still looking like Dr. Kapel'son, that ardent believer in castor and
cod-liver oils from my childhood. Beria now, however, looked like a
heavier, fatter paediatrician, weighted down with many consultations
and demands on his time. He was followed down the stairs by a tall,
scraggy man with a melancholy horsey face. This was not a face from
my childhood, but from the period when I studied at the State
Security Service school. I had seen the scraggy man, whose name was
Khodov no more than once or twice. I knew his son Volod'ka very
well, however. He was younger than I, a tall, slim, blond fellow with
blue eyes of childlike innocence. You might have thought he would
not hurt a fly. Volod'ka Khodov did not, in fact, hurt flies, being busy
with other matters.

In the war years when there was an acute shortage of policemen in
Moscow since most of them had been conscripted into the army,
courses were arranged to train women police officers. To quote
Volod'ka's words, 'There were some quite nice bits of stuff on these
courses, and even the odd virgin, but not very many.' Volod'ka
amused himself with them in his father's large empty flat. A drop of
alcohol, a few physical preliminaries and there you were. It was like
they used to say in Odessa,

> She was a maiden—
> She became a lady.

If everything did not go smoothly and the women police cadets made
a scene then Volod'ka remarked in a carefree way, 'Not to worry.

Viktor Nikolaievich[1] will write this one off as fair wear and tear. He's one of us.'

Volod'ka's parents really were 'on the bandwaggon' in every sense of the expression, particularly Khodov *père*. He worked as Malenkov's assistant (Stalin's deputy for Party matters). I recalled Volod'ka with warmth and gratitude, because it was at one of his parties that he had introduced me to my green-eyed doctor, murmuring as he did so, 'Handle it yourself from here, you're a big boy now.'

All these thoughts flashed through my mind as I caught sight of Khodov *père* with Beria, surrounded by my bosses. They went towards the cars, and the huge Horch with cream curtains on the rear windows moved off at high speed. In front was a black Mercedes 'compressor', with a hotted-up engine. Behind was a second 'compressor'. 'Khodov *père* looks pretty ghastly,' I thought to myself. In that kind of physical state I would never have entrusted him with the operation of 'turning' maiden police cadets into ladies.

The Horch, and for that matter the Maybach too, were objects of my, and all my young officer colleagues', great admiration. They were alas not motor-cars for first lieutenants, nor for that matter for any odd general. The bonnet was an enormous length and the engine had eight cylinders. They moved as silently as a thief at night. I knew this because I'd tried one out myself. Not, of course, the Horch that swept Beria away, but one like it, belonging to the Commander of the Second Air Army, whose house was just below our building in Mauer. Sergeant-Major Badamshin, the colonel-general's chauffeur, let me sit at the wheel myself and drive the car along neighbouring deserted roads. Putting the car into reverse, I miscalculated both my own strength and that of the engine, and pressed too hard on the accelerator. The Horch's engine roared and it bumped lightly into a tree at the side of the road. I was very embarrassed and Sadyk Badamshin was somewhat frightened. Fortunately the Horch's nerves, or rather its bumpers, turned out to be very tough. The only evidence of the collision was a small scratch on the bumper.

'The old bag's bound to notice it!' Sadyk exclaimed.

'Who, the boss?' I asked, meaning the Commander.

'Lord, no, the boss is one of the best. He couldn't care a damn about anything. But Sylva is an absolute bitch.'

Sylva Rudolfovna, a Baltic German, was the general's devoted spouse and known as the scourge of all adjutants, orderlies and chauffeurs. She staged, for example, a real 'Jewish wedding' for a soldier

[1] Viktor Nikolaievich Romanchenko—Moscow Police Chief. See Chapter 7.

orderly, some country bumpkin, because by mistake he called her Alma Rudolfovna, confusing her name with that of the general's favourite long-haired dachshund.

It was while I was living in Mauer that for the first time in my life I really felt that I was in a different world. The shady parks and gardens, with their marble statues and fountains, Maria Thérèsa furniture, or at least some kind of antique furniture, noiseless black limousines, silent sentries and patrols of MVD troops at every step.

One day I was walking along the edge of a shady street when I saw a grey open car, of a make I didn't recognise, parked at the edge of the road. The bonnet was open. Somebody was bending over the engine. I coughed and went up. The woman had dark blond curly hair. She remarked indignantly how unreliable western motor-cars were, especially British ones. It was a Sunbeam Talbot, with red seats, which were, I think, inflatable. Endeavouring to look like a man who had spent the greater part of his life riding about in British cars, I joined her and we leaned over, and peered at the engine together. Now I know as much about engines as a chimpanzee knows about the Foundations of Leninism. I hemmed and hawed a little, and suggested that there was perhaps some dirt in the carburettor. This turned out to be correct. I tried to show an air of modest surprise. Heaven knows whose daughter she was. At any rate, there weren't any working men's daughters in Mauer.

It all came out very quickly. Her husband (that was all I needed!) Kostik had given her this car when she arrived from Moscow. She'd only just come and wanted to go for a ride and try it out.

'It's ages since I did any driving.'

'And I wonder whether you've ever done any,' I thought.

She then told me that she was an ex-student of the Moscow ballet school. She had just got married to Kostik. I don't remember when, but not long before. My spirits improved. I'd seen Kostik, who was one of the bosses of the Administration of Soviet Property in Austria, an old Bolshevik, well past his first youth, if not his third, who looked rather like an old peasant woman who had struck it rich. The reason he needed a wife like her was his secret! When I learned that Kostik was at that moment in Paris dealing with some economic matters I became really quite happy. I eyed her firm buttocks and then thought of the major who was chief in our group.

There was no chance of mistaking this major for the Caucasian lieutenant-colonel. They were as different as chalk and cheese. After working with the major for several weeks I heard no more than thirty or forty words from him. I am certain that he was no more a major than I was a pilot. I knew nothing, of course, about his past life, except that he was an old professional Chekist from Moscow, and I had made no effort to discover his real rank. Any such curiosity on my part would have been very frivolous and out of place. If he wanted to be a major, then that was his affair. Even Chekist majors, however, didn't talk to their seniors in rank in the way he did, particularly senior officers from the same service. I remember him once picking up a telephone in my presence and saying, 'Comrade Chugunov, it's Major so and so here. One or two things aren't clear. I'll be right over.' He then hung up. Although this may appear a very ordinary and unspectacular way of speaking, we should remember that Chugunov was a colonel in the MGB and chief of the counter-intelligence branch of an air army.

Of course, the group which the major headed was unusually important. We were working for really big people like Voroshilov, and Beria. That wasn't all. Though none of my Chekist colleagues were particularly coy in their dealings with other people, this major radiated a special sense of quiet authority, and seemed convinced that people would prefer to agree with him rather than enter into an argument.

The sort of things he usually said to me were remarks like, 'Take care of this', 'Take note of that', 'Find out about the details', 'Let me have a breakdown'. He never became irritated, never raised his voice, was never rude. He listened in silence to reports, without interrupting the person who was speaking.

Looking then at Diana, which is what I shall call her, I wished that my major would have pointed to her and said, 'Take care of that.' Alas however, although one admits that in theory almost anything can happen, there was a better chance of the Emperor Franz-Josef stepping out of the picture in our villa than of the major saying that.

It is noble to take a risk. I agreed with Diana that we should make a trip south of Vienna to try out the Sunbeam Talbot. We went on the next day. I went along as a specialist on western motor-car engines. As far as Diana was concerned, I was a staff officer of a bomber corps who had come to Army HQ for a couple of days to iron out some technical matters. In Mauer I dropped in to visit a telephonist officer, who came from my own part of Russia. The major assented to my trip to Wienerneustadt to clarify information received on, I think, Soviet citizens repatriated from the west and now working in our group of forces. This was in fact the truth. I asked him also to consent to my dropping in to Baden on the following day for one or two items of clothing from my flat, which wasn't quite true.

I met Diana the next morning, and seated myself resolutely at the wheel of the Sunbeam Talbot. It wasn't a Horch, but nevertheless an excellent motor-car. Diana was all right too. She had taken off her slacks and replaced them with a skirt. I flew into our building in Wienerneustadt as if I had wings. For peace and quiet, Diana waited in the car a few blocks away. Having told the captain I was dealing with that I would call in for the information that evening, I ran back to Diana.

She and I began to exchange information of a different character; the latest news and jokes from Moscow. I became convinced that in many ways Diana and I were kindred spirits. For a long, long time, perhaps never since I had said goodbye to Yoska, had I felt myself so much at my ease and oblivious to my surroundings and my job. Diana literally never stopped talking. First she told me all the latest news about acquaintances we had in common, in whom I was interested. The daughter of the late commander of my Front, Vatutin, had got into certain difficulties, happily not financial ones. Both she and Radik, the son of Marshal Konev, my second commander, were studying at that time in the Military Institute of Foreign Languages. I knew that many places in that Institute were permanently reserved for the GRU of the General Staff and the MGB foreign-intelligence Administration. Konev's son's studies were going very badly, as he preferred to chase about on a powerful motor-cycle. She then told me a lot of jokes which I hadn't heard before.

Actually the State Security Service was an excellent place for collecting jokes. If today the Politbureau and the KGB were to publish in book form all the anti-Soviet anecdotes which are kept in their investigation archives, and to sell this book in all the countries under communist domination, they would make a vast sum of money. There would be sufficient money to allow all the Soviet leaders to retire and live the comfortable lives of capitalist plutocrats. Should this not appeal to them, the money would come in useful to help build communism in that part of the world which as yet is still free from it. The archives contain a vast number of Jewish jokes. Even today, years afterwards, I am still literally brimming over with Jewish jokes, which I remember from the days when I had access to these archives. I owe the Jews a debt of gratitude for these.

I can remember another joke from that period, or perhaps it's a true story? A student from the ballet school, like Diana herself, went into the best fur shop in Moscow to buy a mink coat. The manager of the shop was rather suspicious that such a young girl should have such a large sum of money. Perhaps she was a spy! He sent for the duty Chekist. The young girl was invited into a room behind the shop and an interrogation began. She refused to answer any questions and demanded to be allowed to make a telephone call. She gave the Chekist the number, and he at once realised that it was a Kremlin number. The girl screamed indignantly into the telephone, 'You stinking old goat! I told you I should have the coat delivered. But you wouldn't have it. You said I should buy it myself, you old idiot!' She then passed the receiver to the Chekist, who heard the words, 'Kalinin speaking.' It was the aged President of the Soviet Union.

One last anecdote about us Chekists. What a good job Diana didn't know who I was! Three officers, two tank officers and a Chekist, were fighting their way through some open country in a terrible blizzard. They managed somehow to find their way to a lone peasant's hut. The tank officers were in front. An old Russian peasant opened the door.

'My poor boys, come in quickly. Come inside and get yourselves warm,' he said.

'But we're not alone,' the officer answered. 'There's a Chekist with us.'

'That's all right, that's all right,' the old man said, trying to put them at their ease. 'You come into the house and tie the Chekist up under that canvas by the pigsty. I'll give him a bone to gnaw. Dogs are God's creatures too, you know.'

We got out of the car in a secluded wood away from the road, and I took the cushion out of the back seat. Diana produced a couple of very old bottles of white wine, obviously good ones, clearly something Kostik had laid his hands on. I had no pangs of conscience as far as he was concerned. The old ass shouldn't have got married to a young girl. She must have been completely wasted on him. There was a saying which was popular at the time:

> General for treasure
> Lieutenant for pleasure

On the return journey Diana suddenly became very serious and said to me, 'Don't you think that I'm some whore, who married her husband just for his money, and for her own ends. It's not true. I don't need much for myself, but you ought to realise how dreadful life at home was after the war. My father was in the army and got killed, my mother's a sick woman. I'm the eldest child and I've got two little sisters and a brother. Kostik keeps the lot of us.'

To take Diana's mind and mine off gloomy reality, I began to sing comic songs. We stopped at some Gasthaus and had something else to drink. For the rest of the journey we sang a duet:

> Mummy I love a pilot
> He flies high, but not just for the view
> They give him a lot of money.
> And I give him something too.

If you served in the Soviet forces of occupation you could earn a lot of money without flying high. In those years many officers, and generals among them, made real personal fortunes, though not, of course, the ones who commanded infantry companies and battalions. Take the chief of the Army Trade Branch *Voentorg*, who lived not far from Mauer, at the bottom of the hill. He dispatched to the Soviet Union about two railway waggons full of grand pianos, cameras, watches, suit lengths, dresses and other very useful trifles which happened to be in short supply. I knew that particular major quite well. Often, as he sat in the officers' restaurant, drinking vintage wine of which he was very fond, he would sing pensively and reflectively, 'If I were one of God's little birdies . . .' It was absolutely impossible to listen to him. He was about the size of Peter the Great, and must have weighed nearly 300 pounds. No kind of atmosphere could have supported a 'little birdie' like that. Both the army political branch and the military procuracy supported him for a long time, however. Even when he was at last obliged to leave for the Soviet Union he travelled as a free man and held on to most of his ill-gotten gains. The major's name was Lozovsky and he was the nephew of a deputy Minister of Foreign Affairs, who had been one of the controllers of the Sovinformbureau during the war. Lozovsky senior wasn't at all like his nephew in either content or form, and was shot during the purge of the cosmopolitans when I was already in the west. He was silly enough to have been born a Jew. Other officers in our HQ and officials of the Administration of Soviet Property in Austria operated on a more modest scale. A few

cameras or watches, a score or so of suits, a carpet or two, fur coats
for their wives and in some cases not for their wives.

Officers' leather overcoats were a special status symbol. Everybody
who could tried to acquire such an overcoat. My minister, Abakumov,
came to Baden with good reason, and made a big fuss about this
with the chief of the Baden garrison, Major General Dubinin.

'What do you think this is, Hitler's HQ or the base of an SS
Death's Head division?'

After that the owners of leather overcoats became more careful.
Of course, most of our soldiers were constantly sending parcels
home, both by legal and not so legal channels.

I did possess a brown leather overcoat, but didn't send any
parcels home. To whom should I send them and why? My parents
were in need of nothing and anyway my father would have been far
from ecstatic to receive that kind of parcel. He was a product of
quite a different school. I inherited from him my loathing and
scorn for unnecessary things. In any case these methods of getting
rich were very much frowned on within the State Security System.
When I was still in the State Security school one particular axiom
had been planted deeply in my mind; a Chekist should want for
nothing. All his wants should be supplied by the Party and the
State. I recollected that the creator of our service, Dzerzhinsky,
had been particularly harsh towards venal Chekists. They had been
expelled from the Cheka and if they were lucky they ended up in
prison. If they were unlucky they found themselves on the wrong
end of a bullet. Strictly speaking, one can hardly describe as felons
those of our staff or army officers who showed acquisitive tendencies
in eastern Europe. They did it all more or less legally. How could it
be described as a crime if you had a note from a military representative—and these were everywhere—to some Austrian, Hungarian or
Czech factory or warehouse, which entitled you to get an overcoat,
or a suit, or a motor-cycle. Everything depended on an officer's rank
and position. There were a host of such factories and warehouses.
All one had to know how to do was to pick friends in the right
places.

As a matter of fact I acquired certain things for Gilda in this way.
I also got several suits of clothes for myself, but them I needed for
my work. As a rule the MGB took no part in the campaign to stop
our military getting rich. This was the affair of the army political
bodies and the military procuracy. In the MGB we'd got more than
enough to do without that.

Two words which one did not usually come across all that frequently, gonorrhoea and syphilis, were becoming more and more common among the personnel of our group of forces. Initially only a few unlucky cranks could boast of such an acquisition. People said of them, 'He was unlucky and an unlucky fellow would catch clap from his own sister.' If one caught syphilis, one was known as a 'general', with clap one qualified for the title of 'colonel'. Even military medical personnel amicably addressed sufferers in this way. 'Comrade General, or Colonel, it's time you took some treatment.'

Soon, however, the matter was no longer a joke. The number of patients grew at a catastrophic rate. In the main they were young officers, frequently pilots. Not for nothing did people say 'Where aviation begins, discipline ends.' There were, however, among the sufferers representatives of other arms of the forces. Slaves to the new fashion appeared among the ranks of the State Security Service too. Any of our people who succumbed were given urgent treatment and dispatched to the Soviet Union, with the appropriate note in their personal file. It was just about a certain guarantee of demotion and being appointed to one of the most remote provincial MGB administrations.

I remember particularly well one case, which was very tragic and depressing. A young lieutenant, who'd only just graduated from one of our schools, and who spoke excellent German, including various Austrian dialects, without any accent whatsoever, came to our administration with a young wife he had just married. She came from the western Ukraine, and it had been no easy matter for the young lieutenant to convince his superiors of her political reliability. During a trip to our branch on the Hungarian frontier the lieutenant spent the night with a waitress from the officers' canteen, a Soviet girl who had been repatriated from the west. A few weeks later the lieutenant realised with horror that he had become a 'general', and his blameless wife a lady general. It was particularly unpleasant for her, as she was in the early stages of pregnancy. Up to this moment everybody had literally doted on them. They were both young, handsome, and very much in love with one another. The poor fellow was expelled from the Party and sent back to the Soviet Union with a ruined personal file. The waitress who had conferred general's rank upon him swore in hysterics that she was not to blame, as she didn't know that she had syphilis. By way of an extra detail I can say that as she was a young woman of liberal views, this waitress created a number of other 'generals' one of whom was the representative of counter-intelligence in an army unit stationed nearby.

My young officer colleagues and I were shattered by the misfortune of our friend the lieutenant, and acquired a number of medical textbooks. We made a serious study of such details as were of interest to us. I wish I had not done so! Moreover, with Pythagorean expressions on our faces, we would often count on our fingers the days and weeks since certain dates of which only we knew. I promised myself that I would not fool around, but stick close to Gilda. I was very young, however, and around me was the whole of Austria, Hungary and Czechoslovakia, with hordes of girls, all different and each in her own way attractive and desirable. In addition, my work continued to invite a lot of travelling, meaning that I was away from Baden for days on end. I travelled at that time in a service car, an Opel Kapitan. This increased the range of my activities still further. Whenever the opportunity afforded itself, and I had finished my business, I would go into Slovakia from Vienna, which is not very far at all.

In TsGV whole hospitals for 'generals' and 'colonels' appeared, many of which were situated in large, multi-storey buildings. There was one such hospital in Baden which was part of the Air Army Hospital and was known as 'Chvanov's outfit'. The fact of the matter was that there was a severe shortage of penicillin, which was required to treat these noble ailments. It was only issued in extreme cases, either to one's friends or through some recommendation. Most of the patients were treated by old-fashioned methods which, as I heard from many sufferers, were unpleasant and took a long time. By this time I had read so many medical books that I might have been mistaken for a middle-flight specialist in venereal diseases. I often felt obliged to stage 'practice alerts' after striking up certain new friendships on my travels. I still remember the magic intervals: up to a week 'colonel', up to a month 'general'.

The time for me to get home leave was drawing near. I impatiently started packing my things. There were all sorts of bad rumours about post-war life in the Soviet Union. I remembered what Diana had said, 'Life there is terribly hard.' Army officers coming back from leave said the same sort of thing. Some of them landed in the cellars of the Baden administration of the MGB for 'putting about provocative and hostile propaganda among the occupation forces'. Investigations were going on. One captain got caught in a very stupid fashion. After a drink or two he told, 'A sergeant came back to the collective farm with a chest full of medals. His family met him. "Father!" shouted the sergeant, "so you're still alive." "Yes, my boy. As you see." His mother went up to him. "Mother!" the warrior exclaimed, "so you're still alive too!" "Yes, my boy." "Christ," said the sergeant in horror, "how am I going to feed you both!" '

My father wrote to me far more frequently than I did to him. One couldn't say much in letters, though, they all went through the censorship. I consoled myself by thinking that I would soon be able to have a talk with my father and find out how things really were back home.

IO

The war sleeps not,
beneath the mist she shelters from the light
But we'll deceive her now, this very night.

L. Pervomaisky

MY FATHER WAS DOING something very unusual for him. He was resting in a government sanatorium in a small village on the Dnieper. The rest was enforced because his heart was playing up. I discovered, not of course from him, that quite recently he had suffered a heart attack. His appearance made my own heart miss a beat. Undoubtedly typhus in the Civil War and a life full of tensions and cares, which would have been more than most men could cope with, right up to this last war, had made their mark. I felt very ashamed when I thought that my own bad behaviour had caused my father a whole lot of extra worries and annoyance. My mother was living separately in Moscow. She had apparently had enough of my father's nomadic life. 'Where the Party sends me I go.'

We sat on the bank of the Dnieper, well away from other ears. My father was far from delighted with my career as a Chekist. He said that if I had stayed on and graduated from the Gorky gunnery school then he could have fixed me up in a university so that I might complete my higher education. This was not impossible. In an effort to set his mind at rest I said that I had already had a higher education, albeit of a somewhat different kind. My father simply brushed this suggestion aside in annoyance. Well, of course, there was no point in arguing. He knew the life and work of a Chekist officer in peacetime much better than I did. Strictly speaking, I hadn't yet found out what it was like, since my service in KRU MGB in eastern Europe could hardly be called a normal peacetime routine. I shared my father's views completely, though. He was quite right. The nearer we got to peacetime, the less I enjoyed my service.

In some ways I even hankered after the war itself. Then, things were clear. The fascists, who were bringing death and mockery to us all, were the enemies of all the peoples of the USSR. They had to be hit and destroyed, which was what I and others like me did as best we were able. Now there was no longer an overt war. I had learned by heart the statements of my Chekist bosses, that for us Chekists the war went on, and had simply acquired new guises. But in my heart, I was far from sure that the British and Americans wanted to attack us. After all, I had through my work learned a lot about these countries. What was happening there in the first post-war years didn't look at all like preparations for war. Both my father and I knew that there could be no question of my leaving the MGB to work in some other field. This wasn't done or even heard of, and no connections, even in the highest circles, could be of any help. Any such attempts would only cause any Soviet citizen to raise his eyebrows and might even lead to consequences a good deal worse than that. My father nevertheless advised me to go to Kiev State University, simply to familiarise myself with the academic programmes and details of the course for external students. No harm could come of this. During my leave I visited the university more than once, but I swear that I was drawn there by something other than programmes or courses.

I got to know a number of others about my own age in the university. They were all officers who had served at the front, and been invalided out of the army. They had been demobilised in a completely legal manner, so that they could take up their studies. They weren't all from the army either. It was then that I met the Komsomol organiser of the university, Boris Shul'zhenko. During the war Boris had been doing more or less the same job as I had, and had been wounded several times, on one occasion very badly. He had been released temporarily from the State Security bodies and appointed Komsomol organiser of one of the largest universities in the country. This step had a logic of its own. A Chekist officer is a tested man. He must, moreover, never experience need. The job in the university carried responsibility and was well paid. He also had his Chekist disablement pension, which was far bigger than that of an ordinary disabled soldier.

Quite recently, while I was working on this book, I read an obituary of the First Deputy Chairman of the Ukrainian KGB, Major-General Shul'zhenko. Boris was older than I. When he died he was just over fifty. Apparently the State Security Service had drawn him back into its system. They'd probably decided that he was fit or perhaps they were simply short of people. Boris Shul'zhenko became a Chekist general at forty odd, the age I am now. The post of First Deputy of the Chief of the Ukrainian KGB is a very important one. The Ukrainian KGB is the second most important in the Soviet Union.

I remember Boris as a wiry lad with unruly hair in an officer's uniform, without shoulder boards. His eyes were intelligent with a touch of irony.

At that time Kiev was like a huge ant-hill that had been disturbed. There were an enormous number of disabled ex-servicemen, real and phoney. The latter and also the so-called citizens of the Second Tashkent Front had crept out of all the cracks where they had been hiding during the war. There used to be a joke which was current during the war. A hefty youth, a picture of health, who was trying to avoid being sent to the front, arrived in Tashkent and sent a telegram to his mother: 'I'm ready to go even further away.' Now they were all enjoying life, working in the supply network, trading, speculating, and so on. Many even had decorations, medals, and stripes too to show that they had been wounded. You could buy all these things at the famous Kiev bazaar, 'Yevbaz'.[1] There were people there selling brand-new American suits, penicillin and gold. They also had decorations with the appropriate citations, and papers to show that one had been wounded in action. All one needed was the money to buy them. A decent man's suit, for example, cost 3000 to 4000 roubles. An average soldier's or sergeant's disablement pension was 150 to 200 roubles a month.

Over and above all this, both in the Ukraine and in other major agricultural areas, there had been a catastrophically poor harvest. My father just waved the questions aside and said, 'What's the point of talking? You can see for yourself.' And I saw. There were hordes of beggars, disabled people and people who were simply starving; hungry peasants who'd come to town to look for bread. For disabled ex-servicemen the situation got worse every day. At first, immediately after the war, they had wandered from town to town, buying and selling things and food. What you bought more cheaply in one place you could sell dearer in another. In this way they made a living. The authorities however, soon began to force them to live in one particular place, and they were driven either into a collective farm or a factory settlement. Only a few isolated individuals were prepared to go to these places voluntarily. The reason was all too plain. It was impossible to scrape a living at all in a collective farm, particularly

[1] 'Yevbaz' (*Yevreisky Bazar*)—Jewish bazaar.

if you had a family, and the situation in the factories was not much better. The police consequently staged round-ups in the town, confiscated whatever people were trying to trade with, and shoved them on trains and deported them from Kiev under surveillance.

In the haymarket I saw a real battle, between the police and disabled ex-servicemen. The invalids were belabouring the police with their crutches and sticks. The police were loath to use firearms. They were, after all, a different kettle of fish from MVD troops. There were plenty of ex-veterans among the police themselves. A small bearded figure suddenly leapt up on to a trestle table where milk was being sold. He was wearing an astrakhan papakha, and his overcoat was unfastened, revealing its red general's lining. He had a chest full of medals, including the Gold Star of a Hero of the Soviet Union. It was Major-General Kovpak, the former commanding officer of a large partisan detachment, but not a Chekist. Stalin himself had made Kovpak a general because of his special abilities in partisan warfare and his immense popularity with the people. In his trembling old man's voice, Kovpak called for order, both from the disabled and the police, particularly the police. He reminded me very much of the middle-aged Ukrainian soldier who had sung the blue songs with the choir in the military hospital where I had had my affair with Rosa. The battle subsided and both sides went away, nursing their bruises. There had been no need for the MVD troops that time, but sadly this wasn't always the case.

The MVD troops had more than enough to do without street battles. In the western Ukraine, Belorussian and Baltic states there were frequent shots and explosions. Sometimes what amounted to a minor battle would flare up. The struggle went on to wipe out the Ukrainian nationalists and the Baltic partisans, who were called the Forest Brothers. Amongst both there were quite a number of Russians, sometimes former Vlasovites, who had survived, and sometimes simply men who had deserted from the Soviet army. In Russia proper things were by no means quiet. Cases of local soviet representatives being murdered were frequent and sometimes Chekists were murdered as well. In many large towns organised groups emerged which were known as 'Black cats.' They robbed banks and state shops, stopped the more well-to-do citizens, i.e. the representatives of the authorities, and took the clothes off their backs. They often killed them.

Through my service in the MBG I had known about all this while I was still abroad. I now filled in the details. Everywhere mass purges were being conducted. Collaborators with the Fascist occupation forces, anti-Soviet insurgent bands and their relatives, anti-Soviet agitators, persons sabotaging the establishment of normal Soviet conditions on liberated territories and enemies of the new five-year plan for the development of the economy, all were constantly being arrested and deported.

Among the people themselves, a mass of new anti-Soviet jokes and rumours were circulating. In the western Ukraine an old peasant is alleged to have said to a representative of the authorities at a meeting, 'Before the Soviets came, my arse lived in darkness, but when the Soviets came, it saw the light,' and he showed his last pair of trousers, which were all but threadbare on the seat. The words of this joke were a sort of parody of the official slogan, 'Communism bears light to the masses.'

There was another joke, which was widely current in Moscow. A delegation of collective farm workers came to President Kalinin. One of them asked Kalinin, 'What is progress?' Kalinin went to the window and pointed towards Red Square. 'Do you see that single car going across the square? Well, when they cross the square one after the other in a long line, that'll be progress. That's where we are heading.' The peasants returned home to their village. One of them was asked, 'What is progress?' He went over to the window, and pointed at the village street. 'Do you see,' he asked, 'Vas'ka (the village beggar) there by himself? Well, when we've got a whole line of Vas'ka's walking down the street after one another, that'll be progress. And that's where we're heading.'

It was said that in a Russian village collective-farm girls sang a *chastushka*.[1]

> People say that Lenin's popped off
> It ain't true I saw the man
> Yesterday without his trousers
> Chasing after five-year plan

If you sang any songs or were reported for telling a joke like that, you could count on ten to fifteen years in a labour camp for anti-Soviet propaganda under Article 58 of the Criminal Code.

During that home leave it wasn't just all the shortages and the destruction which made a particular impression on me. I knew that

[1] *Chastushka*—a two-line or four-line folk verse, usually humorous and topical. Sung in a lively manner.

the peoples of the Soviet Union had undergone great deprivation during the war, but they had thought then that there was hope of a better, quieter life in peacetime when the war was over. Now there was no such hope. For me, a Chekist, there was even less peace and quiet in the air than for other people. We had to give top priority to making the atom bomb, to get ready for a war with our former allies, to rearm our forces, to fit them out with the latest weapons and equipment, to fight all the Party's enemies within our country and, in accordance with the Party's will, carry on with the building of communism throughout the whole world.

It is hardly surprising that all the Chekist friends and acquaintances whom I met during my leave looked yellow and exhausted, and never laughed or smiled. It wasn't surprising either that my father had said, 'You wait a bit, until you've served here in peacetime, then you'll realise what it's all about.' I couldn't get these words out of my head. If I didn't want to wait and see, what then? Chekist colleagues working in post-war conditions on Soviet territory told me all kinds of details about their work, what was going on in the provinces, how the people lived, what sorts of things they, as Chekists, had to fight against, that I had soon heard more than enough. I didn't want to be a peacetime Chekist at all, either in the Ukraine, or in Russia, or anywhere else.

I was ashamed to admit it, but it's true, that during that leave, for the first time in my life, I regretted having come back to my own country. I wanted to be somewhere else, anywhere else. Perhaps I had been corrupted and spoiled by life in the former capitalist countries of Europe? I don't really think so. Even then in Kiev, I personally wanted for nothing. I had good clothes, plenty of money, I ate, when I was alone, in closed Chekist canteens and restaurants. I had wonderful student girls, both Russians and Ukrainians. There was a tremendous shortage of suitors of my age, many of them had either shared the fate of Yoska, or been crippled. I had my pilot's uniform on, two decorations and my medals, and the stripes on my chest to show that I had been wounded. My purse was bursting with money, even the most critical young woman could hardly call me an unprepossessing suitor. In that leave however, even nights of delight with pretty student girls did not evoke my usual reckless mood of elation. For me this was something new and I began to take a good look at myself with critical interest.

Saying goodbye to my father was a pretty miserable business. He was totally exhausted. He had seen a tremendous amount in his life.

He was by no means a stupid man. He was in fact, much more intelligent than his son, a straight, just man, a revolutionary of the old type. I didn't bother him with unnecessary questions about what he thought of the situation in the country, or the plans for the future. I knew all about the plans for the future through my own work, from my own bosses. All the rest was perfectly clear and there was no need to ask any questions. I never saw my father again.

I came back to Baden by plane, as it was quicker. Here too there was news. My administration had just received an order from GUKR MGB telling us to screen all returnee Soviet citizens who were working in our army units as servicing personnel or in our non-military institutions in eastern Europe. Most of these people were women and girls. It was impossible to keep the first part of this order completely secret, as our own military and of course the civilians who were concerned knew about it. They were summoned both by day and night to our KR branches and sections for interview. By this time, of course, many of the girls and women had acquired permanent boy friends, largely among the army officers. Several had found time to get married to some of those same officers. Some of them had even had children. Life seemed in fact to be following its normal course. In the order our KR administration got from Moscow however, there was a second, secret section, only for Chekists. The gist of this section was as follows. 'After screening, all returnees are to be dispatched to the Soviet Union with all speed, in categories which will depend on the results of the screening.' In other words, the ones who passed our screening satisfactorily went home to the places where they had lived before. They would of course be escorted to the Soviet frontier by special Commandant's groups. Those for whom the screening ended unsatisfactorily, i.e. who were suspected of anti-Soviet attitudes or even activities, would be arrested and travel back to their homeland, but not to their homes, in MVD prison carriages.

When the screening and arrests were completed, our operational branch embarked on the second and concluding phase of the operation. In Baden and the surrounding area this was done in the following way. Between two and three o'clock in the morning, patrols of MVD internal troops appeared in all the streets. They stopped army officers, who had probably stayed late or been detained somewhere or other, checked their documents and advised them to go home as quickly as possible. Then a number of lorries with tarpaulin covers appeared. They stopped outside houses marked on a list of addresses. As a rule, the women and girls who were being sent home lived with their soldier husbands or friends in Austrian houses. A Chekist from the MGB operational branch entered the house with two MVD soldiers, roused the family he needed, and suggested to the wife or girl friend of some army officer, that she get ready to travel without delay. They were then taken off to special assembly points and from there to special trains. That was all there was to it.

During those days and nights, there were many tragedies, particularly in families where there were young children, because they too were sent off with their mothers. There were plenty of tears and plenty of hysterics. The officer-husbands stood shaken by all that was happening and looking as if somebody had spat in their faces.

Often the Austrian householders, particularly in cases where there were tears or screaming, took the nocturnal visitors for robbers or raiders. Their Chekist guests calmed them down with the magic letters, NKVD. The Austrians, like the Hungarians, understood the meaning of those outdated letters only too well. I can remember the morning when the operational branch captain sitting beside me at breakfast, said to me in great mirth, 'You can guess what a laugh it was. Some old Austrian chap shouted out to me, "Go away. What do you think you're doing, causing all this upset at night. Frightening women and children! I shall send for a patrol from the Commandant's office." And I said to him,' the captain went on, 'Take it easy, Dad. We're not robbers, we're just from the NKVD.' I was in no mood for laughing, however.

On the following morning the news of the women and girls who had disappeared that night spread through the whole garrison. We had been unable to dispatch them all in one go. There were neither enough waggons nor enough room at the assembly points. We had to repeat the operation either two or three times I think. You can imagine how the wives and husbands who escaped the first and second rounds felt. The officer husbands in every branch ran to their senior officers. They all got the same answer: 'It's an MGB order, and there's nothing we can do for you. If you want to go with your wife, go to the Personnel Branch or Administration, but our advice is that you should think this over very carefully.' There was a good reason for careful thought. After all, these officers already had one note in their personal file, which said, 'Married to a woman who spent a period of time on enemy territory.' Any person who had been there without express bidding of either the Party or the government was automatically regarded as a second-class citizen. Many doors were closed to them for ever. They would never be given a good job, which carried a degree of responsibility. They would not be allowed to live in certain towns, etc. Marriage to that kind of person usually held out little promise for the husband. The army political bodies and personnel branches looked askance at such liaisons. Friendly efforts were often made to dissuade an officer from taking such a step. The marriages were not, of course, forbidden, because the girls were Soviet citizens and not foreigners.

Love, however, did not always accept either the sober dictates of reason or the friendly advice of the authorities. I had one close acquaintance from the engineering branch of TsGV headquarters, a captain from Minsk, whose name was Vitaly. He had married a Russian girl called Nina, who had been deported for forced labour in Germany from her home town when she was a seventeen-year-old schoolgirl. I enjoyed myself at their wedding and often visited them at their flat afterwards. We used to read the verse of our favourite poets and sing songs together. I really liked going to their home because there I was able to relax completely. Vitaly and Nina knew that I served in the MGB, though they knew no details of my work, as nobody would have thought of asking us about that. This is something one does not do, as every Soviet schoolchild knows.

I wasn't in the least surprised to see Vitaly that morning. He looked very pale and down in the mouth and was wandering up and down waiting for me, not far from my administration. I simply asked him, 'Is Nina still at home, then?' He nodded and we went off into a park, where we were less likely to be overheard. Vitaly told me that Nina was still at home but there was little room for doubt that something would happen either that night or the one following. Vitaly had already been to see his own immediate superior and he had also been to the personnel branch. Without asking I knew what they had told him there. Vitaly now looked at me in silent hope and entreaty. And what could I do? I had already helped him to get a nice flat in the centre of the town, which would usually have been reserved for some more important comrade whose wife was one hundred per cent Soviet. I remember the occasion. All I had to do was to put the wind up some major from the Accommodation Branch.

On that morning, however, every thought that went madly racing through my head came up against a blank wall. Should I go to my Caucasian lieutenant-colonel? What could he do? The times when he could easily make arrangements for a musician, in the same situation as Nina, to be fixed up in a military band had long since passed. The war was getting further and further away. We were now living in 'normal peacetime'. I suppose for some people it might have been normal. In any case, my lieutenant-colonel himself had changed very significantly. He had become pensive and preoccupied and only rarely cracked a joke. I had, after all, myself seen the order about Nina and people like her. It had on it the signature of Abakumov, the Minister of State Security for the USSR. Who would dare to question his word, to interfere, to intercede for someone?

All orders in fact which came through the MGB were very different from the army orders, destined for the generals and officers of our forces. Their orders always began with long preambles: 'In view of the continuing links between our officers and the officers of the Anglo-American forces. . .' or 'In view of the growing harmful contacts between our armed forces and the local population . . .', etc., etc., in the same vein. Abakumov's orders were always absolutely clear, and never had any kind of introduction: 'Carry out such and such an operation in such and such a period of time and report to me or my deputy on such and such a date.' That was all there was to them.

When he saw my funereal expression Vitaly realised there was no point in counting on my help.

'You know what,' he exclaimed in despair, 'I'll put in a report to Krainyukov!'

I shook my head negatively and said, 'I shouldn't bother.'

What could Lieutenant-General Krainyukov, a member of the Military Council of TsGV, who represented the Party in the group, do? Even if he had wanted to, how could he take issue with the orders of someone like Abakumov, the leader of the vanguard, the elect, the élite detachment of that same Party, the leader of the Chekists, who were responsible for the safety of all Soviet people, regardless of whether or not they were Party members? 'Chekists should not waste their time on trivialities, or enter into the feelings and experiences of individual people. A single life and a single fate play no part in the sacred task of building the bright future of Communism for the whole of humanity.' This is what I had been taught in the State Security school. 'The death of one man is a tragedy only for his relatives. The death of tens and of hundreds of thousands of people are statistics for history.' Stalin said this more than once and I remembered it, since it had often been quoted to me by my bosses in the MGB. There was no actual death in Nina's case, but nevertheless. . . .

I suddenly recalled the kind eyes of a small elderly gentleman in a baggy grey civilian suit. Voroshilov! He would have interceded on Nina's behalf. But he was no longer either in Budapest or Mauer, but was now living permanently in Moscow. Moreover, I knew from working with him that the old marshal was literally snowed under with hundreds and thousands of requests of this kind.

Vitaly was not afraid of being transferred from the forces of occupation to a reserve regiment of officers in a remote area of the Soviet Union. Hope of entering the Military Engineering Academy and a brilliant career was gone for ever. On the other hand, he had Nina with him. They might be stuck in a small corner of somebody else's flat in the Soviet Union, near the military township where he was based, but nevertheless they would be together.

Our MGB administration had a whole lot of new worries. They weren't altogether new as they had come into being immediately after the end of the war. I knew from my work in the Third Branch of KRU, that in the period from the end of the war to the time of my own departure to the west about fourteen thousand soldiers, including officers of various ranks, had gone over to the British, Americans and the French, from our troops stationed in Germany and Austria alone. Many of them concealed their ranks and their jobs from the allies, considering that this would reduce the chances of their being extradicted into the hands of the Soviet authorities.

By this time I had already managed to lose a certain amount of my former firm belief in human powers of reasoning and deduction. This belief had been instilled into me by my late grandfather when I was still a child. Much of the behaviour of the Germans during the war had surprised me a great deal, but thanks to my grandfather once again, I was not particularly shaken by them. My grandfather, after all, had often said that the Germans had had a very unfortunate historical development. They had been favoured with dull-witted, short-sighted leaders, whose ideas were unreal and nonsensical. A hard-working people, which had grown up in conditions of over-crowding and poverty, willingly followed any leader who promised them earthly blessings and more land. The British, my grandfather used to say, were an altogether different kettle of fish. They had a great world-wide empire and the sweep of their reason was equally broad. In addition to this they have traditions of decency, recognition of human dignity, humaneness etc. I had it's true been greatly taken aback, and I wasn't the only one, that the British had preferred the relatively obscure Clement Attlee and his Labour Party to Britain's wartime saviour Winston Churchill, a man to whom even Stalin showed a certain respect, accepting that he and Churchill were people of a similar calibre. Not to worry, I thought, everyone has their own way of going mad.

The enforced repatriation of our citizens from the west continued. MGB (KRU) bodies made full use of these extraditions for their own purposes in two particular spheres. In the first place they served to put the wind up our own people and convince them that there was no escape from Soviet power. And secondly they were used to persuade our citizens that the western allies were not to be trusted and were the venal whores that our propaganda made them out to be. They were in addition so afraid of Soviet power that they were ready to do everything they could to get into its good graces.

In those days KRU MGB made wide use of oral and visual propaganda among our troops. Certain of our soldiers and officers who had been handed over by the British and Americans and often been beaten to a pulp on our side, were taken under guard from one unit to another. In each unit meetings were held. The political officers spoke to the assembled people, 'Just take a look at him! This character thought he'd hide himself under the skirts of our allies. He fancied some democracy, ha, ha! Just take a look. This is what will happen to everyone who dares to betray the cause of our Party, the cause of great Stalin.' The appearance of the beaten-up officer spoke volumes. Of course nobody thought of mentioning who had beaten them up or where it had been done. Let people think the worst. Let them think the British and Americans did this for the greater glory of Comrade Stalin. Subsequently, the returnees disappeared into labour camps for periods of from twenty to twenty-five years. Even there however they continued their involuntary and often silent propaganda against the west. The man had run away? Yes, he'd run away. And they had handed him over? Yes, they had handed him over. Well, there you are, you didn't believe our propaganda, kept on talking about western democracy and humaneness. There's your democracy for you!

The French deservedly had the best reputation about extradition They hardly extradited anyone at all. They concealed and assisted people, regardless of the fact that both in the French government and in the Military Intelligence apparatus, there were more than a few communists. Perhaps this was because France had experienced German occupation and the French understood better than the British and the Americans the meaning of striving towards freedom and justice? I don't know.

There were certain items of news in my private life too. My lieutenant-colonel, the Caucasian, was appointed to a new post in the Ministry of State Security in Moscow. He was promoted to the rank of colonel. It was a very sad farewell, in spite of the shashlik which he cooked himself, the Armenian brandy, which I didn't drink, and the vintage white wine, which was superb. There were only two Chekist guests at this celebration, a major from the Third Branch and I. The remainder all came from army circles, the bandmaster, the Baden Commandant's assistant and one or two other people. The colonel, as he had now become, took me aside and told me that he'd put me in for promotion to captain.

'You're an odd chap. Aren't you pleased? You're not twenty-five yet, you know. To be a captain in the State Security Service at your age is not bad going. You'll be past the rank of major before you're thirty. You'll be a great man!'

For a short time he became the old Caucasian lieutenant-colonel of the war years and told me a Caucasian joke.

A young Caucasian dashed into a maternity home. His wife had just had a child. Without any exploratory questions the happy father grabbed the baby, and tossed it high in the air, over and over again, shouting loudly as he did so. 'You'll be an engineer! You'll be a scientist! You'll be a general! You'll be a great man!' Suddenly the child's wrappings came undone and the lower part of its body was exposed. When he saw what there was to see the young father cried in horror, 'You'll be a whore!'

My Caucasian boss had gone. Another kindred spirit had vanished. There was no time however to be bored or lose oneself in thought. There was plenty of work to be done collecting information on the number of unreliable persons arrested and dispatched to the Soviet Union, and other things; compiling bulletins for the Main Administration in Moscow, receiving from them new orders and briefings. But I did find time for some thinking, and some very hard thinking. In our club, which was a former ballroom, with parquet and mosaic floors, there was a meeting of the staff of our administration. Everybody there was a Chekist. There were no outsiders at all. After our lieutenant-general, who was soon to leave for Moscow, had made a speech, our minister, Colonel-General Abakumov, who had flown in from Moscow, took the rostrum. He was wearing a superbly made dark suit and a dark blue tie with a red stripe. He spoke in his customary deliberate, confident voice. Certain things he said I can remember very clearly. Abakumov spoke of the great difficulties

which our Party and our country were experiencing at that particular
time; colossal destruction, famine because of the failure of the harvest,
widespread unrest among the people, often taking active forms. At
the same time it was of paramount importance to create the atomic
bomb, and the most up-to-date conventional weapons and military
equipment as quickly as possible. Factories must also be built for
heavy industry, and iron discipline must be maintained both in the
army and among the population at large.

Abakumov was not in any way urging us on or calling on us to
carry out any epic deeds. He was simply giving us dry facts and plans
for our future work. It was just like being at an operational conference. Strictly speaking, that's exactly what it was, except that the
audience was bigger than usual. His tones remained calm and even.
Just at one point in his speech, he rephrased a famous pre-war
statement of Stalin's. His face became stern, and his hand with its
magnificently polished nails, cut decisively down through the air. I
was sitting in one of the front rows and had a very good view.
'Comrade Stalin once said that if we don't manage to do all these
things very quickly the British and Americans will crush us. After
all they have the atom bomb, and an enormous technical and industrial advantage over us. They are rich countries, which have not been
destroyed by the war. But we will rebuild everything, with our army
and our industry, regardless of the cost. We Chekists are not to be
frightened by problems and sacrifices. It is our good fortune,'
Abakumov went on, 'that the British and the Americans in their
attitudes towards us, have still not emerged from the post-war state
of calf-love. They dream of lasting peace and building a democratic
world for all men. They don't seem to relise that we are the ones who
are going to build a new world and that we shall do it without their
liberal-democratic recipes. All their slobber plays right into our
hands, and we shall thank them for this, in the next world, with
coals of fire. We shall drive them into such dead ends as they've
never dreamed of. We shall disrupt them and corrupt them from
within. We shall lull them to sleep, sap their will to fight. The whole
"free western" world will burst apart like a fat squashed toad. This
won't happen tomorrow. To achieve it will require great efforts on
our part, great sacrifices, and total renunciation of all that is trivial
and personal. Our aim justifies all this. Our aim is a grand one, the
destruction of the old, vile world.'

Abakumov then turned to the Chekists' specific work and tasks.
There were many of them, for the speech was long. I am no lover of

long speeches, but Abakumov's conclusions were as clear as crystal: 'We shall destroy without mercy all who stand in our way and sear with a hot iron any signs of activities which are hostile to us and any hint or thought which comes into conflict with our plans.'

There was an outbreak of cases of suicide among our officers, which was something new and unknown there in peacetime. The reasons for them were all the same. People found that their lives had reached a complete dead end, devoid of all hope or glimpse of light. There was one particular first lieutenant, a duty assistant of the Transport Commandant's Office, who I knew very well. He had gone through the whole war, been more than once wounded and been decorated. At home in the Soviet Union, he had a family; elderly parents and a young wife. They had only just got married when the war broke out. The small town where they lived soon fell into German hands. His father was employed in some minor capacity in the local burgo-master's administration. When our people came back, the father was sent off to a labour camp as a collaborator and the old lady was thrown out of her flat and deprived of her food ration card. Heaven knows how she managed to live, begging here and there and being helped by kind folk. The young wife was seduced by an employee of the Muni-cipal Party Committee. He put her in the family way. The first lieutenant told his friends about all this when he came back from a home leave. He then went to his quarters put his gun inside his mouth and pulled the trigger. The story of this officer's family is depressing but far from unique.

I experienced no such tragedies as these. I simply came to the firm conclusion that I no longer wanted to work in the MGB system. I no longer wanted to assist in the realisation of our magnificent aim, in the cause of destroying the old world and creating the new. Let those who would get on with the job. I had no wish to and that was all there was to it.

The extradition of our people who went over to the west con-tinued, although on a somewhat smaller scale. Many prominent people in the west, one of whom was Eleanor Roosevelt, the widow of the late president, protested and demanded that an end should be put to such extraditions. All this I knew from what was published in the western newspapers and broadcast over the radio and from the bulletins which were compiled regularly in KRU. Such bulletins have always been compiled, though not of course for general circula-tion. I don't know what caused Mrs. Roosevelt to take this stand.

Perhaps it was her conscience trying to neutralise the activities of her late husband. I personally believe that President Roosevelt was irresponsible because without having the slightest understanding of the Soviet social structure he dared to become president of the most powerful nation in the world.

For a long time Stalin could not understand Roosevelt, he could not understand whether Roosevelt was putting on an act, or whether God had really made him the way he was. I think that Stalin must often have wanted to ask Roosevelt, as we used to joke in school, 'Are you really like that, old chap? And what did you have for your breakfast this morning?'

The fact that I had no wish to be extradited into the hands of the MGB restrained me from fleeing to the west at the first possible chance. There were other restraining factors, such as my parents, in particular my father. Of course no one, even in the MGB, could accuse him of collaborating in my defection to the west, but even so . . . It is this 'even so' which has tormented me all these years. Even when I was sure that my father was no longer alive, I was unable to rid myself of a feeling of guilt.

There were other problems of a purely technical nature. I decided not to make any sensational disclosures. In the first place I was thinking about my parents, and in the second place, I already knew certain facts about the western allies and was inclined to think that although my disclosures were unlikely to change the world, they could well bring misfortune down on my relations. In fact I knew the MGB better than I knew the west.

I decided that I would escape, not as a Chekist officer, but as an ordinary Soviet citizen. For this I needed a separate set of personal papers, but that was not the main problem, for I often went into the western sectors of Vienna in civilian clothing, carrying papers in a different name and a different occupation from my own. There was nothing at all illegal about this. I would hardly have been likely to go into the western sectors on some service mission with Third Branch KRU MGB papers in my pocket. This situation was not really much different from when my Chekist colleagues and I flew to the partisans behind the German lines, with equally false papers in our pockets. I prepared my new papers lovingly, with my own hands, taking special steps to make them look slightly dog-eared. When I had finished writing, I sent for the sergeant-major clerk, who looked after the seal, and opened the pages of the new papers in front of him. He slapped his seal down on each side of each page. This took place at the HQ of one of our corps. I was often there on official business and often used that same seal for similar business purposes. A little later I handed this document to the Americans.

Without much fuss, and without arousing anyone's suspicions, I also fitted myself out with a green card, the identification of a civilian employee of one of the Soviet administrations in Austria. These administrations were mushrooming: oil, textile, leather dressing, etc. It was just as easy for a Chekist officer to acquire such a document as it was for him to possess a pile of warrants for arrest and imprisonment, complete with the signature and seal of the prosecutor of the RSFSR, and an empty space into which some client's name could be inserted when necessary. No, my difficulties were of quite a different sort. How should I effect the operational side of my defection to the west? There I had plenty to think of.

As a result of grandfather's influence, I still tended to favour the British. I knew however that as far as operational intelligence techniques were concerned, the Americans were on a better footing in Vienna and I had more chance of being flown out to their zone unobserved. This turned out to be correct. I decided that it really didn't matter very much and that I would first go to the Americans and then slip over to England. I had no urge to cross the ocean. Even today I am grateful to God and my grandfather that I made this choice.

Next came points of detail in the general plan. What I would do and what I shouldn't do in which situations? I wanted to have at least forty-eight hours in reserve so that nobody started to look for me at once. I wanted to leave behind me all personal documents in any way connecting me with the State Security Service and I also wanted to leave a set of false tracks, so that when my own people began looking for me, they would look in completely the wrong direction. I needed to have on me a loaded pistol, the reason for which should be self-evident, and not to take anything at all with me, to avoid attracting attention. I also had a list of 'do's and don'ts'. I must not enter any American institution in Vienna, as they were all under surveillance by our operational groups, either through their own or their Austrian agents. I must not take with me a single kopek or article belonging to the Soviet service, or meet anybody at all on the day of my defection. There was also a series of purely technical and operational points.

I thought with great warmth and gratitude of my teachers and instructors in the State Security school at Babushkin. I am sure that without the knowledge which they had imparted, things would have been a great deal more difficult.

I decided to say that after bathing and spending a long time lying on the grass by the river, I had developed a dreadful cold and was running a high tempeature. I informed my boss about this. He advised me to lie up at home and take aspirins, followed by hot tea with lemon and honey. My cold was of course non-existent, but I now had at least forty-eight hours to play about with. I placed my personal MGB officer's identification card in the drawer of my desk at the administration, and handed the key to the administration duty officer in accordance with the rules. Now nobody would think that I had run off to anyone, anywhere, with an MGB document. I sat in my flat and wrote a letter. This was the gist of it.

'Dear Tadpole, [Imagine trying to find out which of the thousands of officers in our group was nicknamed Tadpole].

I am sure that I can help in the matter of getting permission for your mother to come here. [At that time officers were allowed to bring wives, children and sometimes other members of their families to live with the occupation forces. It's true that where mothers were concerned things were not quite so straightforward, but with good connections it was not altogether impossible. In the context of the letter I was just such a good contact]. Unfortunately I am very busy. To get to you I need at least a couple of days. [Let them work that out! Two days meant further away than either Austria or Czechoslovakia i.e. either Hungary or Roumania. Let them look for me there!] I envy you being married. I myself am thinking about uniting my destiny with that of a delightful water nymph, who dwells on the banks of the Volga. We are very fond of one another. In August I'm going to ask my superiors for urgent leave. I shall bring her back here and don't you try to pinch her. [Excellent. I want to get married. I'm dreaming about meeting my intended. I want to go on leave. Let them read it and think it all over.] For the present I can't wait to see you and your charming little curly-headed wife. What splendid cabbage soup and pies she cooks! I'll bring a drop of rather special booze with me.' [I wish them luck trying to find who's got a curly-headed wife who cooks good pies.]

I went on to write that I was hoping to nip over and see Tadpole for a couple of days or so in the near future. 'And if I can't get leave,

I'll just take my chance', I joked. I then added that if I managed to get news to him of the day of my arrival through some officer who was going in his direction I wouldn't bother sending that letter. 'After all, by the time it gets there through the post . . .' [Let them find out which officers were travelling in which direction.] I screwed the letter up slightly and threw it into the waste paper basket by my desk, making sure that the writing was visible. I then took two narrow strips of tissue paper, which burns very quickly. I printed an English sentence neatly on each [I didn't know any English, I obtained a dictionary, then got rid of it.] On the first paper I wrote: 'Please call CIC, very urgent-important. Let me sit in your back room.' On the second piece: 'Please take me with you. It's very important. I am from Soviet Staff Administration. But don't take me to your official building or residence.'

I took a box of matches, and folded the strips of paper up very small. I made a small mark on one of them with my fountain pen so as not to confuse them. I then put the tiny rolls of paper in among the match heads, so they weren't noticeable. In case of emergency I would put a cigarette in my mouth, light one of the matches and contrive to set the box on fire, so that the paper would burn up, together with the match heads. This was something that happened quite often anyway. To complete the effect of distracting people's attention, one could grasp one's hand and wave it about as though it had been burnt.

I changed my clothes and put on a greeny-grey civilian suit, a light grey shirt, a greyish tie and black shoes. Nothing must stand out or attract attention. Even my shoes should not be too shiny. My hair was neatly combed, but I took care not to have a parting or wear any hair dressing. In my inside pocket I had my new papers, but they didn't look too new. I had a wad of Austrian notes in my other pockets, but not too much. In the right-hand pocket of my trousers was my Browning with a full magazine. I also had a block of my favourite plain chocolate and the usual trifles like a handkerchief a fountain pen and a comb.

I sat on my bed and suffered agonies of apprehension. It was already past mid-day. It was summer and the evenings were long. I wanted to arrive at the right place just as twilight was descending and everything had a grey look about it. The trip to Vienna on the electric train went off well enough. None of our people saw me on the way. I spent the journey with my nose in an Austrian newspaper, like most of the rest of the passengers. I left the newspaper on the carriage seat, so as not to be cluttered up with unnecessary objects. I spent some time riding round the western sectors in tram cars, then I sat for a while in a park, surrounded by Austrians, chewing my chocolate, smoking and thinking.

My girl friend in Baden, Gilda, should not suffer in any way because of my defection. I had told her the week before that I was making quite a long journey on service matters and would be away for a week or two. I had said that an officer friend of mine would be in my flat temporarily and asked her not to call there, as he was far more handsome than I, and I feared for her honour. Gilda was indignant, but I calmed her down, saying that when I got back from my trip, I would call round at her home. In any case I had been careful not to advertise my contact with Gilda in any way in the administration. The only person who knew about it was the Caucasian colonel and he was over the hills and far away in Moscow. The owners of the house where I lived saw me very rarely anyway, as I had my own key and separate entrance. The key I had left in the summer house in their garden, with some other keys and tools. It was rather rude, but what else could I do? I tried not to think about either my parents or my homeland, but couldn't quite manage it. I also tried to banish thoughts of my own person and what might happen to me quite soon. The sun set and everything around became grey. I was on my way.

While I was in Vienna, after I'd decided to defect, I had explored mentally thousands of possibilities, trying to find the most suitable place. The place needed to have two particular features. There must be direct contact with the Americans, without an Austrian intermediary, and it must not be under observation by our services. This didn't seem much to ask for, but oh, how difficult it was to find. In a corner of the American sector, well away from the main streets, was a branch of the American information service. It was a completely innocuous place. Austrians used to go there if they wanted to find out how to make contact with relatives in the USA, what papers they had to fill in to request a trip to the USA, and so forth. There were two rooms in the hut, a large workroom or office, and behind it a small cubby hole. Two Austrian officials worked permanently in the large room with an American supervisor. He wasn't there all the time. I plucked up courage, took the first strip of paper out of the matchbox and held it in my hand.

'The American's hardly likely to phone the Soviet Commandant's Office,' I thought. 'But who knows? I'll have to wait and see.'

I went in and muttered, '. . . *uten Abend*' and handed the American my piece of paper. He ran his eyes over it and his face began to look serious, but not hostile. He said something to me quickly and nodded towards the door into the small room. I quickly took my piece of paper back from him, which caused him to look at me in surprise although he didn't say anything. I followed him into the small room, sat down and nodded my head at him. I lit a cigarette and burned the first piece of paper. He went back into the large room. I hadn't paid any attention to the two Austrians who were sitting there with him. There was nothing more I could do now.

I strained myself to hear all that I could through the open door. There was a brief telephone conversation in which I didn't think I heard the words 'Commandant's Office'. The American came back into the room and said something from which I only recognised the words, 'Fine . . .' and '. . . OK' and something else about minutes. Soon I heard the noise of a car engine outside. The vehicle drew right up on to the pavement. I put my hand in my pocket for a box of matches. Two young Americans walked in. I remember they were both wearing raincoats, though heaven knows why, because it was very warm. The first one took my second piece of paper. He asked about something or other. I shook my head and nodded towards the street, to suggest that he get a move on. One of them went out of the hut, came back and waved with his hand for us to follow him. We went out and I flopped into the back of a covered jeep.

The jeep got off the spot no slower than Beria's Horch and dashed through the dark streets of Vienna. I asked them in German not to take me to any official building. They answered in German of about my standard, that they understood and wouldn't do that. Then they asked me whether I was from Zheltov's or Kurasov's part of Soviet Admin HQ.

'Actually,' I said, 'I worked under Anisimov.'

They nodded. 'Well,' I thought, 'that's another Nikolai Petrovich that God's sent me.'

Lieutenant-General Nikolai Petrovich Anisimov was a Deputy Commander-in-Chief of TsGV, chief of the second echelon of the group. This echelon was mentioned in my new, home-made papers. The Americans wouldn't be disappointed in me however, I knew every branch and administration and almost all the generals and officers in Anisimov's outfit in Modling. And how! After all, they had always been the reserve next door to them and other things too, first of all Smersh and later KRU MGB. And that wasn't all I knew.

We could talk about everything, except of course, Korolyov's outfit.

I remember other Americans asking me afterwards in Vienna, 'Have you heard anything about Lieutenant-General Korolyov?'

'Not very much,' I answered.

'Is it true,' they asked, 'that he got the name Korolyov from Korol' meaning king, because of his important job as chief of the MGB?'

I nearly burst stifling my laughter, but I just shrugged my shoulders and said I didn't know anything about things like that.

I was put to live in an average-sized hotel, not far from one of the small stations in Vienna. I had a comfortable room with a bathroom, etc. I spent a whole month there. I had everything I needed, good food and service, from a silent servant girl, piles of American magazines with long-legged beauties in the illustrations. There was only one thing missing. Peace. I was never free from the constant dread that suddenly the door would open and in would come Soviet soldiers with sub-machine guns. Of course, I had my Browning . . . First one for myself, or how would it be? I thought my way through it all over and over again.

An amiable, friendly American came to see me many times. I can still remember his name, or his code name. In answer to my questions about how and when, he used to answer, 'Not yet, but soon now.' On one occasion he told me, 'The Soviet authorities are looking for you, you know. They asked us whether we'd seen anything of you.' That didn't frighten me particularly. I had after all signed for having received the green card of the civilian administration in their office, indicating its number and adding, 'For service reasons.' This is how it was always done for the purpose of the administrations records.

I had no doubt that my bosses in the MGB would go through everything connected with my person in methodical detail, all my trips, all my service connections, operational documents which I had used earlier. This was also routine. I was far more interested in something else, which was why I quickly asked the American, who spoke excellent Russian, 'And what answer did you make to this request by the Soviet authorities?'

He winked at me cheerfully, 'We told them that we didn't know anyone of that name.'

Then there were more days of tortured anticipation before the flight in a small aeroplane across the Soviet zone of occupation, to the west.

Epilogue

FOR A LONG TIME I could not make up my mind whether to publish this book, even when I was quite sure that I had no close relatives still alive in the Soviet Union. What's the point of turning up a whole lot of things that are over and done with, I thought. Some of my close friends, however, used all their powers of persuasion to urge me to do so.

'There are after all,' they said, 'only a handful of people in the west who graduated from the same finishing school as you did. It's your duty to tell people here what it was like.'

In the west there is far too much loose and inaccurate writing about Soviet Russia. I'm not put out by the ordinary western traveller. Let him write what he can within the limits of his experience. I do think however, that western politicians, diplomats, journalists, professors, in other words anyone who earns his daily bread or a part of it by writing or teaching Soviet affairs and, what is more important, thereby influences and instructs the major part of his fellow citizens, really should ask himself constantly, 'Am I really writing accurately? Do I understand the situation in the USSR?' and finally, 'Who is harmed by, and benefits from what I write and teach?'

People will claim that I think everyone except myself in the field of Soviet studies is an uneducated fool. This is not true. They are not at all badly educated, but how and by whom were they educated? Is it really from the west's point of view, a useful exercise to antagonise the whole Russian nation with a constant barrage of insults and denigration? The Soviet communist regime, after all, has never nurtured, nor does it now nurture, any feelings of warmth towards the west. On the contrary, it works actively and by no means ineffectively for our destruction. What will happen to the west and to democracy if the Russian people begin to hate us and all we stand for, and begin to support the Soviet regime, as the mass of the German people supported Hitler?

How many ordinary people here in the west know, for example, that the Russian people never elected the communists to power by normal democratic methods such as those by which Hitler or for that matter all the western governments, however stupid, were elected? How many people here know that the communists seized power in Russia by force, that a civil war against them began immediately, and in some places went on for six years? That the fight against Soviet power in Russia never stopped, but kept on flaring up first in one place, then in another? Who in the west is aware that Soviet power is maintained in Russia by brute force, because it has created an apparatus of terror and coercion such as history has seldom before seen?

Up to and during the last war, the Russian people believed fiercely in the west, thinking that it understood their incredible difficulties and their yearnings for freedom. Unfortunately after the war, these natural feelings were allowed to degenerate.

Professors have taught generations of western students of Russia about 'bloody Czarism' and the inveterate brutality and dull-wittedness of the Russian people. The pupils of such professors are to be found today among western specialists in Sovietology, teachers, lecturers, diplomats, officers in the armed forces, in intelligence and counter-intelligence, journalists, and of course, in the new generation of professors.

The west today is hardly in a winning position, either from the diplomatic, political or strategic points of view, even at the most optimistic assessment. I do not discuss economics, because it is not my field, but even here we haven't any great achievements to register. Admittedly the western standard of living is higher than that of the Soviet Union. But the Soviet regime does not remain in power in Russia by dint of the quantity of refrigerators, televisions, motor-cars, butter, meat and other things it produces for its citizens. It remains in power through terror and brute force. Only in the most exceptional circumstances, when the authorities are having a particularly difficult time, are they forced to make certain concessions or improvements of an economic nature from which their citizens benefit. As a rule Soviet power spends vast sums of money producing articles of which the Russian people may have no need whatsoever, but which are very useful for strengthening Soviet influence in the world and destroying the west. Even after long, long years of experience this is not understood here.

The KGB MVD system still blossoms in all its former glory. Self-conscious, Orwellian camouflage titles like 'The Ministry for the

Preservation of Social Order' have been cast aside. As in Stalin's time the top leaders of the KGB are elected openly to the Politbureau and the Central Committee of the Party. The KGB has been having a prolonged honeymoon in the west for many years now. No one seems anxious to emulate the brave deed of my fellow Britons in expelling 105 Chekists. On the contrary, many in the west have taken offence at what we did. The behaviour of Belgium, where the NATO HQ is situated, is a case in point. The Belgians quietly, almost apologetically, expelled a group of KGB officers, stating as they did so, 'We are after all anxious to improve contacts between east and west, and are in favour of European security.' The KGB too is in favour of contacts, and security. And not only in Europe at that! Not for nothing is it called the Committee of State Security.

But the aims of the KGB are a little different from those of the west. It is time our leaders and opinion-formers realised that the fundamental aims of the whole Soviet regime have not altered since 1917, and are not likely to do so in future.

Index

Compiled by F. D. Buck

ABAKUMOV, COL.-GEN. V. S., 60 fn, 65,
  69, 93, 99, 130, 144, 169, 172,
  178, 183–92 *passim*, 210, 212, 220,
  234, 237–9 *passim*
air raid, first, 36
Alexander, Field Marshal, 154
Allenstein Training Area, 200
Allied Control Council in Vienna, 171
Alliluyeva, Nadezhda, 213
Alma Ata, 140
Anders, Lt.-Gen., 138, 139
Andrasi, Count, 206
Antipenko, Lt.-Gen. N., 132
Appollonov, Col.-Gen., 141
Attlee, Clement, 235
Austrian Communist Party, 149, 158

BABI YAR, 116
Babushkin, 46, 49, 67, 241
Badmanshin, Sgt.-Major, 215
Baltic Front, operational branch, 126
Bandera, Stepan, 126
Baumanovka, 192
Bel'chenko, Col.-Gen. S. S., 93, 191
Belgorod-Kursk, battle of, 134
Belkin, Lt.-Gen. M. I., 192
Beria, Lavrenti, 55, 61, 64, 67, 120,
  138, 141–4 *passim*, 173, 177–81
  passim, 185, 187, 191, 192, 210,
  212, 214, 215, 217, 245
Berlin, 128, 130, 133, 134, 142, 150
  attack on, 131
'Black Death', 176
Bolshevik-communists, 57
Bolshoi Theatre, 66, 78 fn
Boyarsky, Colonel, 150
Brauder, Yosif Abramovich (*see* Yoska)
Brezhnev, L. I., 30 fn
British Security Service, 160
Budapest, 192–5 *passim*, 200–1,
  passim, 205, 211
  transit station, 196

'Budeonnovka', 14, 14 fn
Budyonny, Marshal S. M., 14, 16
Bulganin, Nikolai, 181

CAPITULATION, THE, 142
Central Group of Forces (see TsGV)
Cheka, 212, 221
Chekists, 16, 26, 27, 31, 33–5, 38, 46,
  52, 53, 55–60 *passim*, 67, 71,
  77, 86, 89, 96, 99, 101, 102, 109,
  110, 112, 116, 118, 127, 143, 144,
  146, 170, 179, 181, 182, 185, 202,
  204, 210, 211, 213, 219, 221,
  225, 226, 228, 230, 231, 232, 237,
  238, 240
  agents, 123
  Badge of Merit, 56
  circles, 146, 189
  demolition squads, 87
  discipline, 92
  generals, 132
  identity document, 207
  investigators, 193
  officers, 145, 154, 171, 173, 175,
    178, 180, 192, 197, 209, 210,
    226, 227, 240, 241
  operational, 34, 146
  partisans, 99
  personnel, 117
  professional, 90, 93, 94, 95, 142,
    217
  regular, 72
  secret agents, 89
  soldiers, 167, 168
Chernyshov, Col.-Gen., 60, 69, 165,
  192
ChON, 135
Chugunov, 127
Churchill, Winston, 29, 141, 147,
  154, 196, 235, 236
CIC, 160, 243
CID, the, 77, 78

Clausewitz, Karl von 170
Committee of Liberation of the
    Peoples of Russia, 127
Communist Party(ies), 161
    foreign, 59
Corrective Labour Camps, 64
Council of People's Commissars of
    the USSR, 170
counter-intelligence, 160, 161
    German, 53
    Hungarian, 54, 194
    military, 60 fn (*see also* Smersh)
    (see also Smersh GUKR)
'Crazy Rosa', 12, 83
criminal(s), 80, 82, 85
Criminal Code, 50, 198, 229
criminal jargon, 75
'Crossed Arrows' party, 194

DEATH'S HEAD DIVISION, 221
demobilisation, 148, 163
Diana, 217, 219, 220
dog-training school, 140
Dresden, 118, 128, 148, 152
Dubcek, Alexander, 150
Dubinin, Maj.-Gen. N., 221
Dzerzhinsky, Division, 135
Dzerzhinsky, Felix, Edmundovich, 60,
    135, 185, 221

EHRENBURG, ILYA, 213
Eisenhower, Gen. Dwight, 134, 135
El'Registan, 146, 147
Evtushenko, Evgeni, 179

FEDOTOV, LT.-GEN., 54, 119
Field Security Service, 160
First Belorussian Front, 128, 132,
    133, 134, 142
First Circle, The, 187, 188
First Ukrainian Front, 87, 116, 127,
    129, 133, 134, 142, 143, 147,
    148, 150
    Rearguard Administration, 101
Fourth Ukrainian Front, 134, 150
Franz-Josef, Kaiser, 162, 217
French Security Service, 161
Funk, Chief Justice, 96

GEHLEN, MAJ.-GEN. REINHARD, 126
Georgia, menshevik government,
    181
German Ministry of Eastern
    Territories, 119

German School of Military
    Engineering, 142
Gestapo, 124, 127, 152, 194
Gilda, 154, 156–7, 159, 162, 169,
    200, 208, 221, 223, 244
Goebbels, Dr. Paul Josef, 123, 125
Golikov, Col.-Gen. P. I., 170
Gorky, 42, 49, 50, 62 fn, 87 fn, 213
Gorky Gunnery School, 225
Gorky, Maxim, 104
Grebennik, Lt.-Gen., 205
GRU, 119, 130, 137, 138, 139, 218
    agents, 125
    Main Intelligence Administration, 170
    MGB, 180
GUGB, 137, 138
    Foreign Intelligence Administration,
    137
GUKR (*see* Smersh)
GULAG (*see* Corrective Labour
    Camps and NKGB)

HASEK, JAROSLAV, 21
Hero of the Soviet Union, 73, 110,
    162, 228
    Gold Star of, 22, 73
    Order of Lenin, 73 fn,
Heydrich, Reinhard, 152
Himmler, Heinrich, 52, 107, 125
Hitler, Adolf, 25, 52, 53, 54, 107,
    116, 118, 122, 126, 144, 148, 152,
    157, 158, 196, 221
Hungarian pro-fascist party, 194
Hungary:
    Allied Control Commission, 209
    Security Service of, 205

ILGEN, GENERAL, 95
Intelligence-Sabotage (see NKGB,
    Fourth Administration)
Investigation Administration (*see*
    Smersh, Fourth Admin.)
investigators, 71
Ivashutin, Lt.-Gen. P. I., 191

JUDICIAL *troikas*, 71

KAGANOVICH, LAZAR, 21
Kalinin, President Mikhail, 229
Kamanin, Nikolai Petrovich, 21,
    22, 23, 161, 162
Kapel'son, Dr., 214
Katyn, 136
    affair, the, 137

Kemelharito, 54, 194
KGB, 135, 140, 191, 218
  archives, 136
  frontier troops, 140
  Ukrainian, 227
Kharkov, 115
  region, 83
Khodov, 214, 215
Khomenko, Maj.-Gen., 176
Khrushchev, Nikita, 33, 90 fn, 101,
  102, 103, 104, 181, 190, 212
  bodyguard, 103
Kiev, 26, 86, 87, 102, 108, 115, 227,
  230
Kiev State University, 226
Kirov, Sergei Mironovitch (Kostrikov),
  10, 10 fn, 15, 26, 26 fn, 30
Koch, Gauleiter Erich, 96
Komsomol(s), 21, 26, 36, 51, 90, 92,
  97, 117, 226
  badge, 22, 23
  local, 92
  meetings, 51
  Municipal Committee, 22, 26
  organisation, 71, 90
Komsorg, 51
Konev, Marshal Ivan Stephanovich,
  103, 121, 132, 133, 147, 153, 165,
  218
Korolyov, Lt.-Gen., 93, 120, 134, 144,
  153, 206, 214
Kostik, 216, 219, 220
Koval'chuk, Lt.-Gen. N., 134
KR Branches, 231
Krainyukov, Lt.-Gen. K. V., 104, 132
Krasnov, General P. N., 126, 153, 154,
  169
Kravchenko, Commissar, 138
Kremlin, 141, 145, 146, 180, 214, 219
KRU, 239, 245
  Administration, 205
  MGB, 196, 198
    First Branches, 204
    Third Administration, 198
  Third Branch, 195, 235
Kruglov, Col.-Gen. S. N., 141, 177,
  184, 191
Krupskaya, Nadezhda Konstantinova,
  15, 15 fn
Kurasov, Col.-Gen. V. V., 160, 214,
  245
Kuznetsky Most, 66
Kuznetzov, Col.-Gen. F. F., 33, 93,
  119, 130

LABOUR CAMPS, 73, 78
Lebedenko, Lt.-Gen., 159
Lemeshev, Sergei, 78
Lenin, Vladimir Ilyich, 15, 33, 86,
  87, 135, 147, 159, 229
  death of, 22 fn
  statue of, 33
Lenin days, 22
Lenin Mausoleum, 87, 111, 145, 146,
  148, 166
Leningrad (Petersburg), 9, 10, 16,
  25, 46, 129
  battle of, 176
  blockade, the, 26
Lidice, 152
'Little Star', 106
Lobachevsky, N. I., 182
London, 211
Lubianka, 183
Lukin, Lt.-Gen. Mikhail, 81 fn
Lvov, 87, 100

MAKAROV, 26, 27
Malenkov, Georgi M., 215
Maryjka, 205, 206, 208
Medvedev, Colonel, 99
Mein Kampf, 157
Mendelyeev, Dmitri, 182, 186
Merkulov, Commissar V. N., 48, 55, 61,
  138, 173, 187, 190, 212
MGB (*see* Smersh)
Mikhailovna, Elizaveta, 47, 83, 84, 85,
  86
Mikoyan, Anastas I., 210
Military Institute of Foreign
  Languages, 218
Military Intelligence, 236
Military Red Banner, Order of, 52
Minim, Kuzma, 87
Ministry of Propaganda, 119
Ministry of State Security, 237
Minyuk, General, 146
Mironych (*see* Kirov)
Modling, 159, 204, 245
Molotov, V. M., 49, 210
Molotov Gunnery School, 42
Montgomery, General Bernard, 134,
  135
Moscow, 25, 45, 61, 66, 68, 82, 93,
  95, 97, 99, 103, 130, 131, 141,
  144, 145, 149, 150, 154, 159, 160,
  165, 170, 179, 181–3, 186, 187,
  191–3, 217, 225, 231, 244
  battle of, 133, 134, 176

City Commandant, 81
defence district, 63
defence of, 141
Military Commandant of, 142
Police Administration, 182
Munnich, Ferenc, 204
MVD, 178, 194, 196
  frontier troops, 210, 211
  internal troops, 140 fn, 231
  prison camps, 124
  prison carriages, 231
  soldiers, 193
  troops, 195, 205, 206, 209, 216,
    228

NAPOLEONIC WARS, 9
nationalism, Hungarian, 54
Nedosekin, Col.-Gen., 64, 138
Nikolaievich, Viktor, 215
Nina, 233
Nizhni-Novgorod (*see* Gorky)
NKGB, 61, 63, 70, 73, 75, 81, 90,
    91, 93, 101, 117, 123–4, 127, 130,
    135, 138, 151, 163–4, 177–8
  Administration, 72, 80
  agents, 154
  counter-intelligence, 64
  Economic Administration, 172
  Foreign Intelligence Administration,
    119, 120
  Fourth Administration, 62, 93,
    119, 124
  GSPU, 170
  Industrial Administration, 172
  Intelligence-Sabotage (*see* Fourth
    Administration)
  Main Administration, 69, 138
    Foreign Intelligence, 130, 138
    Secret Political, 170
  Main Operational Administration,
    135, 141, 145
  military counter-intelligence, 62
  Municipal, 86
  Operational Administration, 172–3
  personnel, 67
  regional administration, 85
  school, 73, 112, 179
  Second Operational Group, 145
  Secret Political Administration, 119,
    172
  staff, 70
  system, 167, 177, 178
  Ukrainian, 116
NKVD, 16, 26–8 *passim*, 32, 34, 38,

44–8 *passim*, 55, 56, 61, 64, 73,
    80, 87, 90, 99, 102, 130, 134–41
    passim, 177–8, 206, 232
  Administration, 15
  agents, 125
  Auxiliary Group, 27, 31, 34
  auxiliary police group, 92
  chain, 177
  club, 26, 60
  communications forces, 72
  Demolition Battalion, 36, 37, 42,
    45, 49, 86, 92
  field communications, 39
  forces, 67, 70, 131
  guards, 34
  GUGB, Special Branch, 183
  GULAG, 138, 177
    Third Administration, 73, 173
    Investigation Administration, 173
  link men, 91
  Main Administration, 136, 141
    Operational Administration, 136
  network, 141
  Police Administration, 173
  prison camps, 124
  Regional Administration, 26
    Operational Branch, 33
  school, 46, 49, 50, 51, 58, 63
  Secret Political Branch, 34
  Special Branch, 41
  subversive groups, 38
  system, 46, 61, 167, 177, 178
  troops, 88, 130, 135, 140, 142, 149,
    154, 168, 172, 176, 191
    escort, 139
    frontier, 70, 139, 174, 191
    internal, 61 fn, 73, 139, 142,
      145, 153, 167, 174, 177
    motorised, 134
Nonna, 20, 21, 23, 24, 25, 27, 35, 86
Novikov, Lt.-Gen., 141
NSDAP, 158

ODER, 129
Odessa, 113
Onyanov, Lt.-Gen., 138
Order of Lenin, 73 fn, 197
Order of the Patriotic War, 106, 117
Order of the Red Star, 106, 117
Organisation of Ukrainian
    Nationalists, 100
Ostarbeiters, 169, 172
OUN (*see* Organisation of Ukrainian
    Nationalists)

PANFILOV, GENERAL, 139
'Partisan of the Patriotic War', 108
partorg, 51
Party meetings, 51
Party organisation, 71, 90
Paulus, Field-Marshal, 213
penal battalions, 74
People's Commissariat of
    Communications, 139
People's Commissariat of Defence, 69
Peter the Great, 9, 40
Petersburg (*see* Leningrad)
Petofi, Sandor, 202
Petrov, General, 131, 132
Petylura, Simon, 107
PKF, 124
Pitovranov, Lt.-Gen. E. P., 119
Politbureau, 21 fn, 48, 55, 101, 179,
    180, 209, 212, 218
Potsdam, 141
Pozharsky, Prince Dmitri, 87
prison(s), 73
    camps, 124
    carriages, 231
Public Security Service, 160

RADIK, 218
Raichman, Lt.-Gen. L., 137
Red Army Personnel Administration, 81
Red Banner of Labour, Order of, 52 fn
Regional Defence Committee, 34, 41
Repatriation of Soviet Citizens, 170
Reserve Formation Units, 72
Revolution, the October, 9–11, 18,
    32, 60, 105, 183, 213
    parade, 31 *et seq*
Ribbentrop, Joachim von, 25, 125
rights, prisoners loss of, 77 fn
ROA (*see* Russian Army of
    Liberation)
Rockets, VI & V2, 99
Rokossovsky, Marshal K. K., 132,
    133, 147, 165, 166
Roman Catholic Church, 59
Romanchenko V. N., Police Commissar,
    186
'Romanov, A. I.':
    at university, 35
    becomes member of NKGB, 61
    childhood, 11 *et seq*
    commissioned, 66
    defection, 244
    demobilisation work, 163
    family, 9 *et seq*

first action, 39
goes to Kursk, 87
in Baden, 148
in Budapest, 192
investigation work, 149
involved with jews, 31
military hospital, in, 40
mobilised, 37
NKVD, joins, 27
NKVD school, 45 *et seq*
promotion, 144
return to Moscow, 82
Smersh, joins 65
transferred to State Security, 45
victory parade and, 145
wounded, 209
youth, 20 *et seq*
Roosevelt, Eleanor, 239
Roosevelt, Franklin D., 141, 147, 240
Rosa, 109–18 *passim*
Rosenberg, Alfred, 123, 125
Rotmistrov, Marshal, 134
RSFSR, 241
Rudolfovna, Alma, 216
Rudolfovna, Sylva, 180, 215
Russian Army of Liberation, 126
Rybalko, Marshal, 134

SARATOV, 77
    Region, 67
Saska, 211, 212
Second Baltic Front, 82
Second Belorussian Front, 132 fn
    124, 147
Second Soviet Strike Army, 126
Second Ukrainian Front, 150
Secret Services of Mussovat, 181
Security Service, 192, 204
Semyonovich, Viktor, 212
Serov, Col.-Gen. I. A., 134, 142, 184,
    190, 191
Shafirov, Capt., 48
Shakers, the, 59
Shandruk, Lt.-Gen., 126
Shatlosh, General, 95
Shcherbakov, Maj.-Gen., 198
Shkuro, Lt.-Gen. A. G., 154
Shul'zhenko, Maj.-Gen., Boris,
    226, 227
Sikorski, Wladyslaw, 139
Simonev, Konstantin, 114, 115
Sinilov, Lt.-Gen. K. R., 142
Smersh, 44, 60, 65, 67, 69–72, 80–1,
    83, 88–9, 93–4, 97, 103, 106, 109,

118–19, 126–7, 131–2, 134–5, 143, 149, 151, 153, 155–6, 158–9, 161, 164, 167–8, 170–1, 175, 187–8, 191, 193, 245

Administration, 93, 95, 99, 100, 129, 153, 163, 165, 174, 176

of the Front, 95–7, 99, 119, 144

agents, 169

auxiliary servicing administration, 71

Communications section, 116

Counter-Espionage Branch (DKR), 105

demobilisation and, 164

end of, 192

Fifth Administration, 71, 193

First Administration, 68, 80, 127

First Branch, 118, 163, 164

Fourth Administration, 71, 193

Front HQ, 116, 152

GUKR (Counter Intelligence), 62, 64–6, 68, 79, 89, 92–3, 95–6, 116–17, 119–20, 136, 138, 145, 148, 159–60, 165, 169–70, 172, 175, 178, 181, 183, 185

administration, 205

investigator, 205

provincial administration, 222

Main Administration, 192

MGB, 178, 180–2, 185–6, 189, 191–4, 196, 204, 209, 217, 218, 221, 223, 225, 228, 231–2, 234, 239, 240, 246

reserve. 83

Third Secret Administration, 178

identifiers, 185

in Vienna, 159

Intelligence-Sabotage group, 95

Main Administration, 71, 84, 86, 96, 108, 118–19, 145, 161, 163, 237

Military Council of the Front, 101

Operational Section, 101

personnel, 101

Military Police, 70

officers, 71, 77, 78

OKR, 129, 192 (*see* Counter-Espionage Branch)

Operational Administration, 70, 80

Technical Branch, 80

Operational Branch, 99, 153

Operational Groups, 72, 102, 150, 152, 158, 159

Operational Records Section, 99

Operational Reserve, 82, 87, 88

operational-sabotage groups, 80, 95

Second Section, 88, 89

permanent regiment representation, 167

PFK (*see* Vetting and Screening Commissions)

Second Administration, 70

Special branches, 182

technical communications, 72

Third Administration, 70, 136, 155

Third Branch, 130, 143–4, 149, 164, 173, 194, 205, 237

Vetting and Screening Commissions, (PFK), 172–4 *passim*

Smolensk, 136

Solzhenitsyn, Alexander, 187–8

Soviet Army, Main Political Administration, 204

special services:

American, 58

British, 57

German, 53

Hungarian, 54

Special Soviet Mission to London, 170

Stalin, Joseph, 16, 19, 24–6, 49, 51–2, 55–6, 60, 67–9, 73, 76, 79, 102, 110, 128, 130, 133–4, 138, 141–2, 145, 147–8, 150, 166, 170, 176–81 *passim*, 185, 189, 209, 212–13, 215, 228, 235–6, 238, 240

death of, 142, 178, 181

personal bodyguard, 145

Stalin, Svetlana, 179, 180, 181

Stalin, Vassili, 180

Stalingrad, 59, 60, 61, 131, 165

battle of, 133, 134, 176, 213

front, 170

State Committee for Defence, 34, 35, 55, 67

State Security, 51, 54, 59, 191

network, 207

Service, 19, 27, 35, 52, 63, 66, 69, 90, 99, 118–19, 136–9, 163, 178–9, 189–91, 199, 210, 213, 218, 222, 226, 237, 241

Main Administration, 45

of Special Branches, 68

personnel, 61

school(s), 45, 53, 60–1, 67, 91, 118, 178, 214, 221, 241

Special Branches, 69

system, 187, 221

Stauffenberg, Count Claus von, 126

Strik-Strikfeld, Capt. Wilfried, 126

Strokach, Lt.-Gen. T. A., 25, 93
Sudoplatov, Lt.-Gen. P. A., 93, 119
Szalasi, Ferenc, 194

TASHKENT, 227
Tatishchevo, 67, 68, 72, 73, 76, 82,
    92, 148
    Military Transit Formation Camps,
      72
Telegin, K. F., 132, 133
Third Ukrainian Front, 191
Thorres, Maurice, 161
Timoshenko, Marshal Semyon, 33
training schools for partisan warfare,
    99
Trotsky murder, 187
Trukhin, General F. I., 130
TsGV, 148, 155, 157, 159, 163, 165,
    180, 193, 210, 214, 223, 245
    engineering branch, 233
    Third Branch of KRU, 199
Tukhachevsky, Marshal Michael, 164,
    189, 212
Tvardovsky, Alexander, 128

UKRAINE PEOPLE'S COMMISSARIAT for
    State Security, 116
Ukrainian Insurgent Army (UPA), 100
Ukrainian KGB, 227
Ukrainian nationalists, 105
Ulbricht, Walther, 204
UPA (see Ukrainian Insurgent Army)
Utyosov, Leonid, 13, 25

VADIS, LT.-GEN. A. I., 132, 134
Vatutin, General, 101, 102, 103, 218

Vetoshnikov, Major, 137
victory, 144
    parade, 145, 147, 165
Vienna, 159, 201, 209, 240, 241, 243
    Soviet Occupation Zone, 159
Vlasik, Lt.-Gen. N., 145
Vlasov, Lt.-Gen., Andrei, 81 fn, 125,
    126, 127, 150, 151, 152, 164, 169,
    213
Voronezh Front, 170
Voroshilov, Marshal K. Ye., 50, 93,
    166, 180, 198, 209, 211, 212, 213,
    214
Vyshinsky, Andrei, 142, 145

WAR WITH GERMANY, 36
'wicket gates', 120

YALTA, 141
Yefremovich, Kliment, 212
Yeremenko, General, 134
Yevdokimenko, Col. Georgi
    Stepanovich, 144, 157, 191
Yezhov, Nikolai Ivanovich 16
Yoska, 12–6 passim, 19, 21, 23, 25, 27,
    30–1, 35, 43, 47, 83–5, 109, 113,
    148, 161–2, 230

ZAMERTSEV, MAJ.-GEN., 194
Zarubin, Maj.-Gen., 137, 138
Zhdanov, Andrei, 26
Zheltov, Col.-Gen. A. S., 159, 245
Zhilenkov, Brigadier G. N., 126
Zhukov, Marshal Georgi K., 103,
    128–34 passim, 142, 146–8, 165, 212
Zyryanov, Col.-Gen. P. I., 191